THE GAY TEEN

THE GAY TEEN

Educational Practice and Theory
for Lesbian, Gay, and
Bisexual Adolescents

edited by
Gerald Unks

Routledge / New York & London

Published in 1995 by
Routledge
29 West 35th Street
New York, NY 10001

Published in Great Britain in 1995 by
Routledge
11 New Fetter Lane
London EC4P 4EE

Essays by Dennis A. Anderson, M.D., Warren J. Blumenfeld, Jim Brogan, Vincent Fuqua, Pat Griffin, Karen M. Harbeck, Michael J. Koski, Glorianne M. Leck, Arthur Lipkin, Peter McLaren, Kenneth P. Monteiro, Andi O'Conor ("Who Gets Called Queer in School?"), Amy L. Reynolds, Eric Rofes, Hugh Singerline, Gerald Unks, and Virginia Uribe were originally published in *The High School Journal,* Volume 77, Nos. 1 and 2, copyright © 1994 The University of North Carolina Press.

Printed in the United States of America.
Design: David Thorne

Library of Congress Cataloging-in-Publication Data

The gay teen: educational practice and theory for lesbian, gay, and bisexual adolescents / edited by Gerald Unks.
   p. cm.
   Includes bibliographical references and index.
   ISBN 0-415-91094-3 (cloth) — ISBN 0-415-91095-1 (pbk.)
   1. Homosexuality and education—United States. 2. Gay Teenagers—United States. I. Unks, Gerald.

LC192.6.G39 1995   94-44783
371.8'2664—dc20   CIP

Contents

1

THE GAY TEENAGER

1

Thinking About the Gay Teen

Gerald Unks

Homosexuals are arguably the most hated group of people in the United States. While other minorities have gained a modicum of protection and acceptance, homosexuals remain essentially outside the pale. In their public lives, few Americans any longer use words such as "nigger," "kike," "gook," or "wop." Yet, "faggot," "fairy," "homo," and "queer" are used by many without hesitation. Picking on persons because of their ethnicity, class, religion, gender, or race is essentially taboo behavior, but adults and children alike are given license to torment and harm people because of their sexuality. The civil liberties of most minorities are fairly secure; those of homosexuals are tenuous at best, and nonexistent at worst. In spite of mighty gains by other minorities, homosexuals stand alone, outside, despised, and ripe for discrimination.

Unlike most minorities, the majority of homosexuals have the option of hiding their identities from a hostile society. Although the damage to their mental health may be considerable, they can conceal their most-despised status, and act publicly as if they were not homosexuals. Most choose this charade as a way of life, for to self-identify as a homosexual is to invite persecution by society and rejection by family, peers, organized religion, and community. In the past two decades, homosexuality has received increasing governmental, medical, and media attention, and several notable people have identified themselves as homosexuals. The topic, homosexuality, has become the acceptable stuff of public discourse, but there is little to suggest that *the subjects* of the topic—homosexuals themselves—are much better off than they were a generation ago. No longer plagued by the "I'm the only one in the world" syndrome, most homosexuals must still continue to choose to lead a lie as a lifestyle. Secretly all around us, fearing to reveal a part of their being, they are nonetheless there. They are our celebrities, our politicians, our manual laborers, our professionals, our acquaintances, our tradespeople, our religious leaders, our friends, our coworkers, our bosses— and our adolescents.

There is little evidence to suggest that adolescent homosexuals experience any less prejudice and discrimination than is visited on their adult counterparts. Indeed, there is compelling data suggesting that they may suffer *more*. First, as is typical of all youth, their political, economic, and social expression is restricted because of their age. However, unlike their counterparts, they do not enjoy the sort of social allegiances, educational resources, or cultural support that are routinely established by the adult society for other youth subcultures. Second, they are children in a minority that society has chosen to regard as solely adult. The most apparent parts of gay and lesbian culture—particularly bars and social clubs—are highly adult-centered, and there are legal, social, financial, and political barriers that prevent any legitimate adolescent participation in them. The youthful homosexual receives messages, implied and explicit, that suggest that homosexuality is an exclusively adult characteristic or privilege, sort of like voting or getting married. The cry of gay teens, "I have no place to go, nowhere to meet people like me, no one to look up to and learn from, no place to turn," echoes their essentially powerless position.

A cursory search for support systems typically available to adolescent homosexuals reveals that there are essentially none. Further, adolescent homosexuals cannot find comfort in family, church, or peer groups, nor are there role models with whom they can identify. In virtually every way, lesbian, gay, and bisexual adolescents are *worse off* than their adult counterparts. While forces in the larger adult society might hint at political correctness, acceptance, and accommodation, the high school—the center of most adolescent life and culture—stands staunchly aloof and rigidly resistant to even a suggestion that any of its faculty or student body might be homosexual or that homosexuals deserve anything but derision and scorn within its walls. High schools may be the most homophobic institutions in American society, and woe be to anyone who would challenge the heterosexist premises on which they operate.

Heterosexism, an ideology "[t]hat denies, denigrates, and stigmatizes any nonheterosexual form of behavior, identity, relationship, or community" (Herek, 1992, p. 89), permeates the typical high school. Consistently, the very existence of homosexuality is denied—on the faculty, in the student body, and even in the curriculum. There is an extraordinarily narrow definition of what is acceptable male and female dress and conduct (much more restrictive than one would find in the college or the adult community), and those who transgress are likely to be taunted. The array of social conventions, mores, folkways, and institutional norms that support the belief that heterosexuality is the best and only lifestyle is overwhelming. It affects what is taught, who takes which subjects, and who is "in" and "out" in the cultural life of the school.

Within the typical secondary school curriculum, homosexuals do not exist. They are "nonpersons" in the finest Stalinist sense. They have fought no battles, held no offices, explored nowhere, written no literature, built nothing, invented nothing, and solved no equations. Ironically, they were neither Greeks nor Romans, and they did not write poetry, compose music, paint, or sculpt. The lesson to the heterosexual student is abundantly clear: homosexuals do nothing of consequence. To the homosexual student, the message has even greater power: no one who has ever felt as you do has done anything worth mentioning. This omission almost certainly contributes to *homophobia*, "the fear and hatred that heterosexuals experience when around homosexuals and the discomfort *and self-hatred* (our italics) homosexuals have about their own homosexuality" (Weinberg, 1972). The absence from the curriculum of valid information about homosexuality cuts both ways; heterosexual students are given no reasons not to hate homosexuals, while homosexual students are given no reason not to hate themselves. Both groups suffer a loss, for they are denied important information about a significant group of human beings.

Over time, subjects in the high school have acquired dubious gender association; some are "masculine," others are "feminine." In reality, math, auto shop, and science are not male domains; nor are literature, home economics, and music the province of females. Yet in the *unreality* of the school environment, this has become the case. The impact of this gender association on female scores in math has been widely documented. However, coupled with a strong strain of heterosexism, it takes its toll on all students. Only a few females take auto shop, just as only a few males take home economics. Fearing homophobic labels, most students stick to their own gender-defined subjects. Does the male who takes his musical ability seriously fear being called a "fairy?" Does the female who excels in sports invite taunts of "dyke?" Some students consider history to be "male," and they do not like female history teachers, just as some believe that literature is somehow "female." In the context of the high school, anything that might even remotely be considered "queer" is avoided, and this includes the study of subjects which could help all students. The entire student body—heterosexual and homosexual—suffers by being denied access to *all* of the subjects in the school curriculum simply because the school allows heterosexism to go unanswered (see Klein, 1992).

Anyone who studies the culture of the typical high school realizes that the curriculum is only half—perhaps less than half—of the "life of the school." Apart from courses and schedules, there is the rich brew of growth, pride, anxiety, hope, wonder, fear, experimentation, anger, and challenge that is the essence of being a high school student. *Sexuality* is also part of that mix, for it is usually during high school that most adolescents have their first serious sexual encounters. Indeed, the high school culture expects and promotes these liaisons with dances, newspaper gossip columns, yearbook signings, class ring exchanges, locker sharings, and—perhaps above all—the prom. It is, however, *heterosexuality* that is being championed; there is no room for homosexuality in the high school culture, for it challenges the blatant heterosexism that infuses the institution's mores and folkways. Any same-sex affection is closely and carefully proscribed—even in athletics (see Pat Griffin's article in this collection). Should students feel any same-sex attraction, and should they act upon those feelings, they will be vigorously punished with ostracism at best, and physical abuse at worst. There is evidence that adolescents, more than any other age group, are likely to commit violence against homosexuals (Masters, Johnson, and Kolodny, 1992, p. 394;

Greer, 1986). Again, *all* students suffer from a heterocentric high school culture. Certainly, the homosexual student is most abused, but heterosexual students are also losers, for they must conform to rigid standards of behavior that admit no individual differences. These unilateral, unbending expectations may be particularly troublesome for a heterosexual male who is small, quiet, serious, or sensitive, and for the heterosexual female who finds it awkward or difficult to display stereotypic feminine traits.

Another factor contributing to the marginalization of homosexual adolescents is their lack of viable support groups. While virtually all students of any other identifiable group have advocates and support in the high school, homosexual students typically have none. They have no equivalent of the African-American student's protection against hate words, slurs, and discrimination. They receive no special programs or assistance. The guidance office is not the place where they can tell it all (see the Reynolds and Koski article in this collection). There are seldom role models on the faculty, and even the most understanding faculty member may not be an appropriate person with whom to confide "their most secret secret." Indeed, heterosexual faculty members who are empathetic to homosexuals are placed in a particular bind; if they champion gay rights, they may themselves be accused of being gay. And should there be "out" gay teachers on the faculty, and should they work for gay student rights, they might well be accused of "recruiting." Lacking any significant support system, it is not surprising that the homosexual adolescent may achieve poorly, drop out of school, engage in substance abuse, run away from home, or attempt suicide.

The occurrence of suicide among adolescent homosexuals is possibly the most widely publicized data about them. That this is the case is perhaps the cruelest irony in the chronicle of the woes of gay teens. How unfortunate it is that they must make the *ultimate* statement about their condition in order to get a significant cohort of the public to pay attention to them. The reports about a disproportionately large number of suicides among young homosexuals have been beneficial in that they have prompted a positive public response in some areas of the country to the problems of gay teens. These reports, however, have not been without their critics (see Shaffer, 1993), and the issue of how many homosexual adolescents commit suicide has become politicized (see Bull, 1994). Kielwasser and Wolf (1994) have evaluated these arguments:

While suicidal ideation among lesbian and gay youth is not uncommon, the statistical profiles used to document a high rate of suicidality are problematic. Random samples of homosexual youth are impossible to generate, and many studies of lesbian and gay youth suicide are based on convenience samples of adolescents already involved in various counseling, suicide prevention, and delinquency abatement programs. Additionally, and perhaps more importantly, this historic emphasis on the psychosocial problems faced by lesbian and gay youth has frequently obscured any systematic consideration of their particular talents. Certainly, most lesbian and gay youth do survive adolescence. They move willfully into adulthood by virtue of an extraordinarily powerful and creative resilience. At least one research psychologist (Gregory M. Herek, 1993, personal communication) has suggested that we adjust our research agenda to include homosexual youth as gifted children. (p. 59)

Herek's suggestion makes sense. Most teens who feel deficient in one area of development will compensate by being even better in others. And there are few areas of life that are as subject to compensation as is sexuality. Indeed, it would be very useful to examine the "outstanding students" in every field. Almost certainly, there would be homosexual students among them. If, however, there was *a disproportionately large number* of homosexual students among "the success class"—the football captains, the honor students, the Eagle Scouts, the cheerleaders, the school officers, and the rest—(and we suspect that there would be), then it would tend to take some of the focus of public attention away from the negative area of suicide, a condition too long associated with homosexuality. To engage in such inquiry, however, would entail gathering accurate *random* sample data, and this requires honest responses. As long as heterosexism and homophobia reign in the high school, this condition is unlikely to obtain. Finally, the point must be made: irrespective of how many young homosexuals commit suicide, numbers are not what is important. If just one young homosexual commits suicide, that is a problem deserving of public attention and community action.

There are certain themes that run through much of the literature about gay teens—oppression, anger, silence, desperation, guilt, and death. Not all of the themes, however, are depressing and negative; there is also a great deal that is positive. As Kielwasser and Wolf pointed out above, in spite of the staggering figures about misery and suicide, it is a fact that most gay teens do survive adolescence—they make it through along with most other adolescents—and they become useful and well-adjusted adults; this is the life pattern for the majority of homosexuals in America. Further, it is extremely positive to remember the closeted gay *Wunderkinder*—born of sublimation and compensation—who bubble as adolescents and star as adults. Few of them would admit to life's being tragic, and some would cite their adolescent discomfort as a wellspring for their adult accomplishments. Karen Harbeck (see her article in this collection) is correct, however, when she reminds us that, in the main, homosexuals—even adolescent ones—are neither miserable wretches nor superachievers. They are mostly ordinary people who accept the challenges and solve the problems that are the essence of life for everyone. Indeed, a case can be made that gay teens will be truly well off only when these, the average homosexuals, are accepted for what *they* are—outstanding only in that they are human beings. Then homosexuals will have no stereotypes attached to them. They will all be thought of neither as the limp-wristed drag queen, the brutish dyke, nor the genius conductor of the symphony. They will be seen as just plain individuals—possessed of all the same warts and wrinkles or shining complexions as are all people.

Perhaps the most positive themes in the literature about gay teens are the descriptions of what is now being done to assist them. In a growing number of schools across the nation, parts of a gay-friendly curriculum are in place, and they are working (see Lipkin's article in this collection). Certainly, these curricula and units became a reality only after a fight, but—in spite of the flack—they are still in place. Project 10, the Harvey Milk School, Spectrum, and OutRight! are models that are working. They have their critics, but these are usually more vocal than numerous. School officials who wish to ease the plight of gay adolescents in their student bodies do not have to invent the wheel; pioneering efforts are already in place to show them the way. All that they must do is to seize the initiative in their own school district, recognizing that there will be opposition, but also realizing that it may be far less intense than they expect.

Yet gay-friendly curricula and student organizations may be simply too much for some faculties and administrators to imagine in their districts. For them there is still a task: strongly oppose any "epithets of hate," and enact policies against harassment. At the very least, any school system can implement these reforms. They do not broaden the curriculum, they do not "recruit," nor do they celebrate a particular lifestyle. What they do is extend basic civil liberties to a minority of students who do not currently enjoy them. And if some faculty or administrators respond that there are none of "them" in their student body, there is still a reason to institute the reforms.

There *are* several of "them" in the student body, and while fear may keep them in hiding while they are in school, the positive action of passing these reforms may give them a bit of self-confidence.

Still, suggesting that homosexuality and homosexual accomplishments should be a part of the curriculum is usually an invitation to trouble. Accusations will almost certainly be made about the person's own sexuality. There is a heterosexist/homophobic presumption that those who have any interest in homosexuals (other than to ferret them out for persecution) must themselves be homosexual. This absurdity is roughly equivalent to assuming that only African-Americans are interested in matters of race, or that one must be poor to be interested in poverty. Aspersions about their sexuality aside, those who want to consider homosexuality in schools may be accused of "causing trouble" by bringing up a "controversial issue." This is the censor's historic weapon—attempting to destroy an idea by refusing to acknowledge or discuss it. A controversial issue is by definition one on which reasonable people can honestly disagree. However, it is *unreasonable* to claim that homosexuals do not exist or that no homosexuals have accomplished anything of worth. To claim that homosexuals—including adolescent homosexuals—do not exist is equivalent to claiming that baseball players do not exist. To discuss baseball players—how many there are, what they do, what they have done, where they live, their good points and their bad—is not at all controversial in schools. Intrinsically, neither is homosexuality; however, it becomes "a problem" when a society is forced to choose between acknowledging the existence of homosexuality, on the one hand, and holding on to the heterosexist notion that homosexuals do not exist, on the other.

However, in the presence of an avalanche of media attention, it is difficult—even for the most rabid heterosexist—to deny the very existence of homosexuals. Robbed of this position, the heterosexist retreats to name-calling, identifying homosexuals *only* as child molesters, men who wear women's clothing, and dirty old men who have sex in public toilets. Above all, heterosexists cling to three ideas that are apparently crucial to their mind-set: being lesbian or gay is in and of itself evil, homosexuals could "change" if they wanted to, and no lesbian or gay person has ever done anything worthwhile. Most curriculum proposals that suggest the importance of studying homosexuality directly challenge these three ideas, and affront the heterosexist mentality because these plans suggest that the curriculum should acknowledge the legitimate existence of a homosexual community and that it should recognize the contemporary and historical contributions of this community to the larger society. This is not a controversial idea at all—unless one wishes to claim that there is no homosexual community and that its scientists, writers, composers, athletes, public officials, and all of the other contributors to the varieties of human accomplishment do not and never did exist. To make such a claim, in the presence of the scholarship on the subject, is not simply unreasonable; to the extent that it denies reality, it is insane.

Three words—myth, reality, and dream—surround the problems of and prospects for the gay teen in American society. Up to the present, much of society and its schools has embraced an elaborate, unchallenged collection of myths about homosexuality and the gay teen. It derives a sort of perverse security from not talking about it, denying it, and persecuting it—as if a strange combination of uncomfortable silence and selective rage would make it go away. Myths unexamined do not, however, become truths; and those who order their lives on myth are doomed. Still, a great number of Americans seek out and cherish myths. They lament the good old days, and call for a return to values and patterns that had the appearance of utility in the past. They refuse to look at reality; they embrace the soothing balm of the political and religious soothsayer who reinforces their parochial beliefs. Authoritarian societies have many "thou shalt nots" in their lexicon, the most dangerous of which is "thou shalt not think." That the American society and its schools have adopted the posture of not thinking about homosexuality and the gay teen is a perilous course to take. For when one rejects thinking as the foundation of an educational system, one is in reality rejecting one of the most promising ways of disciplining ideas with facts.

It is unfortunate that the literature and scholarship about gay teens does not usually address the issue of the student's right to know. Censoring homosexuality as an appropriate topic for reflective examination in a high school is a breach of a student's academic freedom. It is in the same category as all of the other topics that self-appointed thought police have historically sought to keep out of the classroom—evolution, Communism, and the rest. Powerful arguments as they are, gay teen suicide prevention and establishing the civil liberties of gay teens may be second-order reasons for talking about homosexuality in schools. In a truly democratic society, the primary reason in support of studying about homosexuality in schools may be to assure freedom of thought. Societies are totalitarian to the extent that they have areas of belief and attitude that are closed to reflective examination and thought. The real importance of thinking about the gay teen, and homosexuality generally, is to open up one of those areas which American society has chosen to close. In that, it is a search for truth.

In school—if nowhere else—our youth should sate their desire for reliable knowledge. When society, however well-intentioned, denies its youth this sort of information, it perpetrates the most insidious form of intellectual rape upon its children. However, instructing in realities entails an examination of the controversial and what some might consider the downright unpleasant. But it can also involve suggesting dreams—the possibility of hope and of change. In the final analysis, it is the fusion of these realities and dreams—in a process called thinking—which makes people responsible citizens, and it is thinking about all ideas, including homosexuality, which will make the United States and its citizens—including its gay teens—truly free.

REFERENCES

Bull, C. "Suicidal Tendencies," *The Advocate*, Issue 652 (April 5, 1994), pp. 34–42.

Greer, W.R. (1986). "Violence Against Homosexuals Rising, Groups Seeking Wider Protection Say." *New York Times*, November 23, p. 36.

Herek, G.M. (1992). "The Social Context of Hate Crimes: Notes on Cultural Heterosexism." In *Hate Crimes: Confronting Violence Against Lesbians and Gay Men*. G. Herek and K. Berril, eds. Newbury Park, CA: Sage Publications.

Kielwasser, A.P. and Wolf, M.A. (1994). "Silence, Difference, and Annihilation: Understanding the Impact of Mediated Heterosexism on High School Students." *The High School Journal, 77* (January 2), pp. 58–79.

Klein, S.S. (1992). "Why Should We Care About Gender and Sexuality in Education?" In *Sexuality and the Curriculum: The Politics and Practices of Sexuality Education*. James Sears, ed. New York: Teachers College Press.

Masters, W., Johnson, V., and Kolodny, R. (1992). *Human Sexuality*. Fourth Edition. New York: HarperCollins Publishers.

Shaffer, D. (1993). "Political Science." *The New Yorker*, vol. 69, No. 11 (May 3, 1993), p. 116.

Weinberg, G. (1972). *Society and the Healthy Homosexual*. New York: Anchor.

2

Breaking the Silence

Writing About Gay, Lesbian, and Bisexual Teenagers

Andi O'Conor

Eve Kosofsky Sedgwick (1993) writes, "I think everyone who does gay and lesbian studies is haunted by the suicides of adolescents." I am no different. When the 1989 Health and Human Services report on teen suicide was released, I was struck with despair at the statistics. Gay and lesbian youth comprise approximately thirty percent of all teen suicides. One in three have reported committing at least one self-destructive act. Nearly half repeatedly attempt suicide. Gay and lesbian youth make up approximately one quarter of all homeless youth in the U.S. (Gibson, 1989).

In my mind, this makes gay and lesbian teenagers one of the most significant "at-risk" groups in our high schools today. And it puts a new twist on the term itself. At risk of failure, of underachieving, yes. But these teenagers also face a higher risk of harassment, violence, and suicide than other teens.

As a recent news article reported:

> Adolescence is hard for everyone, but agony if you're gay. You're on your own to learn who you are, to find others like you, to search for acceptance. (*Minneapolis Star Tribune,* 1992)

Homophobia, heterosexism, and high schools are a potentially volatile combination for formal research. Not only do researchers face difficulties with access, parental consent, and confidentiality, but we become, to borrow a phrase from John Irving's (1978) book, *The World According to Garp,* "sexual suspects." Karen Harbeck (1992) writes:

> All too often, both the scholars who might have undertaken such studies and the potential participants in that research have been dissuaded by threats to their tenure, promotion, reputation and personal safety…. Even these [heterosexual] scholars spoke of the hardships they had endured once this research had been published, including one's threatened loss of custody of her children during a bitter divorce. (p. 2)

Most gay, lesbian, and bisexual educators and researchers choose to study and write about issues other than sexuality and homosexuality, at least until they are tenured. Rarely does an educational researcher publish work in this area. As Sedgwick (1993) says, "I look at my adult friends and colleagues doing lesbian and gay work, and I feel that the survival of each one is a miracle" (p. 239).

Gay and lesbian theorists, like gay, lesbian, and bisexual teenagers, live in a world that is hostile to our sexualities. We live in a world that tries to silence and ignore us. We live with gay-bashing, oppressive legislation, and legalized discrimination. We live with the epithet, "Die Queer" ringing in our ears. We live with the sinking feeling that the religious right is hunting us down.

Gay and lesbian theory requires courage. To tread in an arena that combines schools and sexuality, kids and queerness, to bring in and bring out our own sexuality is risky indeed. For us, visibility often breeds contempt. Yet silence can truly equal death, especially for gay teens. Death by visibility, death by invisibility—the catch-22 of our tribe.

Jim Sears (1991) calls gay and lesbian teenagers "sexual rebels." Dorothy Allison (1993) calls gay and lesbian writers "outlaws." While we might not think of ourselves as rebels or outlaws, the topic places us both on the margins of academia and in the center of the firestorm of debate about teenagers, sexuality, and schooling.

In my work studying gay, lesbian, and bisexual teenagers, I too have been haunted by the persistent specter of adolescent suicide. In the youth group I studied last year, several teenagers had wrists scarred from previous suicide attempts. Many spoke of their persistent self-destructive behavior. The statistics were often in evidence in the room.

Speaking out about homosexuality is risky, both for academic writers and gay teens. Yet, as Audre Lorde wrote, "If we wait until we are not afraid to speak, we will be speaking from our graves" (Lorde, 1984, p. 4). Regardless of which side of the debate you are on, it is critical to address this topic. The voices of gay adolescents may have been silenced, but these youths are screaming out in other ways to be heard, notably through suicide. It is a situation that cannot be tolerated, and it is time to open the door to the "classroom closet" (Harbeck, 1992), and begin the debate in earnest.

REFERENCES

Allison, D. (1993). Panel discussion presented at the *University of Colorado Gay and Lesbian Studies Conference*, April, Boulder, CO.

Gibson, P. (1989). "Gay Male and Lesbian Youth Suicide." In U.S. Department of Health and Human Services, *Report of the Secretary's Task Force on Youth Suicide*. Washington, DC: U.S. Government Printing Office.

Harbeck, K. (1992). *Coming Out of the Classroom Closet*. New York: Haworth Press.

Lorde, A. (1984). *Sister Outsider*. Freedom, CA: Crossing Press.

Irving, J. (1978). *The World According to Garp*. New York: E.P. Dutton.

Minneapolis Star Tribune (1992). "Growing Up Gay." Sunday, December 6, pp. 1–14S.

Sears, J. (1991). *Growing Up Gay in the South: Race, Gender, and Journeys of the Spirit*. New York: Harrington Park Press.

Sedgwick, E. K. (1993). "Queer and Now." In *Wild Orchids and Trotsky*. Mark Edmundson, ed. New York: Penguin.

3

Lesbian and Gay Adolescents
Social and Developmental Considerations

Dennis A. Anderson, M.D.

A great number of teenagers have had, or will have, homosexual experiences. In our society, homosexual behavior among adolescents is quite common (Kinsey, Pomeroy, and Martin, 1948; Kinsey, Pomeroy, Martin and Gebhard, 1953; Rutter, 1980) and includes incidental homosexual activities of otherwise predominantly heterosexually-oriented adolescents. There are, however, adolescents who have already identified themselves as predominantly homosexual, or who will later come to so identify themselves. For these adolescents, social and emotional development during adolescence are likely to differ in significant ways.

There is almost no prospective research on the development of sexual orientation. Most of our information comes from adult lesbians, gay men, and heterosexual adults recalling their past. From this data, models of homosexual identity formation have been described by several different authors (Troiden, 1988; Cass, 1990). The studies of gay and lesbian adolescents seem to confirm that a similar process is taking place (Boxer, Cook, and Herdt, 1989).

HOMOSEXUAL AROUSAL AND BEHAVIOR

According to reports of adult lesbians and gay men, the onset of homosexual arousal, homosexual erotic imagery, and homosexual romantic attachment occurs during adolescence. A majority have these experiences before fifteen years of age (Saghir and Robins, 1973). Gay males tend to be aware of their same-sex attractions somewhat earlier (twelve to fourteen years) than do lesbians (fourteen to sixteen years). A recent study of gay and lesbian adolescents of fourteen to twenty-one years, found the average age of first homosexual fantasies to be similar for both males and females, 11.2 and 11.9 years, respectively (Boxer, Cook, and Herdt, 1989).

HOMOSEXUAL EXPERIENCES

Gay males, on average, experience significant physical homosexual contact (including body-body contact, manual-genital contact, or oral-genital contact) about five years earlier than do lesbians. Saghir and Robins (1973) found that only twenty-four percent of the lesbians had such contact by fifteen years of age, with an increase to fifty-three percent by age nineteen, compared to over eighty percent of the gay males having such experiences by age fifteen. While there is wide individual variation, gay males tend to begin homosexual activity during early or mid-adolescence (Bell, et al., 1981; McDonald, 1982; Troiden, 1979), while lesbian females tend to begin similar activity around age twenty (Bell, et al., 1981). Thus, males are much more likely to act on their homosexual feelings soon after recognizing them than are females who may not begin homosexual behavior for many years after their awareness of homosexual attractions. In the study of gay and lesbian adolescents discussed above (Boxer, Cook, and Herdt, 1989), the differences in age of first physical homosexual experience were in a similar direction. The average age of first homosexual experience was 13.1 years for the gay boys and 15.2 years for the lesbian girls.

For many adolescents, homosexual activity is not merely incidental sex play or experimentation; rather it is an outward expression of an internal homosexual orientation which includes homosexual imagery, arousal, and romantic attachments. The term *homosexual orientation* is defined here as a "consistent pattern of sexual arousal toward persons of the same gender encompassing fantasy, conscious attractions, emotional and romantic feelings, and sexual behaviors" (Remafedi, 1987).

HETEROSEXUAL EXPERIENCES

It is important to realize that gay and lesbian teenagers frequently begin or continue heterosexual activity despite an awareness of their homosexual orientation. Both lesbian women and gay men report doing a good deal of heterosexual dating in their adolescent years. Heterosexual arousal and experience may precede or follow homosexual experiences, but the majority of lesbian women have had a heterosexual experience by their adult years. About half of lesbian women have experienced heterosexual emotional attachments before age twenty in addition to their homosexual attractions, and more than two-thirds reported experiencing heterosexual sexual arousal. A third had actually had intercourse by age twenty, a number similar to that for heterosexual women (Saghir and Robins, 1973). In the more recent Chicago study of lesbian and gay teens, three-quarters had experienced heterosexual intercourse (Boxer, Cook, and Herdt, 1989). Compared to gay men, more lesbians had experienced heterosexual intercourse by their adult years.

AWARENESS OF HOMOEROTICISM

An organized subjective awareness of experiences as "homosexual" may be lacking in early adolescents, who are cognitively immature and for whom development has just begun to allow longitudinal understanding of their personal history and its implications for their future. Studies of older cohorts show that lesbians self-identify as homosexual in their early twenties, whereas gay males more frequently self-identify in their late teens or earlier (Saghir and Robins, 1973; Bell, et al., 1981; Chapman and Brannock, 1987; Dank, 1971; Woodman and Lenna, 1980). There is evidence that teenagers are now self-labeling at earlier ages than they did in the past (Offer and Boxer, 1991), perhaps because of secular changes in our society which allow more discussion of homosexuality, more public and media presentations of gay and lesbian persons, and more visibility of gay and lesbian people in all walks of life.

Gay or lesbian teenagers usually report that between ages twelve and fourteen they first realize that they are much more sexually attracted to persons of their own sex, even though they may not yet self-label as gay or lesbian.

Most teenagers who acknowledge a predominantly homosexual arousal pattern realize almost immediately that words such as "gay" and "homosexual," or derogatory terms are applied to persons with such feelings. Most also report that they have felt somehow different for many years, sometimes beginning in early childhood, but they usually did not relate these feelings to their concept of homosexuality. In Bell, et al.'s study, three-quarters of lesbian women felt "sexually different" by the time they were age eighteen, whereas a much smaller minority of heterosexual women ever felt that way. The boys labeled their "sexual different" feeling as *homosexuality* considerably earlier than girls (Bell, et al., 1981). Gay adult males report the onset of "self-labeling as homosexual" close to the time of becoming aware of homosexual feelings in early adolescence. On the other hand, the age at which lesbians label this feeling of difference "homosexual" increases gradually through the adolescent years, with half self-labeling by age eighteen and most of the rest by their late twenties (Bell, et al., 1981; Saghir and Robins, 1973; Woodman and Lenna, 1980).

Most often, awareness of their homosexuality comes suddenly for adolescents—even for those gay or lesbian teenagers who may have frequently participated in homosexual sex or have had homoerotic experiences earlier in adolescence or childhood. There are many reasons why homosexual adolescents or even preadolescents come to such a seemingly sudden realization of their sexual orientation. Aside from the frequent use, during preadolescence or early adolescence, of denial to ward off the anxiety caused by homoerotic feelings or experiences, many adolescents only gain the cognitive capacity for abstract thought and formal reasoning which enables them to integrate the experiences they have had in the past with their current situation at this stage of development. Further, sexual arousal to particular stimuli, erotic imagery, masturbation, and romantic attachment all increase dramatically as puberty begins, and they are likely to be homosexual in content. In the social arena, gay and lesbian adolescents now see their peers become more interested in opposite-sex relationships and heterosocial activities, in marked contrast to their own indifference to these pursuits.

Whatever the experiences that lead to the growing personal awareness of their homosexuality, most gay and lesbian adolescents can vividly recall a period of intense anxiety when they first realized that they suddenly belonged to a group of people that is often vehemently despised. For the adolescent, an identity crisis occurs. It can be understood as the conflict produced by the juxtaposition of the negative ideas about homosexuality that were learned throughout childhood with the new awareness of homosexual attractions and identity that is developing. This suddenness of homosexual self-recognition contrasts with the lengthy process of actually coming to understand and accept one's sexuality, a process that takes years. This crisis of self-concept occurs because the gay adolescent senses a sudden involuntary joining to a stigmatized group. The stigma occurs because of homophobia, an unreasonable or irrational fear or hatred of homosexuals or homosexuality (Weinberg, 1972), which has been internalized during childhood. Homophobic attitudes may occur not only within individuals, as internalized homophobia, but also within organizations and the society at large, as institutionalized homophobia (Hencken, 1982). The gay or lesbian adolescent may have few resources available to get information about homosexuality. Little information is formally presented in a balanced and unbiased manner in most schools, and most reading materials that an adolescent may seek are likely to be censored, inaccurate, or blatantly homophobic. Another difficulty that gay and lesbian teenagers have in dealing with their homosexuality in adaptive ways is the absence of positive role models. Gay and lesbian teens do not see the same diversity of adults with whom to identify as heterosexual adolescents do, because so many lesbian and gay adults do not publicly acknowledge their sexual orientation. This is a particularly acute problem in the school setting, where gay and lesbian staff may experience the need to completely hide their sexual orientation, or may be unwilling to provide guidance or to support advocacy for lesbian or gay students out of fear of being suspected to be homosexual.

The teenager's management of the experienced stigma and internalized homophobia is crucial to the gay or lesbian adolescent's social and emotional development, and is crucial for school personnel to understand. Homosexual adolescents initially make one of three choices in dealing with their newly acknowledged feelings: (a) try to change them; (b) continue to hide them; or (c) accept them (Martin, 1982). These three strategies usually follow each other sequentially, but this is not invariable. Maylon (1981) reminds us that for some homosexual adolescents the initial reaction is one of denial of same-sex desires or suppression of these desires, with a developmental moratorium through which heterosexual norms are accommodated. This is followed, perhaps years later, with psychological and social integration of the homosexual orientation. Some individuals spend years—or decades—repressing their homosexual orientation while repeatedly engaging in homosexual behavior. From the time they first acknowledge their homosexuality, most gay adolescents go though a period when they attempt to change their sexual orientation or, at least, they hope these feelings will go away. For young persons, the incorrect notion that all or most homosexuals possess traits of the opposite sex is particularly prevalent. Many gay or lesbian teenagers will attempt to provide self-remedies by accentuating gender-typical behavior while avoiding any behavior which may be considered more typical of the opposite sex, or even just gender-neutral. Boys may walk with a swagger, engage in compulsive bodybuilding, or display aggressive, overassertive, or even antisocial behavior, while girls may dress in very feminine clothes, wear excessive amounts of makeup, or use exaggerated gestures. Both sexes may frantically pursue heterosexual dating and heterosexual activity, sometimes with the goal of pregnancy so as to have powerful evidence with which to claim heterosexuality. Masturbation is often avoided, or accompanied with tremendous guilt, because of the homosexual fantasies which occur. Associations with same-sex peers may be terminated or avoided because of the erotic feelings and anxiety-laden temptations that are aroused or because of the anxiety which accompanies the fear of discovery as the relationship develops. Most commonly, attempts are made to use sheer will and self-recrimination to suppress homoerotic thoughts and feelings.

This is often an extremely lonely time for gay and lesbian adolescents, especially for younger adolescents or preadolescents who are cognitively and affectively not equipped to effectively manage these issues. The developmentally normal egocentrism of early adolescence causes all adolescents to feel as though they are at the center of others' attention; they often believe that others are observing them, and that others are almost able to read their thoughts (Elkind, 1978), or "find them out" through their body language and interactions. At this time gay or lesbian adolescents feel very vulnerable to the potential for rejection or antihomosexual bias. Certain endeavors—for which the adolescent may have considerable talent but which run counter to peer group ideals of gender appropriate interests, such as dramatics, singing, dance, or the creative arts for boys, or athletics or mechanical arts for girls—are sometimes purposely avoided. In some settings, academic achievement itself may be viewed as unmasculine behavior, and it is thus avoided by a boy who is attempting to maintain a positive image amongst his peers. The self-conscious, almost constant internal dialogue that develops may have marked deleterious effects upon personal relationships, particularly on the development of intimacy and friendship. Gay and lesbian adolescents are forever monitoring themselves: "Am I standing too close? Is my voice too high? Do I appear too happy to see him/her?" Activities that should be spontaneous expressions of affection or happiness become self-consciously controlled behavior or moments of agonizing fear or uncertainty. Particularly painful moments for many gay or lesbian adolescents are hearing an antihomosexual joke or seeing another individual being ridiculed or called some epithet which is commonly applied to homosexual persons. It is not unusual for a gay or lesbian adolescent to join in such activities in order to maintain his or her own "cover." Often, in order to avoid drawing attention to themselves, they will not associate in their schools with other students whom they believe to be gay or lesbian.

The experience of the adolescent whose homosexuality becomes known or is highly suspected varies. Name-calling, baiting, and practical jokes are common in all schools. Physical assault sometimes does occur, not to mention the more subtle but powerful forms of social ostracism. Exceptionally popular individuals or those who are successful in high status activities may not suffer as much harassment, but if they are not open about their sexual orientation, they may experience extreme anxiety about the prospect of discovery and loss of social status. Staff within schools determine to a great extent the atmosphere regarding homophobic bias. In many settings, derogatory statements about homosexuals, or antihomosexual epithets, go unchallenged where similar remarks of a racist nature would clearly not be tolerated.

COMING OUT TO OTHERS AND DEVELOPING A LESBIAN OR GAY IDENTITY

Studies suggest that an adolescent goes through a number of stages in coming to terms with a lesbian or gay identity. A lesbian or gay adolescent is likely initially to be aware of feelings of being different, sometimes dating back to early childhood. They then become aware of being attracted to others of the same sex. This has been described as a time of sensitization (Troiden, 1979). In an effort to understand her- or himself, the adolescent may have both homosexual and heterosexual experiences. This can be a time of confusion for the adolescent. Development of a same-sex love relationship, and disclosure to nonhomosexual peers and family are the final stages, indicating commitment to a lesbian or gay identity (Troiden, 1989). For many lesbians, this final stage of "coming out" to nonhomosexuals may occur many years after homosexual self-definition and same-sex love relationships have occurred. The same is true for gay men, but the available data suggest again that the entire process may occur at earlier ages for men than for women (Troiden, 1988).

CROSS-GENDER BEHAVIOR

Contrary to the common stereotypes, most homosexual adolescents do not exhibit gender-deviant behavior. Some gay or lesbian adolescents may, however, display extreme gender-deviant behavior. This includes cross-dressing in a provocative or defiant manner in situations which they perceive as hostile to their homosexual orientation. This is a defense against threatened self-esteem, and it can be viewed as an identification with the cultural or peer group gender-role expectations for homosexuals. Similar adaptations have been noted in individuals from extremely strict religious backgrounds where crossdressing or even transsexualism may be a defense against homosexuality (Hellman, Green, Gray and Williams, 1981). In some ethnic minority groups, especially Hispanic cultures or others with rigidly dichotomized sex-role differences between the feminine and the *macho*, there appears to be a greater tendency for homosexual adolescents to display more extreme gender-deviant behavior. In fact, those Latino homosexual male adolescents who conform to the social role of the effeminate *maricon* are more likely to be tolerated and less subject to violent harassment than are young homosexuals displaying more typically masculine behavior. Many gay adolescents who do cross-dress gradually drop this behavior once they are exposed to a gay peer group (Hetrick and Martin, 1988). In such gay peer groups, the dominant cultural expectations for cross-gender role behavior for homosexuals are experienced with less force.

PEER RELATIONSHIPS

The peer group provides the context for the formation of a personal identity which incorporates the various needs, values, and proclivities of the adolescent. Most adolescents realize that the expression of homosexual feelings within the dominant peer group, where there is tremendous pressure to conform to heterosexual norms, will result in alienation from peers at best, and violence at worst. Withholding important personal information and suppression of his or her genuine interests results in the elaboration of a false persona in order to gain peer acceptance or to maintain status. This psychosexual duality exacts a high cost in vigilance, self-loathing, and the elaboration of defenses to contain the chronic anxiety which this situation produces. This state inhibits a variety of important social interactions. The most destructive is the restriction of opportunities which promote the capacity to engage in erotic and nonerotic intimate relationships. Adolescents in this situation who are afforded the luxury of a relatively prolonged adolescence, such as college, may have the opportunity to complete the tasks of adolescence. For others, however, a premature foreclosure of identity development—during a period where much internalized homophobia has not been worked through—can result in a very long and unnecessarily painful "coming-out" process.

Gay and lesbian adolescents, whether they have "come out" or continue to hide, experience much of the heterosocial and explicitly, or implicitly, homophobic aspects of adolescent life as extremely isolating. Adolescence is a period of heightened awareness of sexuality, and gay and lesbian adolescents are apt to become frustrated by the variety of heterosexual and heterosocial outlets that are available to others while there are so few outlets available to them. To some gay and lesbian adolescents, the experience of watching boys and girls in school walk hand in hand down the hallway, while their own desires must be kept secret, produces feelings of rage and sadness that are difficult to resolve. In addition to having no opportunity to experience social interactions with gay or lesbian peers, there is little likelihood that they will see gay or lesbian adult role models in their day-to-day lives. Low self-esteem, academic inhibition, truancy, substance abuse, social withdrawal, depressed mood, and suicidal ideation are not unusual, and may be difficult to differentiate from depressive disorders. It is not surprising that gay and lesbian adolescents, wanting involvement in a peer group that accepts them and offers the possibility of establishing intimate relationships, often begin to search for other gay persons. Gay and lesbian teenagers in large cities may call telephone hotlines, search for gay newspapers, or contact agencies that serve gay people. Gay boys are much more likely than lesbian girls to travel to areas where they believe gay people are to be found to have sexual encounters (Paroski, 1987). Unfortunately, this search may take the adolescent to areas where they are placed at risk (Roesler and Deisher, 1972). An adolescent who is lonely and sexually frustrated may interpret the release of tension, the supportive environment, and the physical affection of another person as love, an assumption which likely is premature. It is also possible for gay adolescents to feel so comfortable in the first gay supportive environment that they find that a premature foreclosure around a particular kind of lifestyle within the gay and lesbian community may follow.

In most large cities there are a variety of gay and lesbian services, but many of these are directed to adults and actively exclude gay youth because of their fear of reprisals if they serve young people. Services specifically for gay and lesbian youth are being developed throughout the country, and at least one national directory of services has been published (Hetrick-Martin Institute, 1992). Of course, in small towns or rural areas, none of these services are available. In large cities it is extremely difficult, and in most parts of the country it is impossible, for gay adolescents to succeed in meeting other gay adolescents in a positive and supportive environment.

SUMMARY

The proscriptions against homosexuality remain strong within the adolescent's world, especially the *early* adolescent world. Gay and lesbian adolescents whose sexual orientation is self-recognized typically experience intense conflicts with their social environment, particularly in the school environment. Adolescents who hide their sexual orientation from others expend enormous amounts of energy monitoring and restricting their interactions with others. The process of coming out often has deleterious effects on family life, peer relationships, and the development of intimate relationships with others. When school personnel encounter them, gay or lesbian adolescents may be at any stage of self-acknowledgment regarding their homosexuality. This acknowledgment may range from no awareness of their homosexuality, to full awareness and active hiding of it, to being publicly out of the closet and managing to develop a supportive social network. Staff or policies that trivialize the adolescent's homoerotic feelings, or view the behavior as a mere phase of normal development that will pass, are likely to do great damage to the self-concept of the homosexually-oriented teenager. Recognizing the complexity of the individual, family, and social dynamics of adolescent development can be invaluable to gay, lesbian, and "straight" students alike.

REFERENCES

Bell, A.P., Weinberg, and M.S., Hammersmith, S.D. (1981). *Sexual Preference: Its Development in Men and Women.* Bloomington, IN: Indiana University Press.

Boxer, A.M., Cook, J.A., and Herdt, G. (1989). "First Homosexual and

Heterosexual Experiences Reported by Gay and Lesbian Youth in an Urban Community." Presented at the *Annual Meeting of the American Sociological Association*, August, San Francisco, CA.

Cass, V.C. (1990). "The Implications of Homosexual Identity Formation for the Kinsey Model and Scale of Sexual Preference." In *Homosexuality/Heterosexuality: Concepts of Sexual Orientation*. D.P. McWhirter, S.A. Sanders, and J.M. Reinisch, eds. New York: Oxford University Press.

Chapman, B.E. and Brannock, J.C. (1987). "Proposed Model of Lesbian Identity Development: An Empirical Examination." *Journal of Homosexuality*, *14*, pp. 69–80.

Dank, B.M. (1971). "Coming Out in the Gay World." *Psychiatry*, *34*, pp. 180–197.

Elkind, D. (1978). *The Child's Reality: Three Developmental Themes*. Hillsdale, NJ: Etlbaum.

Hellman, R.E., Green, R., Gray, J.L., and Williams, K. (1981). "Childhood Sexual Identity, Childhood Religiosity, and Homophobia as Influences in the Development of Transsexualism, Homosexuality, and Heterosexuality." *Archives of General Psychiatry*, *38*, pp. 910–915.

Hencken, J. (1982). "Homosexuality and Psychoanalysis: Toward a Mutual Understanding." In *Homosexuality: Social, Psychological and Biological Issues*. P.W. Weinrich, Jr., ed. Beverly Hills, CA: Sage.

Hetrick, E.S. and Martin, A.D. (1988). "Developmental Issues and their Resolution for Gay and Lesbian Adolescents." In *Integrated Identity for Gay Men and Lesbians: Psycho-Therapeutic Approaches for Emotional Well-Being*. E. Coleman, ed. New York: Harrington Park Press.

Hetrick-Martin Institute (1992). *You Are Not Alone: National Lesbian, Gay and Bisexual Youth Organization Directory, Spring, 1993*. New York: Hetrick Martin Institute.

Kinsey, A.C., Pomeroy, W.B., and Martin, C.E. (1948). *Sexual Behavior in the Human Male*. Philadelphia, PA: W.B. Saunders Co.

Kinsey, A.C., Pomeroy, W.B., Martin, C.E., and Gebhard, P.H. (1953). *Sexual Behavior in the Human Female*. Philadelphia, PA: W.B. Saunders Co.

Martin, A.D. (1982). "Learning to Hide: The Socialization of the Gay Adolescent." *Adolescent Psychiatry*, *10*, pp. 52–65.

Maylon, A.K. (1981). "The Homosexual Adolescent: Developmental Issues and Social Bias." *Child Welfare*, *60*, pp. 321–329.

McDonald, G.J. (1982). "Individual Differences in the Coming Out Process for Gay Men: Implications for Theoretical Models." *Journal of Homosexuality, 8*, pp. 47–60.

Offer, D. and Boxer, A.M. (1991). "Normal Adolescent Development: Empirical Research Findings." In *Child and Adolescent Psychiatry: A Comprehensive Textbook*. M. Lewis, ed. Baltimore, MD: Williams and Wilkins.

Paroski, P.A. (1987). "Health Care Delivery and the Concerns of Gay and Lesbian Adolescents." *Journal of Adolescent Health Care, 8*, pp. 188–92.

Remafedi, G. (1987). "Adolescent Homosexuality: Psychosocial and Medical Implications." *Pediatrics, 79*, pp. 331–337.

Roesler, T. and Deisher, R.W. (1972). "Youthful Male Homosexuality: Homosexual Experience and the Process of Developing Homosexual Identity in Males Aged 16 to 22 Years." *Journal of the American Medical Association, 219*, pp. 1018–1023.

Rutter, M. (1980). "Psychosexual Development." In *Developmental Psychiatry*. M. Rutter, ed. Washington: American Psychiatric Press.

Saghir, M.T. and Robins, E. (1973). *Male and Female Homosexuality: A Comprehensive Investigation*. Baltimore, MD: Williams and Wilkins Company.

Troiden, R.R. (1979). "Becoming Homosexual: A Model of Gay Identity Acquisition." *Psychiatry, 42*, pp. 362–373.

———. (1988). "Homosexual Identity Development." *Journal of Adolescent Health Care, 9*, pp. 105–13.

———. (1989). "The Formation of Homosexual Identities." In *Gay and Lesbian Youth*. G. Herdt, ed. New York: Harrington Park Press.

Weinberg, G. (1972). *Society and the Healthy Homosexual*. New York: Anchor.

Woodman, N. and Lenna, H. (1980). *Counseling with Gay Men and Women*. San Francisco: Jossey-Bass.

II

EDUCATIONAL PRACTICE AND LESBIAN, GAY, AND BISEXUAL TEENAGERS

4

The Case for a Gay and Lesbian Curriculum

Arthur Lipkin

INTRODUCTION: THE POLITICAL CONTEXT

The debate about New York's "Children of the Rainbow Curriculum" was a rallying point for public discourse about the nature of sexuality and families. The battle over the inclusion of gay-positive instruction in a broad multicultural curriculum evinced a homophobic barrage from a multiethnic chorus, informed with religious zealotry and other biases of the right. Some reporters observed a redeployment of troops from family-planning clinics to school yards.

For gay progressives, the Rainbow controversy was the first national arena in which to take on social conservatives on the issue of education. For those who see schools as a crucial site for antioppression education and for social change, the New York engagement held the promise of being a Stonewall for the nineties. They understood that getting at the roots of homophobia required more than the public relations campaigns prescribed by some critics within the gay community (Kirk and Madsen, 1989; Stafford, 1988); it required early intervention, conscientious curriculum change, programmatic staff development, and student support. Though some may have strategic differences with their cohorts in New York, they welcomed the clash over the Rainbow as a first significant and possibly galvanizing engagement in their campaign to re-make schools into gay-supportive environments.

Unfortunately for these progressives, a historical accident made military service the temporary focal point of the struggle for gay rights. The campaign to lift the military ban on gays diverted national attention from the schools. "HEATHER'S TWO MOMMIES" lost its news billing to "GAYS IN UNIFORM." But with the military issue at least temporarily settled, attention can turn again to the matter of Rainbow curricula. And, in refocusing on schools, we ought to be reminded that the adult antagonists in all national debates about civil rights and diversity have spent a considerable part of their formative years in schools, where their understandings of human differences might have been enhanced.

WHY TEACH THESE THINGS?

We can justify teaching about homosexuality on pragmatic as well as scholarly grounds. Since our schools have both social and intellectual objectives, it should be satisfying to ground this reform firmly in both arenas.

One practical reason that the subject of homosexuality is appropriate, especially for high school students, is that they find the topic engaging. Indeed, the entire realm of sexuality can be an obsession for adolescents. One may argue that the mass media contribute to the exaggeration of this aspect of human experience for young people. But even without the commodification of sex—the suasions of MTV, teen magazines, film, and advertising—the protracted coming-of-age process that has developed in our culture would probably find sexual musings and anxieties at its core. Today's students are not only thinking and talking; they are "doing" sexuality at a high rate and at a very young age (Haignere, 1987; Zelnik and Shah, 1983). If schools are going to have any impact on the attitudes and behaviors of their sexually concerned and often active students, they must acknowledge in their curricula the importance of sexuality in our lives and in the lives of those who have gone before us. This academic exercise will not only illuminate the details of sexuality; it will also put it in perspective.

Americans are embarrassed to admit their interest in sexual representations because they fear that their curiosity makes them immoral. For example, they would rather see explicit sex on screen than see violence, but they assume their neighbors would prefer the opposite. Researchers who study this contradiction between natural interest and shame believe that people's notions of public morality have been skewed by the outspokenness of religious conservatives (Donnerstein and Linz, 1991). The widespread misperception that sexual interest is uncommon and sinful may be corrected by including realistic, developmentally appropriate, sex education curricula in schools.

Sexual ignorance in our culture can be a strong rationale for teaching sex education in general, but what about homosexuality in particular? On the practical level, what is it about homosexuality that provokes the interest of students? Adolescents appear to be as much obsessed with conformity as they are with sex. At the same time as youths discover their individual sexualities, they are also intent on conforming to peer group norms. Our culture makes the very personal exploration of sexuality into a process of self-definition in a comparative context. Is it any wonder then, that not merely sexuality, but sexuality *difference* is a compelling concern for our young people?

What are the practical results of ignorance about sexuality differences? We must answer that question vis-à-vis each of two constituencies: first, those youth who are lesbian, gay, bisexual, or confused about their sexual interests and developing identities; and second, those who are heterosexually identified.

HELP FOR GAY YOUTH

The litany of stresses and self-inflicted injuries suffered by gay and struggling youth should be familiar: alienation, depression, substance abuse, and suicide (Hetrick and Martin, 1987, 1988; Gonsiorek, 1988; Hunter and Schaecher, 1987; U.S. Dept. of Health and Human Services, 1989; Remefadi, 1987, 1990). It is hard to believe that any gay kid growing up listening to Phil Donahue, Oprah, or any other of the daily American cavalcade of TV could still feel isolated or think that he or she is the only one. The openness and variety of television discourses on sexuality must have some positive impact, but there are also worrisome effects. First, the often sensationalistic nature of television talk programming indicates the importance of ratings over accuracy. The images of gay people on these shows could confuse or frighten the ordinary gay kid, who might relate to neither the "motorcycle dyke" nor the "gay weightlifter/model."

Second, an almost universal principle of TV talk on homosexuality—the inclusion of opposing views—is problematic. Having a guest with a different opinion usually means inviting a rabid homophobe. What message does the gay or confused youth take from a show that promotes the expression of undisguised bigotry?

Even a balanced and civil television presentation may evoke discouraging consequences. Though Phil and Oprah themselves often demonstrate an accepting attitude, how many voices of support in the life of the young gay viewer are raised as a result of the TV program? Parents or others may express negative views of homosexuality in response to the presentation. Classmates may do the same in school. How many teachers are prepared or willing to conduct an impromptu class discussion about sexuality? And how many of those teachers who pick up the buzz among students and react to it will express a tolerant view? Young gays' and lesbians' self-esteem is vitally linked to these sources of approval (Savin-Williams, 1990; Weinberg, 1983).

News and public affairs programming can also send alienating and dangerous messages to gay kids. The recent hearing on gays in the military, for example, provided a stream of testimony that portrayed homosexuality—if not gay people—in a negative light. There was almost no testimony to counter the image of gays as predatory, infected, and incapable of promoting group solidarity or providing leadership. Coverage of the HIV epidemic is also skewed. The demography of AIDS in this country insures that most AIDS programming focuses on gay men.

There are exceptions to these characterizations of homosexuality on television. There is the occasional objective discussion, a flattering or good-humored portrayal, and—rarely—an average gay citizen actually speaking about his or her own life. But, for the most part, mass media conflate homosexuality with controversy and suffering. Exposed to these images, gay youth, especially those in remote rural areas, must have a dismal view of their prospects. Indeed one wonders if these young people experience their sexuality very differently from the way most gay people did fifty years ago. Without exposure to a vibrant urban gay community and without the support of family, friends, or school, gay youth can be deeply bruised by these media messages.

Gay/lesbian/bisexual and struggling students can be helped by bringing the discussion of gay issues into the school. All of the researchers who have studied homosexual identity formation have described a developmental stage in which these people consider what they know about gayness in order to see if the label is congruent with what they know about themselves (Herdt, 1989; Coleman, 1988; Troiden, 1988; Cass, 1984). If they are aware only of a limited number of the features of gay life, they may have difficulty in this process of identification. Since many conceptions of homosexuality in our society are inaccurate and stigmatizing, gay youth may rightfully fear the burden that they are taking upon themselves. These are the conflicts and feelings of alienation from their developing identities that cause gay teens to harm themselves (Herdt and Boxer, 1993).

On the other hand, if gay youth are exposed to the diversity of gay identities, to the richness of the culture, and to the long history of same-gender attraction, their development will be enhanced. This is not to say that the homosexual experience ought to be so glamorized that unrealistic expectations will be fostered. However, students should learn that there is more to celebrate in being gay than there may be to fear. We have plenty of evidence—in gay history and literature, as well as in current events—that the gay experience, like that of other minorities, is fraught with risk. But for students who are gay, lesbian, or bisexual, developing a balanced and accurate view of what it can mean to be gay could literally save their lives.

Needless to say, gay youth will also benefit from any increase in tolerance that results from greater understanding. Violence against gay people has a long history, and it appears to be increasing with the advent of AIDS and growing public expressions of homophobia related to political questions. The perpetrators of violence against gays and lesbians are most often young men (Levin and McDevitt, 1993; Herek and Berill, 1992). It should come as no surprise, then, that high schools are a frequent site for homophobic rage and violence.

HELP FOR HETEROSEXUAL YOUTH

School programs about homosexuality help gay youth with their adjustment. In fact, most such programs are conceived for that purpose. The report of the Governor's Commission on Gay and Lesbian Youth in Massachusetts is titled "Making Schools Safe for Gay and Lesbian Youth" (The Governor's Commission on Gay and Lesbian Youth, 1993). Perhaps the first such state-sponsored effort in the country, this laudable report calls on schools to be sensitive to the needs of gay youth, to prevent the harm these students do to themselves, and to curb the violence that is often directed at them. Implicit in the Massachusetts report and others like it (Seattle Commission, 1988; McManus, et al., 1991; Schoenhals, 1992) is the unspoken notion that gay youth will be the *only* beneficiaries of the recommendations. It is crucial to this effort, however, also to acknowledge the benefits to heterosexual people that come with a better understanding of homosexuality.

First, it can be argued that any learning that eliminates prejudice not only helps its target but also frees the bigots themselves from victimization. Hate is a debilitating burden to carry around; letting go of prejudice, on the other hand, allows a stunted mind to grow to a more inclusive understanding of the human experience. This was a consequence ignored by the *Brown vs. Board of Education* decision. Perhaps because it was ruling on the grievances of blacks in a separate and unequal system, the court limited itself to the observation that such separation harmed the black students' interests. It did not point out that lack of contact with black people resulted in a poor education for whites. Segregation hindered the white child's understanding of the breadth of human experience by limiting his contact with his black neighbor. Integration can prevent that by stimulating new dialogues about race. And that discourse can lead to unforeseen recasting of the meanings of race itself.

Getting over homophobia—the misunderstanding, fear, or hatred of homosexuality—can have direct benefits as well, analogous to those of a racially integrated education. Antihomophobia education can help heterosexual people to understand better their own sexualities. The requirements of heterosexual identity in our culture are narrow and rigid. Much anxiety is created over the need to live up to these requirements, and too many young people, especially young women, are hurt in the process. Learning about the range of expression of different sexualities can take some of the pressure off these students.

Ironically, understanding homosexuality—which is one extreme of sexuality in the Kinsey sense—may give people at the other extreme more latitude. Heterosexual students may recognize that they share none of the homosexual experience and are not gay, or they may accept the homoerotic feelings they have experienced as nonthreatening to their heterosexuality, or they may come to believe that sexuality labels are arbitrary markers on a continuum. One heterosexually-identified student recently expressed his new view after studying a unit on the history of gays and lesbians in the U.S.:

> The more we talk about homosexuality in class, the more comfortable I am with the idea, with gay people, with my own sexuality, and with my own male

identity. Is/was this curriculum and these discussions important? About as important as the desegregation of schools in the fifties and the abolition of slavery in the 1800s. We are in the *middle* of a *huge* societal movement, a tremendous change, one more step to a better society. (White male public high school senior, 1992)

Presenting homosexuality without embarrassment or condemnation signals a teacher's acceptance of sexuality in general, an attitude that may facilitate important communication with heterosexual students. Openly gay and lesbian teachers have told how heterosexual students have come to them to discuss sexuality and relationship issues that they would not discuss with others. These students explained that they chose the gay teachers to talk to because they perceived them to be more understanding of different people's sexual experiences than they thought others would be (Ferreira, et al., 1993).

WHAT CAN SCHOOLS DO?

Schools can have an impact on how students construe differences among them. In the areas of racial, ethnic, and gender difference, the mere presence of visible minority group members in a school can lead to experiences and conversations that promote greater understanding. With the addition of a multicultural curriculum, learning about these kinds of differences is greatly enhanced, but learning about sexuality differences remains problematic. First, there are many communities where religious, moral, or political objections prevent teaching about homosexuality. And even where such barriers are absent, the likelihood of gay/lesbian/bisexual students or teachers being open about their sexuality is small. Pressure to remain closeted persists. Therefore, opportunities to interact with openly gay people in school activities are rare, as is learning about the gay experience informally from people who are part of the school community. Most schools that commit to inclusion of gays under the rubric of multiculturalism have to depend on a deliberate curriculum and guest speakers.

As has been illustrated in New York, gay curriculum seems to be even more controversial than gay civil rights. Because children are directly involved, stereotype-based hysteria rises quickly. Public figures want to avoid the accusation of "teaching kids how to be a homosexual" that inevitably flies whenever curriculum is suggested. In fact, during the New York battle, the *curriculum* recommendations of the Governor's Commission on Gay and Lesbian Youth in Massachusetts were quietly dropped from its report, as it made its way from the governor to the state's commissioner of education. On May 20, 1993, the front-page headline in the Boston Herald read "There'll be no gay school lessons," and the governor was quoted as saying, "I don't personally favor teaching a gay and lesbian curriculum in the schools."

Some level of controversy may be avoided by interpreting the notion of curriculum broadly. At a minimum, the forbidding of homophobic name-calling (a part of the Massachusetts plan) is the beginning of curriculum. It implies the teaching of the value of tolerance in a particular context. Some, however, appear to believe that a teacher or administrator can ask a student not to call another "faggot" without having to explain who is being harmed by such language and why it is wrong to defame those people. Enforcement of a name-calling policy without explanation is shortsighted. The rule is important in setting a tone for the school, and it can create some value dissonance within the offender. But if the only rationale for the rule is the seemingly arbitrary authority of the school, then the behavior will likely be stopped only in the school. It may be resumed on the street. If, however, the name-calling rule is contextualized within a fairness discussion, in which gay/lesbian people are given their humanity and misperceptions are challenged, tolerance may be internalized and practiced beyond the schoolhouse walls.

The next level of curriculum is the general sensitivity unit, in which students are explicitly taught that they should be nice to gay people. Usually included with other kinds of difference, the category of homosexuality may also be considered independently. Though it may seem safer to include gays and lesbians in a larger litany of minority groups when teaching respect for differences, that approach can have its limitations. Despite the importance of mentioning gays in lessons on tolerance, teachers must also be prepared to discuss gay issues separately. Explicit classroom references to gays are rare enough that students will naturally be inquisitive about their inclusion. Some students, particularly members of other minority groups, may not understand or may even resent the apparent equating of the minority statuses. Thoughtful amplification is, therefore, required, both to avoid glib superficiality and to clarify similarities and differences among oppressions.

Teachers should also be prepared for questions to arise about their own sexuality. This phenomenon—thinking a teacher might be gay because he or she consistently includes gay people in the American patchwork—is common. Raising the topic of racial oppression does not ordinarily lead to questions about a teacher's racial identity, since racial identity is usually apparent. Mentioning religious or ethnic topics could generate assumptions about the teacher, but it is doubtful that it would have the same impact unless the community is sensitive to certain of those categories. Sexuality, on the other hand, usually does provoke speculation, particularly if the teacher is not known to be married. Because of the pervasiveness of homophobia in our country, as well as the accurate perception that gay people are the most active in the struggle against it, one who repeatedly defends gays is assumed to be homosexual.

As a consequence of raising homosexual issues in the classroom, teachers should be prepared to do three things. The first is to answer some basic questions about gayness—its prevalence, its possible causes, and its practices and cultural features. Second, the teacher must be able to point out features that are common to different forms of oppression as well as the differences among minority groups' experiences. Third, teachers should be ready to respond comfortably to questions about their own sexualities. Stereotypes may be challenged effectively if the heterosexual teacher withholds information about his or her orientation until he or she has asked the students how they might feel differently about him or her if he or she were gay.

When gay/lesbian teachers raise issues of homosexuality with their students, there can be powerful repercussions. If these teachers are unwilling or forbidden to be open with students, their hiding can send a message of shame that is not conducive to healthy adolescent development. On the other hand, the gay teacher must have support in the school in order to undertake an admittedly problematic disclosure. There is no universal answer to this dilemma. In the end, no teacher—gay or heterosexual—should share intimate details of his erotic life with students; however, openness about sexual orientation can be part of a valuable lesson.

BEYOND SENSITIVITY

No one should underestimate the value of teachers' including gay people when they talk with students about cultural diversity. Just hearing the words "homosexuality" or "gay/lesbian/bisexual" in an accepting context sends a powerful message to young people, and creates the potential for a tolerant environment. Further, when teachers are willing and able to discuss some basic facts of homosexuality and gay life, that potential is greatly increased.

But there are still limits to what these minimal curriculum strategies can accomplish. Urging students to be tolerant of gays along with other minorities, spending a few class minutes countering a handful of misconceptions, or even having a special "sensitivity session" about homophobia *separate* the gay experience from the central curricular goals of the school. The gesture could take on the characterization of a "politically correct" thing to do. We cannot deny the political nature of such inclusion nor, I would hope, its rectitude. But we should avoid giving it the aura of a trendy sideshow, conducted apart from the serious business of inquiry in our daily classes. A school rule about name-calling, the direct objection to homophobic harassment, mentioning gays as a legitimate minority group, a multicultural awareness day featuring a segment on gays and lesbians—all of these worthy steps should not relieve the school of its obligation to do more.

What is required is sustained and serious academic discourse within the disciplines of the school. Students need to understand the nature of sexual identity, the long history of same-gender attraction, and how it has been expressed in different times and cultures. They should know about past and current etiological research. They need to analyze how the homosexuality of a historical figure or an author might have influenced his or her life or work. They need to know something about the history of the gay/lesbian community in the United States as well as current issues in gay life. They must appreciate the diversity of gays and lesbians in this country and around the world.

For many years, schools—in their zeal to transmit our common culture—have scanted the experiences and contributions of racial minorities. Homosexuality has been completely ignored. References, even to the gay liberation movement in the sixties and seventies, are almost nonexistent in high school U.S. history texts (Licata, 1980–1981). Ironically, unlike other minorities, many white gay people are featured in history, and gay authors are read, but their sexuality and its implications are not mentioned. If our mission in schools is to cultivate our students' interest in the truth and to give them the skills to begin the search for it, this kind of intentional ignorance through censorship runs counter to our goal. It may be that, some years ago, we could honestly say that scholarship was spotty on the subject of homosexuality, and good sources of material were not available. Today the thriving pursuit of gay studies on the university level provides volumes of respected research and exciting theory. Our work is to make some of this new learning available to secondary school students.

HEALTH AND SEX EDUCATION

One caveat must be given before exploring the possibilities of gay content in the various subject areas: it is the danger of *medicalization*. Mention of homosexuality, if there is any, is most often done in the context of health and HIV curricula. Although it is perfectly appropriate to discuss some aspects of homosexuality in these venues, there is a strong possibility that students' views will be distorted in the process. We run the risk of having them think that homosexuality is inevitably linked with deviance and illness. Even if the teacher is gay-friendly and the curriculum is accurate, placing the matter under the subject heading of "health" or "disease prevention" carries its own message.

The consequences of medicalizing homosexuality can be negative for all students, but we should be particularly concerned about what gay/lesbian youth might experience. Any school that focuses exclusively on the physiological dimensions of homosexuality compounds the societal misconception that gayness is just about sex acts. It objectifies the gay student into a biological subject, reducing his or her experience in the world to his or her sex life. To be sure, sex education in general can result in the same distortion, regardless of the sexuality under consideration. However, curricular representations of heterosexual life outside the health class—in history and literature, for example—offset this effect by countering the impression with other facets of male-female relationships that are not only physical. For the gay student, this curricular balancing is, for the most part, absent.

In the case of AIDS education, gay students can benefit from knowledge that leads to less risk-taking. Nonetheless, a school that examines homosexuality only in the shadow of a tragic illness offers little affirmation to its gay students. It is difficult to make AIDS education a positive experience for gay adults, many of whom have access to support within the gay community. It is even more of a struggle to reach gay youth, who lack community ties, with an AIDS message that affirms their sexuality.

There is a greater possibility for a broader view of gay experience in the area of family life curricula than in health. Presenting the ways that gay men and lesbians construct alternative families will generate opportunities for learning about aspects of gay life. These include spousal relationships, child-rearing, extended biological and intentional family, work-sharing, and financial planning. As with learning about the range of sexuality itself, learning about how gay people make family can have a positive, if not liberating, effect on heterosexual students for whom normative definitions of family might prevent full human development. Young heterosexual women especially could benefit from understanding that there are other ways to thrive beyond conventional marriage. Of course, healthy models of unconventional family life may be provided by heterosexuals too. Still, strong challenges to conservative notions of gender role may often be found in same-gender partnerships.

Family life education offers a natural place for the integration of gay content into standard courses, and this melding is crucial for the success of gay studies in high schools. Courses in gay studies alone are not advisable. On a practical level, who would enroll in an independent gay-themed course? The two types of student who might benefit most from information in such classes would probably stay away. Gay or lesbian students who are not open about their sexuality would likely not enroll for fear of the stigma, and homophobic heterosexual students would probably not cross the threshold. Furthermore, if we want to teach that gay people are a part of the community and that the gay experience is a part of our cultural heritage, then gay studies must not be segregated. We must underscore the value *to all students* of learning about these things. It is too easy for schools to ghettoize minority studies and the people who enroll in them. This process enables school authorities to cover their bases in what they may see as a multicultural game. However, in so doing, they suppress the truth of our national life, which has always been multicultural.

SOCIAL STUDIES

The social studies present fertile ground for the integration of a gay curriculum, particularly in the disciplines of history, political science, sociology, anthropology, and psychology. Of primary interest in these areas are: cross-cultural and transhistorical understandings and representations of same-gender sexuality; the importance of certain gay/lesbian people in various eras; the evolution of the modern gay identity; and current gay issues, including legal rights, medicine, activism, and politics.

An eight-to-ten day curricular unit, "The Stonewall Riots and the History of Gays and Lesbians in the U.S.," will serve as an example for the social studies. It has been used effectively in both U.S. history and sociology classes in the Cambridge, Massachusetts, public high schools. The unit begins with colorful accounts, taken from contemporary newspapers, of the 1969 riots at the Stonewall Inn, a gay bar in Greenwich Village. Beginning a study of gay history with this event pulls students into a vivid conflict. They are then asked to consider questions such as: Who were these people? Why were they there? Had there always been gay people in New York? What is the historical significance of this event—was it a turning point in our national awareness?

How does it compare with other historical events of a similar nature? The unit then recapitulates the history of same-gender expression from the colonial period through the present, with special attention to urbanization, the impact of the world wars, and the ascendancy of science. Economically and racially diverse groups of students have studied this unit from 1991 to 1993. The following are selected observations from their final exams (excerpted verbatim):

> I came in thinking I knew at least something about the gay movement, because I know many people who are gay. Yet I knew barely anything about the Stonewall incident. (White female)

> It is good that people organize a group to help teach kids to understand the values and feelings of gays and lesbians, so they might understand them and know that they too are humans. (Hispanic male)

> I have always thought what people do is their business, but it has taught me that society and its rules for "norms" can do a job on a group of people. (White female)

> It is very similar to the Black Civil Rights Movement. That helps me understand the movement more. The lesson also helped me to be open-minded to homosexuals. (African-American female)

> I was aware that the gay rights movement is still going on. I have always at least within the last couple of years had a concern for human rights. I did know that homosexuals have been around for hundreds of years. In this class I learned the history of homosexual identity. (White male)

A three-to-five day unit, "The History and Nature of Homosexuality and Its 'Causes,'" has been used for three years in biology classes in Cambridge. It is also appropriate to psychology classes. This unit examines the changing understandings of same-gender desire from Ancient Greece to contemporary America. Observations that are more detailed than those in the Stonewall unit are made concerning the changes brought about by developments in science and medicine. Recent psychological and biological theories of etiology are explained. One theme of this unit is the influence of culture and politics on scientific inquiry.

LITERATURE

The question of what is meant by "gay literature" or the "gay aesthetic" has not as yet been answered. Nonetheless, the influence of a gay writer's sexuality on his or her work is worth examining in high school English, foreign language, or world literature classes. The pantheon of writers who invite this analysis include both well-known gay writers such as Auden, Baldwin, Forster, Williams, Woolf, Cather, Whitman, Wilde, Gide, and Verlaine, whose works are already part of the secondary school canon, as well as those, perhaps lesser known, who could be taught successfully in high schools (Radcliffe Hall, Isherwood, Vivien, Leavitt, Mishima, Renault, and so on).

There are other writers whose sexualities are subject to debate. Some of them figure prominently in our schools: Dickinson, G.M. Hopkins, Langston Hughes, Melville, Thoreau, and so on. The crucial point in studying these authors' work from a gay perspective is not to claim them as homosexual, though better cases can be made on that point for some than others. Rather, the purpose in raising the possibility is to gain insight into the writing through hypothesis. We know that gay identity as we understand it today is not a transhistoric means of interpretation (Boswell, 1992; Epstein, 1987; Halperin, 1990; Stein, 1992). But the fact that a particular author might have experienced same-gender attraction and not have identified as gay in the modern sense should not prevent us from examining the importance of this attraction to his or her thinking and its *possible* influence on his or her work. For example, analysis of Thoreau's poem "Sympathy" ("Lately, alas, I knew a gentle boy") is enriched by considering its homoromanticism. Additionally, a hypothesis of Thoreau's homosexuality is an exciting criterion for probing the mindset of *Walden*. This exercise is intellectually satisfying, even if we cannot find explicit reference to gay self-awareness either in *Walden* itself or in the journals (Harding, 1991). As Eve Kosofsky Sedgwick has observed "…no one *can* know in *advance* where the limits of a gay-centered inquiry are to be drawn, or where a gay theorizing of and through even the hegemonic high culture of the Euro-American tradition may need or be able to lead" (Sedgwick, 1990, emphasis hers).

Teachers have taught Willa Cather's "Paul's Case" without mentioning the possible homosexuality either of the character Paul or of the author. Though it may not be critical to know details about Cather's women companions, understanding "Paul's Case" is impoverished without a gay lens. Examination of Cather's early condemnation of Oscar Wilde brings even greater nuance to the analysis (Summers, 1990). A similar argument can be made for studying *Billy Budd* as a story of repressed homoerotic desire and its consequences. The insights gained from this study provide the means for a different understanding of *Moby Dick* or *Bartleby the Scrivener*. Students could sample documentation of the passionate relationship between Melville and Hawthorne (Rowse, 1977). These observations may be commonplace in some universities, but they would be extraordinary anywhere else. The routine unsensationalized inclusion of homosexual possibilities in the high school curriculum would have a profoundly positive effect.

SOCIAL CONSTRUCTION THEORY

Social studies and literature units inevitably lead to the issue of social constructionism. This compelling nominalist theory, propounded by Foucault and others (Foucault, 1978; McIntosh, 1968; Weeks, 1985), posits that categories of identity are completely a creation of culture. Society develops labels and social scripts for the creation of identities which are entirely arbitrary. Social constructionists believe that there are no essential, inborn, and ageless criteria for identity; rather, that certain human features assume importance as a result of society's temporal needs or dictates.

This theory has assumed a central place in modern discourse about sexuality, and one does not have to subscribe to its most extreme forms in order to recognize either its power or its appeal. Whatever the characteristic under consideration—whether sexuality, race, gender, or some other—a social constructionist analysis is a useful one. It is especially appealing to young people, for whom society's dictates are a locus both of self-reference and potential rebellion.

Although one may begin with sexuality, the implications of social constructionism are broad. Discussions of culturally imposed categories of sexual identity can lead to poignant conversations among groups of diverse high school students. In Cambridge, students have struggled over what it means to be Jewish or black in America and what is essential to a woman's identity. One biracial student talked about her inability to choose between being black or being white and her desire to be both and neither. She did not appear to be a pathetic lost soul, searching for meaning in her racial identity. She was a strong, self-respecting person, who expressed impatience with society's narrow categories and perhaps with any category based on pigmentation. Her need to be accepted just as herself was not surprising in a teenager, but her capacity to inspire others to challenge universally accepted racial dichotomies was extraordinary. As a child of mixed parentage, she had doubtless given much thought to the question. However, it was the social constructionist discussion, prompted by the issue of homosexuality, that gave her the incentive to speak out. Through her example, all students were challenged to examine the power of socially constructed labels to determine their lives. Indeed, gay and lesbian youth themselves, for all of the comforts to be found in the safe harbor of a gay identity, may also be trapped to some degree by the limits of its current definition (Sears, 1990).

STAFF TRAINING

Any curricular reform is dependent to some degree on staff development. From the standpoints both of methodology and content, the inclusion of homosexuality is particularly so. Preparing teachers just to broach the subject of homosexuality with their students is the first task. Teachers must work out their own feelings on the issue and must then be trained to handle the discomfort of some students as well as the inevitable "are you one of them" question. We assume that teachers eventually can learn to deal with this issue as they have learned to handle other controversial issues in the classroom. Still, a comfortable willingness on the part of teachers to include homosexuality in their curricula is not the least consideration.

Unlike many other subjects, the content of this area of study is markedly absent from teacher preparation syllabi. A small number of colleges presently offer gay studies courses; a handful may integrate some gay material into broader courses. One has little assurance that incoming secondary school faculty have taken any of these. One can be certain that the vast majority of veteran faculty have had no formal training in gay studies, although they may have read something on their own. Most faculty are dependent on the same sources that inform the general public, and such a superficial acquaintance with the subject is hardly reassuring.

But neither is teacher ignorance about homosexuality surprising. In the 1970s—when curricular diversity required the addition of African-American, Asian-American, or Hispanic-American materials—how many teachers or curriculum specialists were prepared for that task? Indeed, most professionals at that time required some compensatory education. Today, teachers may have brought themselves up to speed on certain facets of multiculturalism; and universities are doing far more than they were twenty-five years ago to prepare beginning teachers for diversity. Nevertheless, as far as sexuality is concerned, the gap between the need and the preparation is still great.

A serious effort to include gay and lesbian curricula in high schools must entail comprehensive staff development. It must include both a general program in "gay sensitivity" and a specific program for imparting substantive information about homosexuality and gay history and culture. Good intentions are not enough. These two programs are the responsibility of the secondary schools themselves and of the teacher training institutions.

If school personnel attempt to bring about change without proper training, there is a great risk of failure. Even the least homophobic teacher may be incapable of answering accurately the most basic questions about homosexuality. It is arguably better not to bring up the subject at all than to repeat even well-intentioned stereotypes or disproven theories. Granted, teachers do not have to be omniscient; on the other hand, sexuality, like race, is one area in which a modicum of ignorance can cause great harm. Similarly, a reluctant or unhappy teacher can be worse than no teacher at all. It would be a mistake at first to require all teachers to teach this subject, especially without proper training. Students are very good at detecting insincerity, and we do not want the message to be "I'm being forced to deal with this subject even though I am uncomfortable with it and don't approve of homosexuality."

All teachers, however, should be required to interrupt expressions of homophobia, if only as a violation of school rules. Even this minimal intervention requires some training, but if a teacher with such training is still uncomfortable with curriculum inclusion it would be better to start with those who are willing. This should not be a top-down reform with mandated curricular change. It is preferable to inspire the changes with encouragement at the building level and the grass-roots. Later, when a critical mass of support has been established among the faculty, further persuasion may be attempted. Even a partial transformation of the personnel and curriculum should have a significant impact.

AGE APPROPRIATENESS

Lastly, it is crucial that the curriculum be age-appropriate. One may scratch one's head over the arbitrariness of grade levels, but there should be no disagreement over gauging the content of the sexuality lesson to the sexual maturity of the student. *Heather Has Two Mommies* (Newman, 1989) was written for the children of lesbians, not for a general children's audience. The book includes an explanation of alternative insemination and is not suitable for all young children. In fact, it was recommended as a teachers' resource in the Children of the Rainbow Curriculum, and was not required for students.

That is not to say that there cannot be materials about gay parents that would be good for all young children. Such a book would describe gay family relationships in terms that a child would understand. It might even, despite the outcries over *Daddy's Roommate* (Willhoite, 1990), include an illustration of two same-gender parents in a bed. The child would be expected to interpret the bedroom scene in the same way he understands the "heterosexual bedroom" as a place where mommy and daddy, daddy and girlfriend, or mommy and boyfriend sleep. As the student's sophistication about sexuality develops at home, in the community, and at school, the gay and lesbian curriculum should keep pace.

THE CHALLENGE

Teachers may be encouraged and supported in antihomophobia work by the passage of legislation protecting gay/lesbian/bisexual youth from harassment and discrimination in schools. Teachers often need some form of official dictum to support them in a sensitive enterprise; they want to have a defense against attack from political foes or anxious parents. Thus far, however, except in Massachusetts, antiharassment law applicable to minors has not covered harassment based on sexual orientation. Moreover, "gay rights" laws do not apply to minors.

Even where policies protecting gay youth exist, they cannot be construed easily as a call for curriculum. As we have seen in Massachusetts, protecting gay youth from assault or suicide and offering them counseling are seen as issues that are separate from presenting gay subject matter. The first three are defended as care-giving, an approved function of schools in the last thirty years; the last is condemned as proselytizing, teaching kids to be gay. One opponent of the gay curriculum, the attorney for the New York school board that rejected the Rainbow, said in a radio debate with me ("Talk of the Nation," National Public Radio, December 22, 1992) that he approved of teaching about homosexuality in schools as long as it was presented alongside drug addiction, alcoholism, and other evils.

It will take great courage for schools to begin including gay and lesbian materials in their curricula. Such innovation may be supported in the end by two powerful arguments. First, we must hold to the fact that learning about gay life does not cause young people to become gay, though it might encourage those who are struggling with their homosexual desires to feel better about their gay identities. This coming to happier terms with one's sexuality will benefit the entire community, for we know of the misery and harm that repression and hiding can bring to both the gay person and his or her loved ones. Second, we must maintain our professional integrity as teachers in our respective disciplines. We will not advance learning, nor will we model honesty, if we persist in ignoring certain facts of history, science, or artistic representation simply because some faction or other may object to them. That brand of political correctness, exercised by the majority, is as much a threat to the ideal of education as is the more often decried "tyranny of the left."

If anyone is recruited in this campaign to cast off one nature and assume another, let it be the bigot, who learns to accept this difference of sexual expression. As proof of that possibility, I offer an excerpt from an examination written by a student at Cambridge Rindge & Latin School, in Cambridge, Massachusetts, in 1992. This student had previously presented an oral class report on discrimination against gays. In it, he admitted to being from a neighborhood in which gay-bashing was common, and to having been a party to it. He wrote:

> One thing that changed me the most, and made me become a better person, and made me understand better, was the topic on homosexuals been discriminated against.
>
> People nowadays, alot of people that I know, don't take this serious. They think it's a big joke to laugh about but in my opinion it is something we all women and men should work on to make people understand the effects of life, so we all could live hopefully forevermore.
>
> I must admit myself. I used to hate even hearing the word homosexual. I used to think that they were not regular people, so they should all get eliminated from our society but now I have a different perspective. And because of the class and studying about this topic in particular changed a great deal. People should not be discriminated against no matter what....

REFERENCES

Boswell, J. (1992). "Categories, Experience and Sexuality." In *Forms of Desire: Sexual Orientation and the Social Constructionist Controversy*. Edward Stein, ed. New York: Routledge.

Cass, V.C. (1984). "Homosexual Identity Formation: Testing a Theoretical Model." *The Journal of Sex Research, 20.*

Coleman, E. (1988). *Integrated Identity for Gays and Lesbians: Psychotherapeutic Approaches for Emotional Well-Being.* New York: Harrington Park Press.

Donnerstein, E., and Linz, D., et al. (1991). "Estimating Community Standards: The Use of Social Science Evidence in an Obscenity Prosecution." *Public Opinion Quarterly, 55* (1).

Epstein, S. (1987). "Gay Politics, Ethnic Identity: The Limits of Social Constructionism." *Socialist Review,* May–August.

Ferreira, A., et al. (1993). "The Contributions of Lesbian and Gay Teachers." Panel at the *Third Annual Conference of the Gay and Lesbian School Teachers Network,* March, Milton Academy, Milton MA.

Foucault, M. (1978). *The History of Sexuality. Volume I: An Introduction.* Robert Hurley, trans. New York: Pantheon.

Gonsiorek, J.C. (1988). "Mental Health Issues of Gay and Lesbian Adolescents." *Journal of Adolescent Health Care, 9.*

Haignere, C.S. (1987). "Planned Parenthood Harris Poll Findings: Teens' Sexuality Knowledge and Beliefs." Paper presented at the *Annual Childrens' Defense Fund National Conference,* Washington, D.C.

Halperin, D. (1990). *One Hundred Years of Homosexuality.* New York: Routledge.

Harding, W. (1991). "Thoreau's Sexuality." *Journal of Homosexuality, 21* (3).

Herdt, Gilbert, ed. (1989). *Gay and Lesbian Youth.* New York: Harrington Park Press.

Herdt, G. and Boxer, A. (1993). *Children of Horizons: How Gay and Lesbian Teens are Leading a New Way Out of the Closet.* Boston: Beacon Press.

Herek, G. and Berill, K. (1992). *Hate Crimes: Confronting Violence Against Lesbians and Gay Men.* Newbury Park, CA: Sage.

Hetrick, E. S. and Martin, A.D. (1987). "Developmental Issues and their Resolution for Gay and Lesbian Adolescents." *Journal of Homosexuality, 14* (1/2).

———. (1988). "The Stigmatization of the Gay and Lesbian Adolescent." *Journal of Homosexuality, 15* (1/2).

Hunter, J. and Schaecher, R. (1987). "Stresses on Lesbian and Gay Adolescents in Schools." *Work in Education,* Spring.

Kirk, M. and Madsen, H. (1989). *After the Ball: How America Will Conquer its Fear and Hatred of Gays in the 90's.* New York: Doubleday.

Levin, J. and McDevitt, J. (1993). *Hate Crimes: The Rising Tide of Bigotry and Bloodshed*. New York: Plenum.

Licata, S. (1980–1981). "The Homosexual Rights Movement in the U.S.: A Traditionally Overlooked Area of American History." *Journal of Homosexuality, 6* (1–2).

McIntosh, M. (1968). "The Homosexual Role." *Social Problems, 16.*

McManus, M., et al. (1991). *Oregon's Sexual Minority Youth: An At-Risk Population. Lesbian, Gay and Bisexual Youth*. Portland, OR: Task Force on Sexual Minority Youth.

Newman, L. (1989). *Heather Has Two Mommies*. Boston: Alyson.

Remafedi, G. (1987). "Homosexual Youth: A Challenge to Contemporary Society." *Journal of the American Medical Association, 258* (2).

———. (1990). "Fundamental Issues in the Care of Homosexual Youth." *Medical Clinics of North America, 74* (5).

Rowse, A.L. (1977). *Homosexuals in History: A Study of Ambivalence in Society, Literature and the Arts*. New York: Dorset.

Savin-Williams, R.C. (1990). *Gay and Lesbian Youth: Expressions of Identity*. New York: Hemisphere Publishing.

Schoenhals, M. (1992). *Youth Survey Report*. Philadelphia, PA: Philadelphia Lesbian and Gay Task Force.

Sears, J.T. (1990). "On Homosexual Communities, Identities, and Culture: Journeys of the Spirit." In *Growing Up Gay in the South*. James T. Sears, ed. New York: Haworth.

Seattle Commission on Children and Youth (1988). *Report on Gay and Lesbian Youth in Seattle*. Seattle, WA: Author.

Sedgwick, Eve Kosofsky. (1990). "Pedagogy in the Context of an Antihomophobic Project." *South Atlantic Quarterly, 89* (1).

Stafford, J.M. (1988). "In Defense of Gay Lessons," *Journal of Moral Education, 17.*

Stein, E. (1992). "Introduction." In *Forms of Desire: Sexual Orientation and the Social Constructionist Controversy*. Edward Stein, ed. New York: Routledge, 1992.

Summers, C.J. (1990). *Gay Fictions: Wilde to Stonewall: Studies in a Male Homosexual Literary Tradition*. New York: Continuum.

The Governor's Commission on Gay and Lesbian Youth (February, 1993). *Making Schools Safe for Gay and Lesbian Youth: Education Report*. Boston: Commonwealth of Massachusetts.

Troiden, R.R. (1988). *Gay and Lesbian Identity: A Sociological Analysis*. New

York: General Hall, Inc.

U.S. Dept. of Health and Human Services (1989). *Report of the Secretary's Task Force on Youth Suicide.*

Weeks, J. (1985). *Sexuality and its Discontents: Meanings, Myths and Modern Sexuality.* New York: Routledge.

Weinberg, T.S. (1983). *Gay Men, Gay Selves.* New York: Irvington.

Willhoite, M. (1990). *Daddy's Roommate.* Boston: Alyson Publications.

Zelnik, M. and Shah, F.K. (1983) "First Intercourse among Young Americans." *Family Planning Perspectives, 15.*

5

Homophobia in Sport

Addressing the Needs of Lesbian and Gay High School Athletes

Pat Griffin

Concurrent with the increased attention to the needs of lesbian, gay, and bisexual students in schools, a number of articles have appeared in the mainstream press about lesbians and gay men in athletics (Cart, 1992; Denney, 1992; Lipsyte, 1991; *USA Today*, 1991). These articles document the hostility and fear surrounding lesbians and gay men in college and professional athletics, as well as the reluctance of people in athletics to acknowledge the presence of lesbian and gay coaches or athletes.

Professional development programs for coaches rarely include information about homophobia in athletics. Virtually no major athletic organizations address discrimination against lesbian, gay, or bisexual people in athletics. With the notable exception of tennis player Martina Navratilova, few lesbian, gay, or bisexual coaches or athletes at the high school, college, or professional levels have publicly identified themselves.

In the post-high school atmosphere, lesbian, gay, and bisexual coaches and athletes endure both subtle and blatant discrimination and harassment in silence (Griffin, 1992a). Some college coaches publicly state that they do not allow lesbian or gay athletes on their teams. Other coaches use antigay slurs to shame or punish athletes, and they allow team members to use antigay slurs to bait opponents. Some coaches employ negative recruiting tactics to encourage parents and prospective athletes to avoid rival schools because of purported lesbian reputations. Lesbian and gay athletes are ostracized by teammates and coaches.

Little of this media attention to homosexuality or homophobia in sport, however, has focused on high school athletics. This norm of intense secrecy about and even hostility toward homosexuality in athletics makes high-school-based sports programs a particular challenge when attempting to make schools safe for lesbian and gay young people. It is reasonable to assume that some high school athletes are lesbian, gay, or bisexual. How are their lives affected by the homophobia evidenced in college and professional sports? More importantly, how are their lives affected by the silence about lesbian and gay people in high school athletics?

The purpose of this article is to describe some unique aspects of heterosexism and homophobia as they affect lesbian and gay athletes on high school sports teams: (a) What accounts for the intense homophobia in athletics? (b) How does homophobia affect gay male and lesbian athletes? (c) What can high schools do to address homophobia in athletics?

WHAT ACCOUNTS FOR THE INTENSE HOMOPHOBIA IN ATHLETICS?

Athletics occupies a special place for men in the United States (Bryson, 1987; Whitson, 1990). Male athletes are idolized, and athletic ritual and performance command attention and reverence. Young boys learn that keen interest, if not aptitude, in athletics is an essential part of gaining acceptance among peers. The role that athletics plays in the lives of young men can be at least partially understood by examining—from a feminist perspective—the social functions of athletics in the United States (Messner and Sabo, 1990).

Sport for men in the United States serves five functions in maintaining traditional gender roles and power inequities between men and women: a) defining and reinforcing traditional conceptions of masculinity, b) providing a context for acceptable and safe male bonding and intimacy, c) establishing status among other males, d) reinforcing male privilege and perceptions of female inferiority, and e) reifying heterosexuality.

Defining and Reinforcing Traditional Conceptions of Masculinity

Sport can be conceptualized as a training ground where young boys learn masculinity skills (Messner and Sabo, 1990). Competitive sports are based on defining hierarchies of performance and skill in public arenas. Team sports such as football, basketball, ice hockey, and baseball are popular in large measure because of their reliance on physical size, strength, and power. Mental toughness, competitiveness, and a will to dominate are valued as important qualities for athletes and coaches. All of these qualities are central to a traditional sense of masculinity and, far from being innate, they must be carefully taught and reinforced. Athletics provides an arena for this learning process.

Conversely, behaviors that are not consistent with traditional masculinity are punished. In sport, boys learn to devalue actions that are perceived to reflect weakness, such as crying or acknowledging injury. Young athletes learn to suppress those emotions that reflect softness, such as compassion, tenderness, or fear.

Providing a Context for Acceptable and Safe Male Bonding and Intimacy

Athletics provides one of the few contexts, other than the family, in which affection between males and the physical expression of emotional closeness is publicly acceptable. Being part of an athletic team invites emotional intimacy among teammates. Athletes spend an enormous amount of time together practicing, playing games, traveling to games, and engaging in social activities. The shared intensity of testing personal physical limits and the emotional highs and lows of competition develop close emotional bonds among teammates. Athletes can hug each other after winning the big game—and even cry after losing—without fear of ridicule, censure, or suspicion.

In addition to the emotional intimacy that is inherent in the athletic experience, there is also a high level of physical intimacy. The expression and admiration of physicality is central to athletics. Many sports require physical contact among men; football, wrestling, ice hockey, and basketball are examples. Moreover, all athletic teams spend time together in locker rooms, showers, and whirlpools, where athletes share the physical closeness inherent in these settings.

The emotional and physical intimacy of participating in an activity that is inextricably associated with traditional masculinity provides an opportunity for men and boys to develop a sense of solidarity around their identities. Because athletics is integral to traditional conceptions of masculinity, the expression of emotional and physical intimacy among men in this context is perceived to be acceptable.

Establishing Status among Other Males

Athletics is the primary arena in which young men can achieve status among their adolescent peers. Because they are too young to achieve status through work or economic accumulation, athletics is the most accessible means of establishing status and, as a result, it takes on special importance. Numerous studies of high school culture report that male "jocks" are perceived to be in a high-status group among school peers, and that boys who are not athletes do not enjoy the popularity or attention that is accorded to boys who are (Palonsky, 1975; Varenne, 1982). Even among preadolescent males, participation in athletics is an important part of developing a masculine identity and in establishing status among peers (Fine, 1987).

Reinforcing Male Privilege and Female Inferiority

In American culture, athletics has always been a male domain. Though progress has been achieved over the last twenty years, women's athletics and women's athletic performance are still marginalized and trivialized (Bennett, Whitaker, Woolley, and Sablove, 1987). Until the last twenty-five years, most women did not have access to school athletics. Even now, despite Title IX, a federal law requiring gender equity in education, women have not achieved equity in athletics. Experiencing the body as powerful and skillful is an important part of feeling empowered. Our society deems it to be essential for boys, but not for girls.

Athletics is one of the primary ways in which boys learn to differentiate themselves from girls and to distance themselves from qualities in themselves that they perceive to be feminine and, therefore, inferior. In fact, comparing a male's athletic performance to that of a female is considered an insult. Losing to a female in sport provokes shame and invites teasing or ridicule from other men. Studies of locker-room talk among men describe consistent patterns of antiwomen and antigay interactions (Curry, 1991). Teammates participating in gang rape and gay-bashing or developing a scoring system to rank sexual conquests are more extreme and disturbing examples of male athletes' bonding around their sense of superiority to and rejection of what they consider to be feminine.

Reifying Heterosexuality

Many young men and women see male, team, sport athletes as the embodiment of the traditional masculine image. Being heterosexual is an assumed part of this image. A gay, masculine, male athlete is a contradiction for most people, and runs counter to the stereotype of the effeminate, silly faggot (Pronger, 1990). For if gay men can be athletes, and can display all of the qualities of masculinity that are valued in athletics, how can other men confidently differentiate themselves from gays?

Studies show that men have higher levels of homophobia than do women (Herek, 1984). In fact, an integral part of the masculinity training that boys receive in athletics is the belief that to be gay is contemptible. Just as being called a woman or being compared to a woman is an insult to most male athletes, being called a "faggot" is a comparable epithet that is also considered highly insulting to one's sense of masculinity.

Maintaining the twin myths that all male athletes are heterosexual, and that sexual attraction among male athletes does not exist, allows men to enjoy the physical and emotional intimacy of the athletic experience without confronting the complexity of emotional and physical ties that men can feel towards each other. These contradictions produce the homophobic atmosphere found on many men's athletic teams. Displaying contempt for gays—through antigay name-calling, jokes, or violence—reassures an athlete and his teammates about their masculinity and heterosexuality in an intimate, all-male context.

In summary, athletics serves several important social functions in maintaining traditional gender roles and power imbalances between men and women. The interconnections between homophobia and sexism (Pharr, 1988) develop a sense of entitlement, superiority, and solidarity in male athletes. Fear of being perceived as gay is a powerful social control in athletics. It keeps men safely within the bounds of traditionally masculine and heterosexual attitudes and behavior in an emotionally and physically intimate setting.

The Threat of Female Athletics

Given the functions of athletics for men in the United States, the presence of women in athletics poses a challenge to the traditional gender order. If athletics is a place where boys learn how to be masculine, develop a sense of superiority to women, and bond with other men, acknowledging that women can participate in athletics with comparable enthusiasm, intensity, and skill threatens the special status of athletics for men. If women, as well as gay men, can be intensely competitive, tough-minded, and physically strong and competent, then our traditional conceptions of masculinity and femininity must be reevaluated. If women discover their own physical prowess, develop a sense of empowerment, and bond with other women in the athletic arena, then the "naturalness" of the traditional gender order must be reassessed (Bryson, 1987).

In order to preserve the special status of athletics for men, women must be discouraged from participation, and, when they do participate, their performance must be stigmatized, trivialized, and marginalized. In the early twentieth century, women were warned about the dire physiological consequences of rigorous athletic activity (Lenskyj, 1986). More recently, women have been discouraged from participation in athletics by institutional barriers such as lack of programs and resources, minimal media coverage of female athletic events, and an assumption of the inferiority of female performance.

The most potent strategy for discouraging female participation in athletics has always been raising questions about the "femininity" of female athletes. Perhaps the most threatening strategy has been to assume that women athletes are lesbians. In the athletic context, the lesbian label is used to discourage women from participation (Griffin, 1992a). Because the lesbian label carries such a heavy negative stigma, most girls and women learn to fear being associated with it. The association of lesbians with athletics is enough to discourage many women from considering participation in athletics. Other women who do choose to participate respond defensively to this label, and they go to great lengths in order to display traditional heterosexual markers through clothing, hairstyles, and mannerisms. As long as lesbians can be stigmatized as immoral, sick, or unnatural, this label will function to control women's athletic participation. As long as women's athletic participation can be controlled, the role of athletics in defining masculinity and in sustaining the traditional gender order is maintained.

Understanding the social functions of athletics in maintaining unequal power relationships between men and women in a sexist society provides a context for describing the experiences of young lesbian and gay athletes. Many lesbian and gay high school athletes experience the isolation and self-hatred that their nonathletic peers do. There are, however, some gay-athlete-specific experiences that are connected to the role that athletics plays in defining and reinforcing sexist gender traditions in our culture.

HOW DOES HOMOPHOBIA AFFECT YOUNG GAY MALE AND LESBIAN ATHLETES?

One of the differences in the athletic experiences of women and men is that men are participating in an activity that enhances both their masculine and heterosexual images. Women, on the other hand, are participating in an activity that often detracts from the perception that they are feminine and enhances the perception that they are lesbian.

This difference can have profound effects on the experience of high school lesbian and gay athletes. Closeted high school gay male athletes are less likely to be identified because their athletic interests and talents run so contrary to popular images of gay men and are so consistent with traditional conceptions of heterosexual masculinity. In effect their identity as an athlete protects them from suspicions about their sexual orientation. This protection, however, carries the cost of extreme isolation and secrecy. The overt hostility toward gays that is displayed in casual locker-room talk and the accepted use of antigay slurs by coaches and athletes make a gay athlete's acceptance contingent on his ability to convincingly pass as a heterosexual. He must constantly monitor how he is being perceived by teammates and coaches in order to avoid any suspicion that he is gay. He must also silently endure the expressions of contempt and hostility toward gays uttered by his teammates and even by his coaches.

In contrast, lesbian high school athletes are participating in an activity that already casts suspicion on their femininity and heterosexuality. Instead of allaying suspicion, their athletic talents and interests—consistent with popular images of lesbians—invite speculation about their sexual identities. Closeted lesbian athletes (as well as their heterosexual teammates) sometimes feel the need for protective camouflage—for example, a conspicuous boyfriend and feminine dress. Unlike her male athlete peers, a female athlete is often perceived to be "guilty" (of being lesbian) until proven "innocent" (heterosexual). She is called upon to actively "prove" her heterosexuality again and again. A male athlete is assumed to be heterosexual unless something happens to create suspicion among his teammates and coaches. Both situations are stressful for lesbian and gay athletes, particularly since they are young people who are struggling to claim and affirm their sexual orientation in a team atmosphere that is at best silently, and at worst openly hostile toward lesbian and gay people.

Because all women athletes must confront the popular association of lesbians with athletics, there is often a conspiracy of silence surrounding this topic. Most lesbian athletes and coaches participate in this silence. Even when some athletes are privately identified and accepted as lesbians, they are expected to maintain a public silence so that the lesbian stereotype does not tarnish the rest of the team. In this silence, it is difficult for young lesbians to develop a realistic and positive sense of self or to develop healthy relationship skills.

In addition, high school-aged women athletes who are planning to continue their athletic careers in college are often warned by coaches or parents about programs with lesbian athletes or coaches. The assumption is that participating on teams with lesbian teammates or coaches would be dangerous. For a young lesbian struggling in isolation to learn to accept who she is, the effects of hearing so many negative messages about lesbians in athletics from peers, family, and coaches can have devastating consequences on self-esteem. It can also reinforce the belief that deception and secrecy are the only options.

Moreover, lesbian and gay coaches are also under a great deal of pressure to maintain secrecy about their identities. They fear losing their jobs, being subjected to public attack, or losing credibility among colleagues or athletes and their parents (Griffin, 1992a, and 1992b; Woods, 1992). As a result, lesbian and gay coaches model silence and denial as the only viable survival strategies. Young lesbian and gay athletes learn that secrecy is the only option if they are interested in pursuing a career in athletics. The invisibility of lesbian and gay high school coaches, combined with the hostility toward gays expressed by some heterosexual coaches, intensifies the isolation that young lesbian and gay athletes experience. Faced with invisibility or hostility from coaches, young lesbian and gay athletes lose access to an important adult in their lives, one who could have helped them sort out their fears and misconceptions about being lesbian or gay.

Though isolation is an overwhelming problem among many lesbian and gay high school athletes, some are able to identify a circle of lesbian or gay teammates who provide mutual emotional and social support. Lesbians may be more successful than gay men in establishing an underground support network of friends in athletics. The overt hostility that is expressed toward gayness in men's athletics is so intense that developing a similar network of support is more difficult. Young lesbians, who are able to find each other in the silence, provide mutual support where adults, in the roles of teacher, coach, and parent, have not.

The destructive coping strategies that are used by lesbian and gay high school athletes are similar to those used by their nonathletic peers. Alcohol and drugs provide ways to escape the sense of isolation and self-hatred. Closeted lesbian and gay athletes sometimes express rabidly homophobic feelings as they struggle to distance themselves from an identity that they fear and hate. Their athletic and academic performance can suffer. They can withdraw from teammates, and lose interest in or even quit teams. Some young lesbian and gay athletes engage in heterosexual dating and sex as a way of denying their feelings to themselves and of hiding their identity from others. Other young lesbian and gay athletes focus their attention on high achievement in athletics or academics as a way to compensate for, and deflect attention from, their homosexuality. How could others guess that the star basketball player, the class valedictorian, or the class president was lesbian or gay?

Some of these lesbian and gay athletes, however, cannot cope with the negative messages they hear about who they are. They cannot conceive of a future in which they will find happiness. These athletes become part of the tragic suicide statistics that illustrate how profoundly schools, teachers, and coaches have failed this silent young minority.

WHAT CAN HIGH SCHOOLS DO TO ADDRESS HOMOPHOBIA IN ATHLETICS?

As a school begins to address the needs of lesbian, gay, and bisexual students, each program within the school must be held accountable to the same standards of sensitivity and fairness. There are several steps that schools can take to address homophobia in athletics, and to address the needs of lesbian, gay, and bisexual athletes. Administrators can:

- Establish a nondiscrimination policy—that includes sexual orientation—for all teams. Make sure that all coaches, parents, and athletes understand what actions are not acceptable and what procedures are to be followed when the policy is violated.
- Establish an antiharassment policy—that includes sexual orientation—for all teams. Make sure that all coaches, parents, and athletes understand what actions are not acceptable, and what procedures are to be followed when the policy is violated.

- Establish nondiscrimination and antiharassment policies in the local, regional, and state athletic organizations that govern high school athletic programs.
- Provide coaches with antihomophobia education and programs that are focused on addressing the needs of lesbian, gay, and bisexual athletes.
- Develop strategies for addressing homophobia among the parents of athletes.
- Work to protect lesbian and gay teachers and coaches from employment discrimination—including that based solely on their sexual orientation.

Coaches can:

- Attend workshops or read about homophobia in athletics, as well as the needs of lesbian and gay young people.
- Stop assuming that all athletes are heterosexual. Some probably are lesbian, gay, or bisexual. Others may be questioning who they are.
- Monitor their own attitudes and actions. Stop behaviors that either encourage a hostile atmosphere for lesbian or gay athletes or condone antigay actions by any athletes.
- Discuss homophobia with their athletes, and address antigay actions and attitudes among athletes.
- Be available and prepared to talk with athletes who are either questioning their sexual orientation or expressing homophobic beliefs.
- Identify school and community resources for athletes and parents who need them (lesbian, gay, and bisexual student support or social groups; lesbian and gay-sensitive counselors; groups for parents with lesbian or gay children; religious organizations that affirm lesbian, gay, and bisexual people).
- Request that coaches' associations provide programs about homophobia in athletics and how to meet the needs of lesbian, gay, and bisexual athletes.
- (For heterosexual coaches.) Support your lesbian and gay coaching colleagues by speaking out against antigay actions and policies.
- (For lesbian, gay, bisexual coaches.) Be as open as you safely can about who you are. *All* young people need to know lesbian, gay, and bisexual adults who are leading satisfying and productive lives.

Athletes can:

- Stop using antigay slurs or making antigay comments about specific people or about gay and lesbian people in general.

- Be a friend to teammates who choose to identify themselves as lesbian or gay.
- Realize that when someone tries to intimidate others by using antigay slurs or by hinting that someone else is gay or lesbian as a joke or put-down, they are expressing fear and prejudice.
- (For athletes who think they might be lesbian or gay.) Talk to a coach, teacher, family member, or counselor whom you can trust, and whom you have reason to believe can be open and accepting of lesbian and gay people.
- Call the national lesbian and gay youth toll-free hot-line (1-800-347-TEEN) or call local lesbian and gay organizations for information about support groups for young lesbians, gays, and bisexuals that are near where you live.

Parents can:

- Challenge their own prejudices about lesbian, gay, and bisexual people, and monitor how they condone antigay prejudice in their children.
- Support school efforts to teach all athletes to respect each other and to discourage antigay attitudes and actions.
- Contact a local chapter of P-FLAG (Parents, Friends, and Families of Lesbians and Gays) for information and support.
- Challenge coaches who use antigay prejudice to motivate athletes to perform better.
- Refrain from attempting to find out about the sexual orientation of coaches in order to avoid coaches who are lesbian or gay.
- Understand that a coach's sexual orientation does not determine her or his ability to be an effective and respected professional.
- Encourage young people to talk about their beliefs about homosexuality, and invite them to learn to respect different sexual orientations, rather than to fear or hate people who are lesbian, gay, or bisexual.

Making schools safe for lesbian, gay, and bisexual young people requires that every school program evaluate its policies and practices. High school athletic administrators and coaches must accept the responsibility that they have for making the locker room and gymnasium safe for lesbian and gay athletes. They must also accept responsibility for addressing the homophobia—in themselves and in heterosexual athletes—that creates a threatening and isolating environment for lesbian and gay people in athletics. Understanding the relationship between sexism, homophobia, and heterosexism and the role that athletics plays in their maintenance can help all school personnel understand both the depth of resistance to and the absolute necessity for change. For it is a commitment to change that is essential if we are to make high school athletics a place where students and coaches of all sexual orientations can participate fully.

REFERENCES

Bennett, R., Whitaker, G., Woolley, N., and Sablove, A. (1987). "Changing the Rules of the Game: Reflections Toward a Feminist Analysis of Sport." *Women's Studies International Forum. 10* (4), pp. 369–380.

Bryson, Lois (1987). "Sport and the Maintenance of Masculine Hegemony." *Women's Studies International Forum. 10* (4), pp. 349–360.

Cart, J. (1992). "Lesbian Issue Stirs Discussion." *Los Angeles Times*, April 6, pp. C1, C12.

Curry, T. (1991). "Fraternal Bonding in the Locker Room: A Profeminist Analysis of Talk about Competition and Women." *Sociology of Sport Journal. 8* (2), pp. 119–135.

Denney, M. (1992). "Homophobia in Sports." *Indianapolis News-Sentinel*, July 15, pp. S1, S5.

Fine, G. (1987). *With the Boys: Little League Baseball and Preadolescent Culture.* Chicago: University of Chicago Press.

Griffin, P. (1992a). "Changing the Game: Homophobia, Sexism, and Lesbians in Sport." *Quest, 44*, pp. 251–265.

———. (1992b). "From Hiding Out to Coming Out: Empowering Lesbian and Gay Educators." In *Coming Out of the Classroom Closet: Gay and Lesbian Students, Teachers, and Curricula.* K. Harbeck, ed. New York: Haworth Press.

Herek, G. (1984). "Beyond Homophobia: A Social Psychological Perspective on Attitudes Towards Lesbians and Gay Men." In *Bashers, baiters, and bigots: Homophobia in American society.* J. DeCecco, ed. New York: Haworth Press.

Lipsyte, R. (1991). "Gay Bias Moves off the Sidelines." *New York Times*, May 24.

Lenskyj, H. (1986). *Out of Bounds: Women, Sport, and Sexuality.* Toronto: Women's Press.

Messner, M. and Sabo, D. (1990). *Sport, Men, and the Gender Order: Critical Feminist Perspectives.* Champaign, IL: Human Kinetics.

Palonsky, S. (1975). "Hempies and Squeaks, Truckers and Cruisers: A Participant Observation Study in a City High School." *Educational Administration Quarterly,11* (2), pp 86–103.

Pharr, S. (1988). *Homophobia: A Weapon of Sexism.* Inverness, CA: Chardon Press.

Pronger, B. (1990). "Gay Jocks: A Phenomenology of Gay Men in Athletics." In *Sport, Men and the Gender Order.* M. Messner and D. Sabo, eds. Champaign, IL: Human Kinetics.

USA Today, (1991). "Sportsview: Homophobia in Sports." September 18, p. 10C.

Varenne, H. (1982). "Jocks and Freaks: The Symbolic Structure of the Expression of Social Interaction among American Senior High School Students." In *Doing the Ethnography of Schooling.* G. Spindler, ed. New York: Holt Rinehart, and Winston.

Whitson, D. (1990). "Sport in the Social Construction of Masculinity." In *Sport, Men and the Gender Order.* M. Messner and D. Sabo, eds. Champaign, IL: Human Kinetics.

Woods, S. (1992). "Describing the Experiences of Lesbian Physical Educators: A Phenomenological Study." In *Research in Physical Education and Sport.* A. Sparkes, ed. London: Falmer.

6

Gay Teens in Literature

Jim Brogan

Gay teens in literature? A quick search of one's memory produces only a few examples. But after rummaging about a bit—with the help of students and colleagues—one finds that material abounds. Only then do we notice that we have been making arbitrary distinctions in this search, culling out fiction which spotlights those aged eighteen or under from a vast body of material that highlights young men and women, who are usually a bit older than eighteen, the "consenting adults" who leave their home towns and families for either college or the big city. While we must make this distinction for the purposes of this article, it comes as a bit of a surprise to me that writers have not. Until this epoch in American life when we have finally faced up to something like the full extent of child abuse in this country, writers have integrated teens quite naturally and unselfconsciously into the total fabric of youthful literary experience. Indeed, in the three decades *preceding* Stonewall, a much higher percentage of the literature about gays and lesbians included teens as part of their subject matter than did publications which came afterwards.

Surely, though, one wants to counter, post-Stonewall literature has been more positive about gay and lesbian themes, has it not? A little, but not to any great extent, one must answer. Even after checking out all the literary sources mentioned in this article, the well-informed high school teacher will still be hard-pressed to be able to recommend, without reservations, very many of these short stories or novels. Yes, we have had a few wily writers who have succeeded in presenting us with happy, victorious, gay protagonists, but just a few. Even more disconcerting is our having to face the inevitable conclusion that Young Adult novels with gay themes have done more than their fair share over the last twenty-five years to keep teen homosexuality a dark and dirty secret.

The whole YA gay/lesbian market reminds me of a 1953 volume called *Twenty-one Variations on a Theme*, collected by Donald Webster Cory, in which the theme, homosexuality, was never mentioned once throughout the entire volume. And yet I have returned to that volume, and have emerged delighted with the literary quality of the stories I discovered there about gay teens, by such fine writers as Henry James, Paul Bowles, Charles Jackson, and Denton Welch. Our aesthetic pleasure in these stories defines the conflict for the teacher interested in gay studies—fine writing, excellent characterizations, remarkably likable archetypal adolescents, but—for the most part—very negative messages about the prospects of being homosexual in Western culture.

We must rely on classical scholars to tell us if there were such creatures as gay and lesbian teens in ancient civilizations. The poetry of Greeks such as Strato and Malaeger assures us that older men were attracted to beardless youths. Modern historical novels do their best to recall specific instances. In Mary Renault's *The Persian Boy* (1972), Bagoas, Alexander the Great's youthful lover, narrates the action. Marguerite Yourcenar's *Memoirs of Hadrian* provides us with the Roman emperor's perspective on the beautiful Bithynian youth, Antinous. Joel Schmidt provides a less weighty, more specific perspective on the same relationship, also from the older man's point of view, in *Hadrian* (1984).

Let us begin our survey of the modern era with several masters of fiction— Henry James, D.H. Lawrence, E.M. Forster, and André Gide. Henry James's

"The Pupil" (1891) offers a fitting prelude to our study by presenting us a nonsexual affectionate relationship between Pemberton, a Yale graduate, who tutors Morgan Moreen, a neglected child with unscrupulous parents who flee their debtors by moving from one European city to another. This story, which was published just a few years before Oscar Wilde's trial, functions roughly in the same way as Whitman's poetry. Homosexual love is there, but only if one wants to see it. Unfortunately, like so many stories of such youth which were to come later, Morgan dies—in this instance of a weak heart, when he panics at the likelihood that his tutor will choose to move away from his disreputable parents.

Most Victorians did not, of course, see any such homosexual undertones, and so the story never became as notorious as D.H. Lawrence's chapter, "Shame," from his novel, *The Rainbow* (1915), which was prosecuted by the Public Morality Council. In that chapter, Lawrence's heroine, Ursula, still a schoolgirl, falls in love with her teacher, Winifred Unger. Their amorous episode in a swimming pool receives a beautiful, sensitive treatment from Lawrence, who was himself highly ambivalent to homosexuality throughout his entire life. Their happiness quickly wanes when Ursula, besieged by guilt and shame, rejects her older lover, whom Lawrence then relegates to a loveless marriage with Ursula's gay uncle.

Meanwhile E.M. Forster had already been writing stories about adolescents who might well be gay or bisexual. For example, in "The Story of a Panic" (1902), the English boy, Eustace—having become uncontrollably exuberant about nature after his vision of Pan—must submit to a potentially deadly confinement in his room *without* a view, an imprisonment perpetrated by his repressed English family. At the story's conclusion, a young Italian man, Gennaro who may have had a physical relationship with Eustace, releases the youth only to fall, sacrificially perhaps, to his own death. In his posthumous collection of stories, *The Life to Come*, Forster includes a trio of stories with such young men. In "Ansell" (1903), a priggish young Greek scholar is awakened to the experience of real life by a young gamekeeper, Ansell, with whom he very well may have had a youthful sexual relationship. (Ansell is named for and based on an actual boy whom Forster knew and played with as a child. He also used the name for an appealing young man in his youthful novel published in 1907, *The Longest Journey*.) *The Life To Come* also includes two later stories with gay adolescents, "The Classical Annex" (1930), and Forster's only historical fiction, "The Torque" (1958), set in early Christian Italy.

At about the same time, Virginia Woolf published "Moments of Being: 'Slater's Pins have No Points'" (1926). As with James's story, we may read as much homosexuality into the situation as we wish, although nothing is explicit. Young tomboy Fanny Wilmot comes to some inevitable conclusions about the sexuality of her music teacher, Julia Craye. The story ends with Miss Craye kissing Fanny while she laughs "queerly" and allows the young girl to pin a flower to her breast with "trembling fingers."

Three interesting works of fiction stand out during the decade of the twenties as groundbreaking novels which deal frankly with the issue of youthful homosexuality: André Gide's *The Counterfeiters* (1925), Claus Mann's *The Pious Dance: The Adventure Story of a Young Man* (1925), and Radclyffe Hall's *The Well of Loneliness* (1928). Gide's novel includes two young students with homosexual proclivities: the illegitimate, unscrupulous Bernard, and the thoughtful, reserved Olivier who, at one point, attempts suicide, only to be revived by his gay uncle, Edouard, a novelist who resembles Gide himself. A complex, highly original masterpiece, *The Counterfeiters* presents too many literary challenges for most adolescents, but it remains a boon to the mature reader, who may well find this work immensely rewarding. In *The Pious Dance*, Claus Mann, barely seventeen, arrives in Berlin in 1923 to explore the underground world of gay bars and sexual ambiguity during the Weimar Republic. Nor has time dulled the rich, sensual portrait of the adolescent, Stephen, one of the heroines of *The Well of Loneliness*, a fine novel with the usual tragic ending.

Perhaps one must beg the reader's patience for suggesting that literary quality may often be found in nonexplicit fiction. Forrest Reid, for example, a friend of Forster, describes the rich textures of the youth of a boy, Tom, who might well be gay, in his trilogy of novels, *Uncle Stephen* (1931), *The Retreat* (1936), and *Young Tom* (1944). Similarly, how many lesbians must see their own lonely adolescence in the young heroines of Carson McCullers's works, such as *The Heart is a Lonely Hunter* (1940) and *The Member of the Wedding* (1946)? And even after all these years, J.D. Salinger's *Catcher in the Rye* (1951) remains a superb example of adolescent sexual ambiguity. Nor can we eliminate homosexuality as a possible submerged theme in John Knowles' classic, *A Separate Peace* (1960).

The years immediately following World War II brought forth a quartet of short stories that were remarkable for their time. Paul Bowles's "Pages from Cold Point" (1949) presents the irrepressible Racky, the sixteen-year-old son of a widower, the narrator, who puts up with the boy's sexual adventures with the male native populace on the tropical island on which they've settled because the boy is able to use his youthful beauty in such a way as to disarm the older man from confronting him about his behavior. Racky parades his lithe, sensual body, full of animal energy and grace, about his father's bedroom and successfully forestalls any reprimands. In the end, however, the boy must leave Cold Point for his own safety, and he decides to set sail for Havana, accompanied by a handsome Cuban. Charles Jackson's "Palm Sunday" (1950) details the narrator's coming to terms with his being seduced by Ray Verne, a singer who is simultaneously just as notorious about town for his sexual activities with minors as he is renowned for his voice. At the end of the story, the now-married narrator and his brother both recall (to themselves) their seductions by Ray, and they decide (out loud) that those episodes now seem long ago and unimportant.

Denton Welch's "When I Was Thirteen" (1949) wins my vote for the best short story about gay youth. On a skiing trip to Switzerland with his much older brother, the young English narrator spends a blissful idyll with Archer, a young man who attends Oxford with his brother. Archer has the wonderful capacity of being able to treat the young boy as an equal. The narrator's spirits soar as he is initiated into the pleasures of male bonding through sharing a ski trek, tobacco, alcohol, and other treats. But the brother returns early and discovers that his younger sibling has not slept in his own bed. He jumps to conclusions (there has been mutual desire in the boy's friendship with Archer, but no sex), and in a frenzy of what most readers would guess to be both sexual envy and self-hating homophobia, he viciously beats the thirteen-year-old while screaming at him that he is a harlot and a bugger. Even so, one leaves this story feeling that Archer and the narrator have had their triumphant day in the sun, achieving a kind of egalitarian camaraderie which Walt Whitman would well understand.

Remarkably, for its time, Gore Vidal's story, "The Zenner Trophy" (1956) ends on an equally positive note. The principal of a prep school wishes to expel two students, Sawyer and Flynn, who were discovered having sex together. Sawyer has already fled the school, but Flynn remains behind, about to be awarded the Zenner trophy for sportsmanship, the school's highest honor. The resolution? Not tragic at all. Flynn informs one of the faculty, Beckman—who is gay himself, but very much in the closet—that he plans to pick up Sawyer at the local inn and proceed on with him to Boston. Because they both have high school diplomas, Flynn feels confident that both he and his friend can continue on to college life together. Finally, this remarkably self-confident lad suggests that he and Beckman might get together socially some time in Boston!

The decade of the fifties also gave us a trio of novels about gay adolescents, the most remarkable, in my opinion, being *Finistère* (1951) by Fritz Peters. He also wrote two autobiographical volumes recalling his boyhood and friendship with Gurdjieff. Young Matthew is a psychologically acute *wunderkind* who—after a schoolboy fling with his roommate André—establishes a remarkably mature relationship with Michel, one of his teachers. For example, he recognizes how Michel's self-destructiveness hurts their harmony, a self-destructiveness based on Michel's lack of self-worth, *not* society's taboo about homosexuality. He sees Michel's envy and jealousy of Matthew's other male friends as a sign of his insecurity, and he tells him that if he has urges to destroy their relationship, then he will probably do so. Just before the novel's tragic ending, Matthew admits to himself that the relationship cannot work because Michel is so emotionally damaged. That is where the book should end, and I would like to believe that is how Peters wanted it to end. Instead, Matthew commits suicide by drowning himself, after his mother tells him she would rather have him dead than homosexual. And, yes, since he tried to drown himself earlier in the narrative, inexplicably, just after Michel first laid eyes on him, I suppose we should regard him as flawed and suicidal. But I don't buy it. Matthew is too conscious, too much in love with life not to bounce back from both Michel's failure as a lover and his mother's moralistic judgment. Perhaps Peters changed the ending because of demands from the publisher—not the first time for such an occurrence.

The adolescents in two other novels published later in this decade, Iris Murdoch's *The Bell* (1958) and Yukio Mishima's *Confessions of a Mask* (1958) are much more obviously self-destructive. *The Bell* dramatizes the aftermath of an intimate relationship between the middle-aged Michael and his previous lover, the adolescent Nick. Years after their breakup, Michael fails to hold to his resolution to keep away from young men, and he slips by having an encounter with the adolescent Toby while residing in a spiritual commune where Nick also lives. Nick revenges himself on Michael by forcing Toby to confess the incident to the head of the commune. Then he kills himself. Iris Murdoch, however, does not leave it there. In a final talk with the abbess, Michael accepts the fact that he had failed Nick by ignoring his pleas for help. The abbess teaches him that all failures are ultimately failures of love, and that the way is always forward.

No such uplifting sentiment mitigates the self-hate of the narrator of Mishima's *Confessions of a Mask*. But the Japanese writer does give us a wonderful picture of the crush he had on Omi, a somewhat older, more physically developed classmate. Omi becomes his first love, his hero, his idol. With this overpowering crush for this vital young animal also comes the fatalistic realization that he can never be like Omi, and that he is doomed to stand on the sidelines to view such specimens of emerging manhood from afar.

Paul Goodman's "Martin" (1968) symbolizes the new freedom that gay literature enjoyed in the late sixties. A man desires to have a relationship with both a woman and her younger brother. At the end of the story, when the shocked woman warns her brother that the man is a pederast, that he makes love to boys, Martin utters a single word, "Gee." The following year, 1969, witnessed the publishing of the first Young Adult novel to deal with homosexuality, John Donovan's *I'll Get There. It'd Better Be Worth the Trip*. Although it represents a breakthough with respect to subject matter, Donovan's story also set some negative precedents for later YA novels which explored the same theme. First, homosexual behavior occurs offstage and out of sight. After all, such books contend, homosexual experimentation may only be part of a confused, lonely stage of adolescence. (Isabelle Holland's 1970 novel, *The Man Without a Face*, also follows this pattern by focusing on a single, troublesome, homosexual "incident.") Thus, the young protagonist almost always ends up "open-minded" about the future, in the sense that he might well become heterosexual as well as homosexual in his adult life.

A second, even more disturbing, aspect of the YA novels is that homophobic acts of violence, such as the attack on one of the male lovers in Sandra Scoppettone's *Trying Hard to Hear You* (1974), are portrayed graphically. In her *Happy Endings Are All Alike* (1978), one of the young lesbians is raped by a demented homophobe, a rape to which we are eyewitnesses. Furthermore, very few of the score or so of the YA novels with gay themes are actually narrated by the young man or woman who has the homosexual experiences. Finally, as we have already seen, the death rate among such youth is so extraordinarily high that these books, cumulatively, carry a most ominous message to the gay teen reader. For example, the token gay adolescent in Judy Blume's *Forever* (1975) attempts suicide. In Paul Covert's *Cages* (1971), one of the boyfriends swears eternal love and loyalty, but his promises are not enough to keep his lover from jumping off a bridge to his death because he cannot accept his homosexuality. In Aidan Chambers's *Dance on My Grave*

(1982), the charismatic Barry is killed in a motorcycle accident minutes after rejecting his lover, Hal, for being too possessive of his free spirit.

On the positive side, Deborah Hautzig's *Hey, Dollface* (1978) dramatizes a wonderfully intimate friendship between two potentially gay or bisexual high school girls. B.A. Ecker's *Independence Day* (1983) concludes with the gay protagonist's best friend accepting his friend's sexuality and pledging life-long friendship. In Nancy Garden's *Annie on My Mind* (1982), the two sophisticated high school girls actually have a sexual relationship which will survive their transition to college. And in my own *Casey: The Bi-Coastal Kid* (1986), Casey's girlfriend experiments with bisexuality and encourages him to do the same with men. At the novel's conclusion, Casey accepts his bisexuality and seems willing to help one of his gay friends come out. Too explicit for most high school libraries, *Casey* suggests—as do Hautzig's and Garden's novels—that teens are capable of sophisticated, loving relationships.

In the last decade or so, a gay press, Alyson, has published several upbeat gay YA books. Two examples are Frank Mosca's novel, *All-American Boys* (1983), and Aaron Fricke's autobiography, *Confessions of a Rock Lobster* (1981). Fricke's volume could be much more complex, but it is one of the few books that a high school teacher could recommend unequivocally to a student. Indeed one should continue to check Alyson's new entries in the genre.

But what about relationships between teens and older adults? One is struck by the fact that several novels published in the eighties which portray such attachments with some sympathy, probably could not be published today. These include Wallace Hamilton's *Kevin* (1980), Ruth Turk's *More Than Friends* (1980), and Margaret Sturgis's *Danny* (1984). (A surprising number of women writers has always been sympathetic to gay love, even man-boy relationships.) Paul Fussell's *Boys of Life* (1991), although not a YA book, represents the perspective of the nineties, in which the younger person is seen as a victim, even though he personally is willing to get involved sexually with the older man. In *Boys*, an American film director (who resembles in some ways both Warhol and Pasolini) recruits a handsome, bored youth from Kentucky to act in his films. The youth eagerly accepts his role both as lover and performer, only to become caught up in the director's debasing, malevolent grip.

When we escape the rather stultifying ground rules of the YA genre, we discover a relatively interesting group of novels in which the gay teen has played a major role over the last couple of decades. Has there ever been, for example, a more delightfully naughty heroine than the schoolgirl Molly Bolt in the first half of Rita Mae Brown's *Rubyfruit Jungle* (1973)? As a self-respecting, assertive young lesbian, Molly always has the perfect retort for any situation—Rita Mae's hindsight, I suspect—which she uses in the most creative possible fashion in this novel. Neither the prom queen nor the head cheerleader can resist Molly's charms, and she brags about her sexual conquests as shamelessly as any male.

Also deliciously naughty is Augustin Gomez-Arcos's *Carnivorous Lamb* (1975), which dramatizes the ongoing sexual romance of two brothers while also satirizing Franco's Spain and the Church. Written originally in French (the author now resides permanently in France), the novel bristles with the younger brother's love for his indulgent older brother. And how they sexually tease the visiting priests, their tutors, and confessors—all of whom are obvious closet cases! As for their indulging in a secret sexual act during the actual moment of the younger's confirmation rite, well I must say I find the whole novel immensely shocking. Yet, they do stay together—they actually participate in a marriage ceremony at the novel's conclusion, a ceremony officiated by Clara, their wise, loving, family servant, who is a much more effective parent than either their disillusioned, left-wing father, or their delightfully self-absorbed mother, who knows all and does nothing about it!

In many ways, Edmund White's *A Boy's Own Story* (1982) deserves to be applauded as the consummate portrait of the everyday life of the typically alienated, but intellectually alive, young gay male. This is fiction, but White has told us that this novel inaugurated a series of four novels based on his own life. Yes, the boy has a few sexual episodes. Yes, he hides his homosexuality for years, but he does come out to his parents while in high school, only to be sent to an emotionally unstable therapist. White, who is a novelist very conscious of his craft, uses the word "betrayal" eight times—it is a critical theme. The narrator does betray one of his teacher-lovers in the final episode of the novel. It is a particularly ugly scene, because we know that the adult Edmund White is acutely conscious of just how self-hating an act it is to betray one of his gay brothers. Still, the youth's need to strike out against adult authority is overwhelming. For example, he relishes identifying with the beautiful adolescent, Tadzio, while reading Mann's *Death in Venice* because, he explains, he wants that same power over older men for himself.

The protagonist of Jeanette Winterson's *Oranges Are Not the Only Fruit* (1987) also accepts her lesbianism, and enjoys having a girlfriend before moving on to college, despite her fanatic, fundamentalist family. Jimmy

Chesire's *Home Boy* (1989) details a likable kid's final term at Father
McFlaherty's Home for Boys in Ohio, circa 1962. There is lots of sex here,
some of it good adolescent fun, some of it abusive. Frederick, the narrator,
exudes masculine charm, and grows up a good deal during the course of his
adventures. Almost as much fun may be ingested from Will Aitken's *Terre
Haute* (1989). Jared McCavety, a precociously cultured teen, lands a job in
the local museum in Terre Haute. Then he gets involved with the new director of the museum: a real kid, a real situation, and no suicides. Michael
Grumley's *Life Drawing* (1991) sketches a beautiful picture of a modern-day
Huck and Jim escaping straight civilization by hooking up with a steamer
bound for New Orleans. The tenderness between white and black satisfies
deep literary needs for many of us. How wonderful to read about something
as sweet and beautiful as this, after so many years of vainly pursuing it in literature. As a final entry on this list of satisfying, if not great, contemporary
works about gay teens, Mike Seabrook's *Out of Bounds* (1992) caricatures
Fritz Peters's "fantasy" of the *Wunderkind*. Seventeen-year-old Stephen Hill,
cricket player *par excellence*, falls in love with teammate and schoolmaster,
Graham Curtis. Stephen is the perfect lover—sensually passionate and
fiercely loyal. They part temporarily, in order to avoid detection, and during that break Stephen stumbles into an affair with Richard, a clever, irre-
sistible classmate. Gifted, like Stephen, he has psychological maturity, so
much so that he understands and accepts Stephen's love for Graham, and he
willingly relinquishes him when the two original lovers flee to France to be
reunited. Not great literature, but one can do worse than to relish Seabrook's
delightfully circumlocutious, very British descriptions of this, that, and the
other thing—in other words, the pace is casual.

The most realistic, yet emotionally satisfying relationship between two
youths still in high school? My vote goes to Matthew Stadler's *Landscape:
Memory* (1990). Set in San Francisco during World War I, this well-crafted
novel dramatizes sixteen-year-old Max's passage to adulthood through his
diary entries. Max's friendship with Duncan, a schoolmate with a Persian
father, dates back to the 1906 earthquake, when they were dramatically
thrown together as kids who are separated, temporarily, from their parents.
Over the years their attraction deepens until, as seniors in high school, they
become lovers. Their initial love scenes work extremely well. Stadler chooses to emphasize their feelings as well as the electric touch between these two
handsome youths, sustaining an erotically charged atmosphere without having to use anatomical terms. After graduation, the young men decide to

attend the University of California at Berkeley together, but not before they spend an idyllic summer together in Bolinas, on the ocean north of San Francisco. The one disturbing note that a reader might pick up involves the increasing obsessiveness of Max's love. He refers in his diary to how he is blind and possessed each night with the desperate hunger of it all, how he just wants to cry out, "I need you. Love me." I mention this undercurrent because Duncan, an excellent swimmer, one day jumps into the ocean right in front of Max and, exhausted perhaps from their hike together, drowns.

As I read that section, all of those years of tragic endings for young gay and lesbian protagonists came back to me, and I put down the book angry at Stadler for killing off one of his lovers in a seemingly meaningless accident. For example, Duncan did have a macho side, which expressed interest in fighting in the war. If he had been killed in the war, at least his death would not have that random quality to it. Stadler, of course, can plot his novels in any way he sees fit. His story, "The Sex Offender," in the volume of short stories called *Men on Men 4* (1992), dramatizes the case of an unrepentant lover of boys who is undergoing a harrowing form of futuristic aversion therapy. That man's sense of loss toward his twelve-year-old friend reminds us of the devastated Max, whom we watch at the novel's conclusion on his long, gray, wintry train ride across the country on his way to Harvard, still very much disconsolate at the loss of Duncan. All in all, this is a fine novel—Stadler does not deserve to be the victim of my frustration. I will simply conclude by noting that I still would very much like to read a similarly well written novel about youthful gay lovers in which both survive happily. (By the way, readers interested in more stories about gay adolescents might cull the back issues of the more important gay literary periodicals—*Christopher Street*, *A Different Light Review*, *Lambda Rising News*, *Lambda Book Report*, and the *James White Review*. For example, I very much enjoyed L.R. Holben's story, "Wallace Among the Gods," about a surprising sexual relationship at a prep school, in the September, 1993 edition of *Christopher Street*.)

Despite my complaints about all of the not-so-covert negative messages in many of these fictional works, I concluded this period of reading and rereading with a sense of exhilaration. Collectively, these writers do a fine job of capturing not only the vitality and exuberance of youth, but its vulnerability as well. Whether graceful or awkward, all youth is beautiful, doubly so because few if any of us realize it at the time. We—and youthful readers— not only can fondly remember Racky in "Pages From Cold Point," Matthew from *Finistère*, Archer from "When I Was Thirteen," Molly Bolt from

Rubyfruit Jungle, and the youthful lovers from *Hey, Dollface, Annie on My Mind*, and *Landscape: Memory*; we can also absorb their qualities and let them become part of our own psyches.

7

Making Our Schools Safe for Sissies

Eric Rofes

I knew I was queer when I was a small child. My voice was gentle and sweet. I avoided sports and all roughness. I played with the girls.

I did not fit into the world around me. I knew the meaning of "heresy" before I entered kindergarten. Heresy was a boy who cried a lot when he got hurt. Heresy was a boy who couldn't throw a baseball. Heresy was a boy putting on girls' clothing. Heresy was me.

As I got older, and fully entered the society of children, I met the key enforcer of social roles among children: the bully. The bully was the boy who defined me as queer to my peers. If they had not already noticed, he pointed out my nonconformity. He was ever-present throughout my childhood, like an evil spirit entering different bodies on different occasions. He haunted me at school, throughout my neighborhood, during synagogue, even at birthday parties. In any group of three or more boys, the bully was present.

I know a lot about bullies. I know they have a specific social function: they define the limits of acceptable conduct, appearance, and activities for children. They enforce rigid expectations. They are masters of the art of humiliation and technicians of the science of terrorism. They wreaked havoc on my entire childhood. To this day, their handprints, like a slap on the face, remain stark and defined on my soul.

When I was a young boy, the bully called me names, stole my bicycle, and forced me off the playground. I was victim to the ridicule he heaped on me. He made fun of me in front of other children, forced me to turn over my lunch money each day, and threatened to give me a black eye if I told adult authority figures. At different times I was subject to a wide range of degradation and abuse—"de-pantsing," spit in my face, forced to eat the playground dirt.

Today psychologists and educators are aware of the deep scars which are borne by children and youth who are victimized by violent physical abuse, sexual assault and incest, and the addiction-based behavior of parents. We see the results in our classrooms on a daily basis. Little analysis, however, has focused on the impact of boy-to-boy abuse as lived out among social peers. The abuse I suffered in American public schools, from kindergarten to my senior year of high school, created deep psychic scars with which I have struggled throughout my lifetime. These same scars are shared by many others. We will never forget that we were tortured and publicly humiliated because we refused to be real boys, acted "girlish," or were simply different. This was the price we paid for being queer.

As I entered adolescence, I noticed that the bully could replicate himself. As part of male rites of passage, all boys were presented with a simple choice: suffer daily humiliation, or join the ranks of the bully. We all had to answer the question, "Which side are you on?" I watched sweet childhood friends become hard and mean. I saw other sissy boys become neighborhood toughs. They formed gangs of bullies that tormented us. I witnessed the cycle of abuse which ensures the constant creation of new bullies, and I vowed that this would never happen to me. Watching the powerless take on the trappings of power, I would shake my head and withdraw into deeper isolation.

The world of children was a cruel place for me.

THE RELATIONSHIP OF SISSIES TO GAY YOUTH

Despite twenty-five years of gay liberation work in the United States, there has been an overwhelming silence about gay men's youthful experiences as sissies. In fact, despite increasingly active work by educators, social workers, and activists focused on gay youth, very little discussion has occurred explicitly focused on the plight of sissy boys in our schools. Few of us want to touch this topic.

Why?

Two key barriers exist which cause professionals and gay activists alike to avoid discussing the horrors which are visited on sissies or creating a plan of action to confront the epidemic of bullying. The first is that people of all sexual orientations who work on lesbian and gay youth issues want to avoid stereotyping gay male youth. To say *sissies = gay male youth* is considered offensive by many in the gay community. Instead we insist that gay youth are fully integrated throughout our schools; they are on the football team as well as the drama club, student council as well as art class, the computer club and the swim team. We tell the world that childhood sissies grow up to be men of all sexual orientations.

The second reason that little attention has focused on the plight of the sissy is that gay male activists and educators alike carry unresolved feelings about their own sissy pasts. When we left home and fled to a safer location, we did our best to leave our sissy identities behind. We never dealt with the deep scarring of our souls which occurred at the hand of other boys. Instead, we threw ourselves into adult lives and tried never to look back. It is too painful to reopen these wounds.

These barriers must be examined, challenged, and overcome because—regardless of future sexual orientation—sissy boys have become contemporary youth's primary exposure to gay identity. Throughout my primary and secondary school years, the words hurled at nontraditional boys were "sissy," "pansy," and "nancy-boy." Today the words are "gay," "faggot," and "queer." In fact, many students, when challenged by teachers on using the word "gay" as an epithet, insist that it has nothing to do with homosexuality. Instead, they are using the word to brand an individual as odd, nontraditional, or "girlish." The links to youthful misogyny are evident. Whether or not sissy boys grow up to be adult gay men, no attempt to prevent violence in our schools will succeed without addressing the attacks on sissies.

Furthermore, interviews with gay men of all classes, races, and educational backgrounds reveal a strikingly large percentage who acknowledge a sissy past when asked. This is true of gay men who exemplify American ideals of masculinity, as well as hypermasculine men in the gay ghetto. Some sissy boys grow up to be nontraditional adult men—androgynous, "effeminate," transgendered, or simply gentle—while others transform themselves into traditional versions of masculinity. I believe the modern gay male community's obsession with images and artifacts of masculinity and femininity is rooted in childhood sissy experiences.

Some gay men have talked and written candidly about their struggles as sissy boys. Early gay liberationists wrote about their sissy boyhoods out of a political framework of ending rigid gender roles (Alinder, 1972; Silverstein, 1972; Vernon, 1972). Seymour Kleinberg (1980), author of *Alienated Affections: Being Gay in America*, in a chapter entitled "Where Have All the Sissies Gone?," discusses the response of urban gay male communities to the sissy stereotype. More recent accounts of sissy pasts appear in John Preston's (1991) anthology *Hometowns: Gay Men Write About Where They Belong*, as well as Paul Monette's (1992) *Becoming A Man*, and Michelangelo Signorelle's (1992) *Queer in America*. Yet the literature of books and academic journals that is focused on gay youth issues frequently appears to bend over backwards to avoid any equating of gay youth with sissies.

Schools must incorporate strategic responses to the bully/sissy paradigm in their work to make educational institutions responsive to the needs of gay youth, and they must eschew any fears that a link between sissies and gay youth panders to stereotypes. In the eyes of youth culture, sissy boys function as gay youth even before the dawn of conscious erotic desire appears.

RESPONDING TO THE PERSECUTION OF SISSIES

When I was in high school, the bully operated with a great deal of autonomy because he knew that teachers would look the other way rather than confront his terrorism. The bully/sissy paradigm was the key element of male youth culture; it occupied separate space from the academic culture. Even when the bullying occurred in the classroom, it was when the teacher's back was turned, or during team sports, or when we broke up into small groups for project work. On the rare occasions when teachers would witness bullying, they uniformly failed to respond, implicitly granting sanction to the persecution of nontraditional boys.

If schools intend to address the pain of sissy boys and its impact on mental health distress, low self-esteem, and poor academic performance, significant teacher training must occur to root out the prejudices and sexist assumptions which are widespread among American educators. *In the long run*, an examination of the roots of power abuses between children (boy to boy, boy to girl, and girl to girl) must take place if we are going to end violence and harassment in our schools. In the short run, however, schools can make a commitment to the following policies:

1. *Teachers and administrators must play an active role in interrupting bullying.* No longer should teachers pretend that this kind of persecution is not taking place and that boys who are named sissies are themselves at fault for their predicament. Boys have the right to choose their relationship to socially constructed gender roles and, for boys who do not consciously choose to be a particular way, there is the right to be different and still be free from school-sanctioned victimization. Interrupting, confronting, and disciplining are within the responsibility of all school staff. Abrogating this task is nothing short of complicity in the dynamic.

2. *Boys who do not enjoy or wish to participate in activities focused solely on boys should be given a range of alternative options.* No place is more frightening to the sissy than gym class. Being the last child chosen for a team or standing in right field are common experiences for sissy boys. Traditional team sports and individual athletic prowess are fraught with opportunities for humiliation and public degradation for sissy boys. The situation is exacerbated when gym teachers themselves participate in the harassment by using sexist taunts to encourage better participation or higher achievement. A rethinking of gym class must occur. It should aim to promote physical activity and health among all students without the gender-specific options that are still offered by most schools and without the rampant sissy-baiting which is integrated into sports in America.

3. *Schools must examine the overt and covert ways in which they honor certain kinds of achievement for boys and ignore other kinds of achievement which are not seen as traditionally male-focused.* Traditional pep-rallies promote very specific expectations and roles for both young men and young women. The men are expected to exhibit athletic prowess and aggressive competitive urges, and the women are expected to be their boosters. Aside from the question of whether sports in schools can be reformed in a meaningful way, until it is as honorable for a boy to be a cheerleader and a girl to be a football player, sissy boys and strong girls will be relegated to a secondary status as misfits. A wide range of academic and extracurricular activities should be offered to both boys and girls, and public honoring of achievement must mesh traditional and nontraditional pursuits with commensurate attention.

Finally, it must be noted that a wide range of nontraditional behavior among boys creates several different persecuted identities. Schools must consider the following categories of boys and the special issues they face in finding safety in our schools and in fulfilling their educational potential: sissies, sensitive boys, nerds, and wonks. Meaningful remedies which foster self-esteem and promote security are a bottom-line responsibility of all of our schools.

REFERENCES

Alinder, G. (1972). "My Gay Soul." In *Out of the Closets: Voices of Gay Liberation*. Karla Jay and Allen Young, eds. New York: Douglas/Links.

Kleinberg, S. (1980). *Alienated Affections: Being Gay in America*. New York: St. Martin's.

Monette, P. (1992). *Becoming a Man*. San Francisco: Harper.

Preston, J. (Ed.) (1991). *Hometowns: Gay Men Write about Where They Belong*. New York: Dutton.

Signorelle, M. (1992). *Queer in America*. New York: Random House.

Silverstein, M. (1972). "An Open Letter to Tennessee Williams." In *Out of the Closets: Voices of Gay Liberation*. Karla Jay and Allen Young, eds. New York: Douglas/Links.

Vernon, R. (1972). "Sissy in Prison." In *Out of the Closets: Voices of Gay Liberation*. Karla Jay and Allen Young, eds. New York: Douglas/Links.

8

Lesbian, Gay, and Bisexual Teens and the School Counselor

Building Alliances

Amy L. Reynolds and Michael J. Koski

Teenagers who are contemplating their sexuality and attempting to understand and integrate their sexual identity are dealing with a typical aspect of adolescent development. However, those teens who are beginning to identify as lesbian, gay, and bisexual (LGB) face a multitude of unique stressors and challenges. Martin and Hetrick (1988) identify three major problems of LGB youth: (1) isolation, (2) family difficulties, and (3) violence. Family difficulties also lead to increased isolation, and many LGB teens experience rejection, denial, and even violence from their families (O'Connor, 1992; Martin and Hetrick, 1988). School environments are often considered hostile towards LGB youth because once their sexual orientation is identified or even assumed, their psychological development and emotional well-being are often thwarted because of isolation and the harassment and violence they experience from their peers (Hunter and Schaecher, 1987; Martin, 1982).

In general, LGB adolescents—and even those unsure of their sexual identity—are at a higher risk for substance abuse, clinical depression, prostitution, AIDS, running away, truancy, academic difficulties, and dropping out of school (O'Connor, 1992; Russell, 1989). They experience more psychological stress and lower self-esteem than other teens their age (Hunter and Schaecher, 1987). In fact, recent studies estimate that LGB youth may encompass thirty percent of the successful suicide attempts in the United States every year (Freiberg, 1990).

Considering their degree of need, and the hostile school environment that LGB teens face, they are clearly in need of a support system within their daily educational environment. They need advocates and supportive professionals. According to Russell (1989), LGB adolescents need "counselors as a source for positive intervention" (p. 333). Unfortunately few school counselors have been trained to work effectively with LGB youth, and even fewer school systems prohibit discrimination and harassment on the basis of sexual orientation (Hunter and Schaecher, 1987; Wakelee-Lynch, 1989). There is a multitude of skills, sensitivities, and roles that school counselors can incorporate into their daily work lives to address the needs of LGB youth, and this chapter will address the strategies and knowledge needed to do so. Until such time that LGB adolescents encounter school counselors who are willing to "promote understanding, tolerance, sympathy, and compassion" (Hunter and Schaecher, 1987, p. 187), they will continue to be at risk.

The goals for this chapter include: (1) to heighten the awareness of LGB students and their issues among those working in secondary schools, especially counselors; (2) to increase knowledge and awareness of effective and necessary strategies to meet the needs of LGB adolescents; and (3) to encourage school counselors and other professionals to advocate on behalf of LGB teens in their schools. This chapter presents a succinct discussion of typical issues faced by adolescents, and highlights the unique issues faced by LGB teens. The general role of the school counselor will be addressed briefly in order to offer a context for what is needed to meet effectively the needs of LGB youth. In addition, this chapter addresses what LGB teens need from their school counselors, and it suggests recommendations for strategies for support, empowerment, and advocacy. Finally, specific resources are offered in terms of literature and national organizations that can meet the needs of both school counselors and LGB adolescents. While this chapter targets school counselors, we are hopeful that all professionals who work in the schools will read and implement these suggestions, so that they can help LGB adolescents develop and grow.

Adolescence is a period of transition from childhood to adulthood. For the "*Sturm und Drang*" theorists, this time is marked by a great deal of turmoil (Blos, 1962; A. Freud, 1969). For others, normal adolescent development is seen as continuous and undisturbed (Offer, 1975). Erikson (1975) has described adolescence as: "not an affliction but a normative crisis, a normal phase of increased conflict characterized by a seeming fluctuation in ego strength and yet also by a high growth potential" (p. 116). Whether or not one sees adolescence as a time of inevitable turmoil, a peaceful transition, or somewhere in between, it is clear that adolescents are faced with complex developmental tasks that can cause stress for even the most balanced and well-adjusted youth.

All adolescents, regardless of their sexual identity, deal with a variety of similar issues, such as coping with physical and sexual maturation and separation and individuation from parents. Blos (1975) describes this process as a "second individuation" phase that is analogous to the separation-individuation phase a young child experiences, and one that establishes a sense of autonomy while retaining a mature emotional relationship with parents and other elders. According to Erikson (1975), adolescents must experience the normative crisis of identity formation in order to form a stable, life-sustaining, socially consistent identity in the world.

As many adolescents begin to separate emotionally from their parents and strive for independence, they often reexamine the personal values that they adopted as children. Shertzer and Stone (1981) characterize the adolescent's search for new values as an active testing of both old and new ideals. The peer group, which is where adolescents experiment with newly developing social skills, becomes the dominant culture for teens.

The adolescent who begins to identify as LGB is faced with all of the tasks and conflicts addressed above. However, many of these dynamics are heightened because of the stigma and confusion that are associated with adopting a sexual identity that is often considered abnormal, immoral, and pathological. Because they typically look like other students, many LGB youth can easily "pass," and they are often unable to express the isolation and loneliness that they feel with their family or friends. While other adolescents are becoming aware of their interest in the other sex, and may openly relish the novelty of those feelings, LGB adolescents are often frightened by their sexual feelings.

Unlike adolescents who are people of color and who can find support and affirmation for being different from the dominant culture in their families, LGB teens often feel that there is no one who will accept and comfort them. The peer group, which for heterosexual youth often provides support for the confusing feelings of adolescence, may often become a source of verbal and physical violence toward the youth who identifies as LGB (Hunter and Schaecher, 1987). This ostracism from both family and friends will often lead to self-blame and further isolation. As stated previously, this isolation may in turn lead to high-risk behaviors such as running away, dropping out of school, substance abuse, unhealthy sexual acting out, and others (O'Connor, 1992; Russell, 1989).

The sense of "being different" is further exacerbated for LGB youth because of the emphasis on heterosexual dating and team sports. LGB teens often experience a major social vacuum in these key domains (Herdt, 1989). Feeling different and alienated can lead to both negative and positive changes. Because of the presumption of the normalcy of heterosexuality in their family, their peer group, and our culture, a dissonance often occurs between how LGB teens view themselves and how others view them. This dissonance can be resolved by accepting society's judgment that heterosexuality is "normal" and that one's own feelings are immoral or sick. Some LGB youth, on the other hand, resolve the dissonance by challenging the norm of heterosexuality and by coming out in a way that allows them to feel comfortable with their sexuality. This coming out process will result, it is hoped, in the development of positive LGB feelings, affirming contact with LGB peers and/or community, and integration of sexual orientation as only one aspect of an individual's entire identity. In order for those positive developments to occur for the LGB teen, however, there are certain strategies and competencies that school counselors need.

RECOMMENDED STRATEGIES AND COMPETENCIES

Traditionally, the high school counselor assumes a number of roles and functions which, while they may differ across school districts, generally fall within the following areas: *individual and group counseling*, which may include helping students in developing decision-making competence, formulating future plans, and dealing with current personal problems; *educational planning*, which may include academic advisement, vocational advisement and planning for post-secondary education; *being available for parents* via conferences and workshops; *consulting with staff* via personal conferences and workshops; *interpreting tests* to students, parents, and staff; *making appropriate referrals* to outside agencies and community-based organizations; and *acting as a liaison* between these organizations and the school (Shertzer and Stone, 1981).

LGB youth do not differ from heterosexual students in their need to make use of these services. Yet counselors may need to adapt their role in order to help the LGB adolescent who may be feeling isolated and stigmatized. The counselor can begin in the most basic way—by being aware of the use of language. When counselors speak with teens or parents about dating, social relationships, and sexual matters, they must not assume that males only date females or that sexual feelings only happen across gender. LGB teens will feel less invisible if they hear the counselor refer to "partner" or hear the counselor talking about a boy's going out with his girl or boyfriend. The counselor should be proactive in offering feedback and suggestions to parents and staff in order to increase their awareness of how the words they use may suggest that heterosexuality is the desired norm.

In order to effectively meet the needs of LGB teens, school counselors must be able to provide the following: (1) support and affirmation, (2) knowledge and accurate information, (3) role modeling, and (4) the ability to be counselor/consultant/advisor. Throughout the literature, it is emphasized that counselors who work with LGB youth need a high degree of self-awareness and sensitivity, and must have addressed their own attitudes and biases (Hunter and Schaecher, 1987; Russell, 1989; Wakelee-Lynch, 1989).

A study examining the perception of LGB youth about educators and counselors showed that many saw their counselors as ill-informed, unconcerned, and uncomfortable when talking with them (Sears, 1992). The study also demonstrated that nearly two-thirds of the school counselors who were surveyed expressed negative attitudes and feelings about LGB people and issues. Although the study was conducted only in the South, the antigay amendment in Colorado and the issue of LGB people in the military are good examples of how widespread homophobia is, rather than being endemic to any particular region of the country.

Counselors who find that they are not familiar with issues that surround LGB youth, or who themselves have unresolved issues around their own sexual identity, should make a concerted effort, through readings and additional training, to develop some competencies in this area. According to O'Connor (1992), it is vital that counselors be informed and be able to provide accurate and essential information on LGB issues: the coming-out process, HIV, and other vital topics. They should also be able to debunk myths for both LGB and heterosexual students. Information about local organizations and resources is also necessary, so that appropriate referrals can be made.

LGB students are in need of role models who can help create a more positive climate in their school (Martin, 1982). School counselors must be willing to be those role models. If a counselor is LGB, self-disclosure of her or his identity must be well timed and appropriate. If a counselor is heterosexual, or is not able to come out because of the climate, she or he can be a role model by actively combating homophobia. The counselor who identifies as being LGB may have some special issues attached to working with adolescents who are coming out as LGB. The counselor who is "out" in the school community can serve as a role model for youth who are coming out. By being visible as a LGB person, the counselor can help dispel many of the myths and stereotypes about LGB people. However, the counselor who is still "in the closet" may be faced with some difficult issues. When a counselor is affirming and supportive of LGB youth, others may become suspicious of the counselor's sexual orientation. Although remaining secretive about one's sexual orientation is not necessarily incompatible with being accessible to LGB youth, one must ask what message is being sent to youth who are struggling with coming out.

Finally, LGB teens need someone to talk with about their concerns and feelings (Martin, 1982; O'Connor, 1992). School counselors are a natural choice for filling this role. Research by Sears (1992) discovered that while LGB students wanted a supportive counselor to talk with, they were often hesitant to take the risk to initiate conversation. If counselors create an office environment that is sensitive and open (for example, one that has LGB related posters and books and has information on local LGB events and community resources), students will develop trust, and eventually may confide in their counselor. LGB adolescents also need a meaningful social environment which can be found in support groups and workshops (Martin, 1982; O'Connor, 1992). In order for such efforts to be effective, however, school counselors must be able to ensure confidentiality and privacy. They also need to offer sensitivity and skill-building training for teachers, administrators, and staff. If counselors do not feel prepared to offer this sort of training, they must be willing to seek out additional training for themselves.

When the counselor develops workshops on current concerns for staff and parents, the issue of sexual orientation should be presented not as a "problem" but as another part of normal development. The stance should not merely be one of tolerance; it should be one of support, acceptance, and affirmation. Misinformation and myths about sexual orientation should be challenged wherever they occur. The high school counselor is often thought of as the repository of mental health in the school community; this position can be used to normalize, support, and affirm different sexual orientations and feelings (Russell, 1989). Just as counselors today are expected not to tolerate a lack of respect for racial, ethnic, and religious differences, so should the counselor be unwilling to tolerate a lack of respect for LGB people and issues, whether it comes from students or staff.

If school counselors are going to attempt to meet the needs of LGB youth, certain competencies are vital. Some of these involve the everyday skills of a school counselor—listening, empathy, counseling, individual and group assessment, consultation, problem-solving, and others. In addition to these, there are some unique skills that counselors will need if they are to work effectively with LGB teens. Counselors must be able to tolerate ambiguity and conflict, both internally and externally. LGB issues are controversial, especially among teenagers, and those who attempt to educate are often challenged (Washington and Evans, 1991). At times, those who speak out will even have their own sexual orientation questioned (Hunter and Schaecher, 1987). One must be willing to confront homophobia and deal with sexuality openly. In general, a school counselor who wants to address LGB issues must be willing to take risks (Hunter and Schaecher, 1987), for regardless of one's sexuality, there are serious risks and institutional barriers for counselors who take a proactive, affirming stance with LGB youth. The controversy over the Rainbow Curriculum, which incorporated LGB issues and led to the firing of the school chancellor in New York City in 1992, is a good example of what may happen when professionals advocate for sensitivity to LGB concerns.

According to Kaplan and Geoffroy (1990), school counselors are in a position to make the difference in creating positive school climates, because they have the necessary attitudes, knowledge, and skills. In fact, they believe that school counselors can become change agents, and they encourage them to take an active role. They further identify eight roles that school counselors should take: (1) advocate; (2) expert; (3) trainer; (4) alternative identifier; (5) collaborator; (6) process specialist; (7) fact finder; and (8) reflector. More specifically, they suggest that counselors offer alternative strategies, solutions, and approaches when the ones that schools are currently using do not build positive and affirming environments. Counselors can provide a necessary support service and leadership role for their school. Finally, Kaplan and Geoffroy state that counselors can serve as catalysts in creating more positive and affirming schools.

In order to be an advocate for LGB teens, school counselors must be willing to be an ally for LGB students. According to Washington and Evans (1991), an ally is one who: "works to end oppression in his or her personal and professional life through support of, and as an advocate with and for, the oppressed population" (p. 195). Although anyone can be an ally in the general sense, it is often more powerful when the advocate is *not* a member of the oppressed group. Being an ally can mean offering support and services to LGB individuals themselves, or sometimes focusing on increasing the awareness and sensitivity of institutions and heterosexual individuals (Washington and Evans, 1991). Being a visible supporter of LGB youth in the schools is often challenging, and many barriers exist. However, the rewards can be endless if one imagines combatting the self-hatred and psychological difficulties of LGB students, as well as challenging the ignorance, insensitivity, and sometimes hatred of their peers, teachers, administrators, and parents. After all, the desire to make a difference and to improve the quality of life of students is why many people decide to become school counselors.

REFERENCES

Blos, P. (1962). *On Adolescence: A Psychoanalytic Interpretation.* New York: Free Press of Glencoe.

———. (1975). "The Second Individuation Process of Adolescence." In *The Psychology of Adolescence.* A. Esman, ed. New York: International Universities Press.

Erikson, E.H. (1975). "The Concept of Ego Identity." In *The Psychology of Adolescence.* A. Esman, ed. New York: International Universities Press.

Freud, A. (1969). "Adolescence as a Developmental Disturbance." *The Writings of Anna Freud.* Volume 17. New York: International Universities Press.

Freiberg, P. (1990). "Sullivan is Criticized by APA Over Report." *APA Monitor,* July, p. 41.

Herdt, G. (1989). "Gay and Lesbian Youth, Emergent Identities and Cultural Scenes at Home and Abroad." *Journal of Homosexuality, 17,* pp. 1–41.

Hunter, J. and Schaecher, R. (1987). "Stresses on Lesbian and Gay Adolescents in Schools." *Social Work in Education, 2*, pp. 180–190.

Kaplan, L.S. and Geoffroy, K.E. (1990). "Enhancing the School Climate: New Opportunities for the Counselor." *The School Counselor, 38*, pp. 7–12.

Martin, A.D. (1982). "Learning to Hide: The Socialization of the Gay Adolescent." In *Adolescent Psychiatry: Developmental and Clinical Studies.* Volume X. S.C. Feinstein, J.G. Looney, A.Z. Schwartzberg, and A.D. Sorosky, eds. Chicago: University of Chicago Press.

———. (1988). "The Stigmatization of the Gay and Lesbian Adolescent." *Journal of Homosexuality, 15*, pp. 163–183.

Offer, D. (1975). "Adolescent Turmoil." In *The Psychology of Adolescence.* A. Esman, ed. New York: International Universities Press.

O'Connor, M.F. (1992). "Psychotherapy with Gay and Lesbian Adolescents." In *Counseling Gay Men and Lesbians: Journey to the End of the Rainbow.* S.H. Dworkin and F.J. Gutierrez, eds. Alexandria, VA: American Association of Counseling and Development.

Russell, T.G. (1989). "AIDS Education, Homosexuality, and the Counselor's Role." *The School Counselor, 36*, pp. 333–337.

Sears, J.T. (1992). "Educators, Homosexuality, and Homosexual Students: Are Personal Feelings Related to Professional Beliefs?" *Journal of Homosexuality, 3/4*, pp. 29–79.

Shertzer, B. and Stone, S.C., eds. (1981). *Fundamentals of Guidance.* Fourth Edition. Boston: Houghton Mifflin Company.

Wakelee-Lynch, J. (1989). "Gay and Lesbian Youths Face Danger and Isolation." *AACD Guidepost*, October 5, pp. 1, 4, 7, 16.

Washington, J. and Evans, N.J. (1991). "Becoming an Ally." In *Beyond Tolerance: Gays, Lesbians, and Bisexuals on Campus.* N.J. Evans and V.A. Wall, eds. Alexandria, VA: American Association of Counseling and Development.

9

Who Gets Called Queer
in School?

Lesbian, Gay, and Bisexual Teenagers, Homophobia, and High School

Andi O'Conor

Discussions of heterosexism, homophobia, and the lives of lesbian, gay, and bisexual youth have been noticeably absent in the educational literature. As Reed (1993) states: "Not only does the group remain invisible, the existence of and problems associated with gay youth are largely denied by public school educators, particularly school administrators."

In 1992, I spent several months observing and interviewing a group of gay, lesbian and bisexual teenagers in a support group setting. The group met at the local gay and lesbian community center, and about twenty to forty teenagers attended each week. Attendance fluctuated a great deal, and while I got to know the core group of youths fairly well, I actually observed over a hundred different teens. Many sought me out to tell their stories; many told their stories to the entire group. Part of my goal in conducting this research project was to give voice to these teenagers. However, having your story printed and published can be very risky for gay teens, many of whom had not disclosed their sexual identity to their parents, friends, or peers.

In order to give voice to these teenagers and protect their identities, I constructed a composite narrative. In the narrative, only two voices are portrayed—one male, one female, named fictitiously "Christi" and "Tommy." Though their names are fictitious, their experiences are not. Each word they utter in the narrative is taken verbatim from my notes or from interviews. Christi and Tommy represent a wide range of teenagers—black, white, Asian, Latino/a, working and middle class. Their conversation reflects some of the most common and important experiences of these teenagers—isolation, alienation, rejection by gay adults, hostility by parents, and problems with homophobia in and out of school. It also portrays some of their humor and heart, their courage and compassion for each other.

A CONVERSATION WITH CHRISTI AND TOMMY

We sit having coffee at a downtown coffee shop, a fast-food place on the main drag in the city. It is filled with businesspeople, street people, waitresses in tired brown uniforms.

Tommy takes a drag of his cigarette; "I don't know which was worse," he says, "home or school." He fingers the ragged scars at his wrists. "My mom, has, um…a drinking problem. After I came out to her, she got drunk and told me I was a faggot and she didn't want no queer in her house. My brother, he called me a sick fag. So I figured it was either stay and take their shit or leave. So here I am." He stops talking and looks out the window again.

"School was a definite hellhole." says Christi. "H-E-L-L hole. No lie. Like, you sit in class, right, and all these girls are talking about which boys they like and all that crap. And you make stuff up, like 'oh, yeah, *he's* really cute. You don't know how many times I wanted to lean over and say, 'Hey, what about Julia Roberts? Some fox, huh…' And class was such a joke. Teachers were such a joke. This one English teacher, all these girls have such a big crush on him. I *know* this guy is gay, he has to be. And he avoids me like the plague for two years. Like he KNOWS I KNOW and I'm going to turn him in or something. Fucking chicken. He could have helped me. He could have talked to me. But nooo…"

Tommy: "When I was about, I don't know, fifteen I guess, people at school decided I was gay. I didn't even know what they were talking about at first. They just started calling me 'faggot' this and 'fag' that, and all of a sudden I didn't have any friends anymore. So when people started calling me faggot and queer and stuff, and I thought, Yeah, I'm gay. That's what I am. I saw what happened to other kids who got called queer at school. I dropped out. I got a job. My mom thought that was cool. I didn't tell her until later, and that's when things got sort of bad."

Christi turns to me. "I used to call guys faggots in school. We thought it was real funny. 'You fag, you faggot.' We used to call guys gay, if they were skinny or nerdy. 'You sissy, you queer.' We'd hit them, punch them in the halls and stuff. I'd get in trouble and they'd call my mom. Poor Mom. She was so clueless. She'd sit me down and say, 'We are ladies, you and I.' I'd say yeah, yeah. And I'd try to be more ladylike. I mean, I wear makeup and stuff. When I came out to my mom she said, 'But you're so pretty!' Like I had to be ugly to be a lesbian!

"Mom and Dad are pretty cool. I mean, they haven't kicked me out or sent me to a shrink or anything. My mom's even gone to P-FLAG [Parents and Friends of Lesbians and Gays] a couple of times. She goes and cries with other parents. My dad just went, 'uh, huh.' He's clueless. He just, like, reads the newspaper and doesn't say anything. Who knows if they talk about it. I think Mom is really bummed because she, like, wanted me to be a Chanel runway model or something."

Tommy gives a sarcastic sigh. "I always wanted to be a Chanel runway model myself." We laugh.

We order more coffee and watch people walk by on the street. A man and a woman walk by, holding hands. "See that?" Christi says. "No way could I do that with my girlfriend on this street. I'd get killed. No lie. It pisses me off, kind of. That Jo and I can't walk down the street like that. Just like everyone else. I mean, people *throw* stuff at you…really. It's not that they just yell stuff, but they really get mean."

"Yeah," Tommy sighs. "I don't have a boyfriend right now, but everywhere I go I think: Am I safe here? Is someone waiting to get me? So many people get bashed. I mean, we can't even go to bars unless we sneak in, so there's no gay places to even hang out, but I'm still afraid. I mean, I don't even look gay. I go to the park and I hang out with my friends, and we have to plan an escape route before we even sit down. It's such a drag. Last summer we were in the park and this car full of guys drove through screaming 'FUCKING FAG-GOTS' and threw bottles from the car. They drove on the lawn, trying to run guys over and stuff. The cops got there later, way later, and looked at us like we were dirt. 'So no one got hurt,' they said. Yeah, right. No one got hurt."

"It's so sad." Christi says. "But I think things are better. I mean, better for us than for people our parents' age. You know, we have this group, we have P-FLAG, we have the center. And there are groups in schools now, in high schools and stuff. We don't have any bars, and that's a drag. And the adult gay community thinks we're babies." "Or jail bait," Tommy adds. She laughs. "Yeah, or like we don't really know we're gay because we're too young. Like they were never young. Like *they* never went to high school. But really, it's better. Since AIDS, people know that we exist, at least."

Tommy lights another cigarette. "But they still hate us," he says. "Our parents hate us, our teachers hate us, straight kids hate us, adults hate us...." His voice falters a little. Christi leans over the table and takes his hand. "But WE don't hate us, dummy. *We* don't hate us."

Christi and Tommy's conversation brings to light many of the problems experienced by gay, lesbian, and bisexual teenagers in high schools today. Tommy speaks of his problems at home, dealing with the hostility of his mother and brother. His brother calls him a "sick fag"; his mother calls him "queer," and "faggot." Unlike teenagers from other oppressed minority groups, gay teenagers find little or no support or understanding at home for their societal difference. Most often, family members are the most difficult people to reveal sexual orientation to, and are often the last to know. Considering the consequences, this is often a wise choice. Many teenagers who reveal their sexual orientation (or "come out") to their parents face extreme hostility, violence, or sudden homelessness. As one gay youth stated, "growing up gay in my family is like being Jewish in a Nazi home" (Friend, 1993).

In contrast, Christi states that her parents are "clueless," even though they know she's a lesbian. Though they haven't kicked her out of the house, they don't discuss her lesbianism. Many parents of gay teenagers refuse to acknowledge their son's or daughter's sexual orientation, and even formerly close relationships can be torn apart.

School is also a hostile and dangerous environment for most gay and lesbian teenagers. As Christi says, "a definite hellhole." A recent U.S. Department of Justice report states that gays and lesbians are the most frequent victims of hate crimes, and school is the primary setting for this type of violence (Herek, 1989). Comstock (1991) writes, "Lesbian and gay crime victims report greater frequency of incidents in school settings than do victims of crime in general (25 percent lesbian/gay, 9 percent general)." People of color and men experience greater incidence of violence in schools than do whites and women.

Silence on the part of teachers and administrators also make schools unsafe places for gay and lesbian teens. While teachers often punish students who make racist remarks, homophobic comments are typically unchallenged, and sometimes even perpetrated by teachers themselves (Friend, 1993). As Tommy says, "I saw what happened to other kids who got called queer at school."

Often in order to survive in school, many gay and lesbian teens have to construct a false, heterosexual self. As Christi says above, "You make stuff up, like, 'Oh yeah, *he's* really cute.'" Some teenagers have sex with members of the opposite sex to prove they are straight, and to avoid being called "queer," or "dyke." Lesbian and gay youth may also engage in antigay violence in an attempt to hide their homosexuality. Christi describes beating up boys who were feminine or different. Others participate in name-calling, or join in the laughter at "fag" or "dyke" jokes.

Gay and lesbian teens are also often isolated from gay, lesbian, and bisexual adults. Because of societal misconceptions about gay people as "recruiters" of youth, gay, lesbian and bisexual adults (particularly teachers) often avoid interacting with gay and lesbian teenagers. Christi describes the situation well when she talks about her English teacher. "I *know* this guy is gay…and he avoids me like the plague for two years. Like he KNOWS I KNOW and I'm going to turn him in or something." Unlike other minority teachers, who can serve as role models to minority youth, gay and lesbian teachers nearly always hide their sexual identity and distance themselves from gay and lesbian youth.

Many youths face exclusion from the adult gay and lesbian community. As Christi and Tommy state, "The adult gay community thinks we're babies…like we don't really know we're gay because we're too young." Gay and lesbian youth are excluded from many community activities as well, since they often lack transportation and are too young for gay bars and social events.

Thus, gay, lesbian, and bisexual youth often go through the difficult period of adolescence ostracized and isolated from family members, teachers, peer groups, and the adult gay and lesbian community. As Tommy says, "Our parents hate us, our teachers hate us, straight kids hate us, adults hate us." As a result, gay and lesbian teenagers often feel they have no place to go, that there is no room in the world for them to exist. As Tommy says, "Everywhere I go I think, 'Am I safe here? Is someone waiting to get me?'"

Fortunately, as Christi says, "things are better." With the advent of groups like Parents and Friends of Lesbian and Gays (P-FLAG), parents can learn more about their gay, lesbian, and bisexual children, and can understand their unique difficulties. Support programs such as Project 10 in Los Angeles and the Harvey Milk School in New York, offer safe environments for gay and lesbian youth. In-school support groups are being started in high schools throughout the country, and many gay and lesbian community centers offer support groups specifically for teenagers. These programs offer a critical bridge between gay and lesbian teenagers, their parents, friends, and the adult gay and lesbian community. They provide buffer zones where teenagers can learn who they are in a positive environment, away from the dangers of home and school. Support groups and programs both in and out of school provide these teenagers with a critical sense of community and self esteem. They provide an alternative to alienation and suicide, a place to learn, as Christi says, that "*We* don't hate us."

I'd like to close with a quote by Aaron Fricke. As a teenager, Fricke sued his high school and won the right to take a male date to his senior prom. As a result, he became nationally known and soon after wrote a book called *Reflections of a Rock Lobster, A Story About Growing Up Gay* (1981). This book is an invaluable source of information for teachers, students, parents, and educational researchers interested in the lives of gay and lesbian youth. In this passage, Fricke reflects on what turned out to be a tense but uneventful senior prom:

> I thought of all the people who would have enjoyed going to their proms with the date of their choice but were denied that right; of all the people in the past who wanted to live respectably with the person they loved but could not; of all the men and women who had been hurt or killed because they were gay; of the rich history of lesbians and homosexual men that had so long been ignored. Gradually we were triumphing over ignorance. One day we would be free.

That freedom, I hope, can be won by speaking out, and by sharing the stories of gay, lesbian, and bisexual youth. By refusing to tolerate name-calling, gay-bashing, and other forms of homophobia, and by recognizing gay, lesbian, and bisexual teenagers as a high school population at risk, teachers, students, parents, and administrators can help break the silence and truly "triumph over ignorance." We can help end homophobia and antigay violence, and work toward a day when no one gets called "queer" in school.

Many thanks to Matthew Goldwasser, Pat McQuillan, Margaret Eisenhart, and Cheryl Schwartz for their valuable input and ongoing support of my work. Special thanks to S.C.

REFERENCES

Comstock, G.D. (1991). *Violence Against Lesbians and Gay Men.* New York: Columbia University Press.

Fricke, A. (1981). *Reflections of a Rock Lobster: A Story About Growing Up Gay.* Boston: Alyson Publications.

Friend, R. (1991). "Choices, Not Closets: Heterosexism and Homophobia in Schools." In *Beyond Silenced Voices.* Lois Weis and Michelle Fine, eds. Albany, NY: SUNY Press.

Herek, G.M. "Hate Crimes Against Lesbians and Gay Men: Issues for Research and Policy." *American Psychologist 44*, pp. 948–955.

Reed, D. (1993). "High School Gay Youth: Invisible Diversity." *Paper Presented at the Annual Meeting of the American Educational Research Association*, April, Atlanta, GA.

III

EDUCATIONAL THEORY AND LESBIAN, GAY, AND BISEXUAL TEENAGERS

10

Moral Panic, Schooling, and Gay Identity

Critical Pedagogy and the Politics of Resistance

Peter McLaren

Human rights, dissidence, antiracism, the antinuclear movement, and the environment are gentle ideologies. They are easy, *post coitum historicum,* after the orgy; ideology for an agreeable generation—the children of crisis, who are acquainted with neither hard ideologies nor radical philosophies.

—*Jean Baudrillard, "The Anorexic Ruins," p. 43.*

MORAL PANIC IN THE AGE OF THE HYSTERICAL HETEROSEXUAL

We are living at a time in U.S. cultural history in which the autonomy and dignity of the human spirit is being threatened rather than exercised. What makes it bearable is what is hidden from us, what is repressively desublimated. The current historical juncture is precisely that perilous mixture of historical amnesia and cultural intensity in which society is attempting to reinvent itself without the benefit of knowing who or what it already is.

This decidedly postmodern combination of extreme wakefulness and forgetfulness has helped to create the contemporary moral panic surrounding sexuality. We rely as a society on perceptions that have been filtered through constellations of historical commentaries rooted in xenophobia, homophobia, racism, sexism, the commodification of everyday life, and the reproduction of race, class, and gender relations. Schools both mirror and motivate such perceptions, reproducing a culture of fear that contributes to a wider justification for vigilance surrounding sexual practices through polar definitions of youth as morally upright/sexually deviant, and approvingly decent/unrepentantly corrupt. This Manichaean perspective on youth further supports a paternalistic and authoritarian politics and policing of the unconscious by limiting access to more progressive and liberatory vocabularies and practices of knowing.

The specter of AIDS reminds us all that death awaits us. While heterosexual and homosexual flesh choose not to mingle in life, in death both will eventually end in the same compost of decay, melting through corruption to reveal the magnificent luminosity of the bones and the mocking smile that adorns each skull wiped clean of life. We are reminded that even the most putrid and decayed flesh tastes sweet to the triumphant worms and maggots and euphorically silent colonies of bacteria who perform in those invisible theaters of death where human "filth" becomes nature's feast. It is when we most fully realize that those taut sheets of flesh produced in our youth inevitably become the sagging shroud that clings chillingly to our brittle frame during the ends of our days, that Death's lurid mockery of the living most profoundly disturbs us. It is then that we seek to give temporary relief to our fears through expulsion of those groups who remind us most of our frail finitude.

Again, what makes our age bearable is that which is hidden from us, and that which we choose to hide from ourselves, including our motivated forgetfulness surrounding the dangerous memories of victimization and marginalization that have haunted human societies through the centuries, from the lynching of blacks, Nazi Germany's persecution of Jews and homosexuals, the systematic violence against women, right up to the hollowed eyes that stare out from behind the barbed wire fences of Serbian prison camps. We remain shaken by the degree to which torture and brutality have assumed the form of law and madness the shape of reason.

SUBJECTS OF THE MEDIA AND MEDIATED SUBJECTS:
THE POLITICS OF FORGETFULNESS AND EXCLUSION

Henri Lefebvre (1990) warns that we are at this present time suffering an alienation from alienation, that is, a disappearance of our consciousness of existing in a state of alienation. This is a world of pure appearances, a self-ironizing world that has completely simulated itself through parodies of itself, such that the media no longer serve as extensions of ourselves. Rather, we serve as the extensions of the media, in terms of our inability to operate outside of what has already been said about ourselves through our positionalities as subjects produced by the narratives and antinarratives of postmodern media conventions. Here we only need to be reminded of the fate of the recent Children of the Rainbow Curriculum that was part of a comprehensive multicultural project created by New York City's Board of Education. Gay-inclusive sections made up part of this curriculum, including respect for gay and lesbian families. However, anti-Rainbow efforts by right-wing affiliations, which included members of the Family Defense Council with active links to the Oregon Citizens Alliance (sponsors of that state's antigay ballot measure), eventually won the day, largely because they went unreported by the media. As Donna Minkowitz notes, the media, in covering the anti-Rainbow rallies, failed for the most part to report speakers who called for violence against lesbians and gay men. For instance, the media failed to mention the presence at such rallies of large contingents from the Society for the Preservation of Tradition, Family and Property, a right-wing paramilitary group active in Latin America. The dominant media fell silent when faced by remarks by elected officials, such as Senator Serphin Maltese, who described homosexuals as "pure evil and wickedness" (1993, p. 12). In fact, most newspaper accounts failed to dispute opponents' charges that the curriculum was designed to teach "oral and anal sex" in the first grade.

Minkowitz rightly notes that the most basic reason for including gays and lesbians in the multicultural education plan was the conviction that a truthful and accurate education means teaching students about the important role gays and lesbians have played—and continue to play—in history, literature, science, and culture. Not surprisingly, there existed in the media a motivated amnesia surrounding this fundamental conviction behind the Children of the Rainbow project. In the midst of such a culture of silence, even the most well-intentioned heterosexual groups frequently choose to ignore the democratic imperatives of a just society by failing to respond to the AIDS crisis, and by unwittingly creating a politics of exclusion and victimization of gay and lesbian perspectives through their own unacknowledged homophobia. Regrettably, in a culture which chooses to motivate its subjects into moral inertia through a politics of forgetfulness and exclusion, even the most progressive liberals insist on turning democracy itself into an empty signifier that points to a better, more tolerant, and less homophobic future only on condition that such a future be eternally delayed.

THE MULTIVOCAL SUBJECT AND THE POLITICS OF DESIRE

In an age which artificially separates mind from the flesh, we do not like to be reminded that our bodies are integral aspects of who we are. Because such a reminder emphasizes that we are both different from others yet connected materially to civil society through intersubjective relations. The notion of the individual subject as an embodied subject that is part of the body politic ruptures the modernist notion of the autonomous agent as disembodied, disconnected, and self-initiating. Our bodies remind us of the complex and heterogeneous configuration of our identity that is differentiated, interleaved, and constructed out of multiple discourses and social practices. The putative stability of identity is shattered when it is recognized that individuals are the *loci* in which various conflictual discourses intersect and compete for dominance. The individual subject is constituted as pluripolar tensions and desires. Our corporeality also reminds us of our civil responsibility to create through intersubjective relations, a society where individuals can be secure in the integrity of their own sexual as well as other social practices. It reminds gay students that our society is one premised on sexual apartheid.

SEXUAL APARTHEID AND SEDIMENTED PERCEPTION:
CRITICAL PEDAGOGY AND THE POLITICS OF RESISTANCE

When we examine the plight of the gay student, our perceptions are shaped by ideological trajectories created largely by the moral consensus that controls and ritualizes the stories we tell ourselves about ourselves as a community of citizens. Our perceptions serve as social acts that summon us into existence in a particular way, and moral acts in which the one who perceives participates in a selective mode of social collectivity, in a certain form of ethical address, in a particular way of engaging difference, such that a voracious center of dominant values works silently and often invisibly to domesticate those constructed as the margins. To understand how we come to perceive and to value, and how objects are brought into existence as "acts" of such valuing, has been one of the goals of critical pedagogy over the last decade. Critical pedagogy is the act of reading the world and the word, as Freire and Macedo (1987) note, by taking the measure of the world's indwelling in us as we are constructed as ethical and political subjects. This is no small feat in an era of multinational capitalism and under circumstances in which time and space have been implosively contracted through new information technologies. In fact, critical pedagogy posits a further challenge to understanding how identities are structured by the cultural logic of late capitalism by asking: In whose interests does the social construction of perception and valuation serve? Whose interests do the social, cultural, and institutional practices which shape (and are shaped by) such values operate? These are wide-ranging questions, and critical pedagogy and feminist pedagogy have worked conjointly to help answer them.

More specifically, critical pedagogy has attempted to situate the process of schooling within the present state of the capitalist formation of society and the reproduction of asymmetrical relations of power and privilege (McLaren, 1989; 1993; forthcoming; Giroux and McLaren 1989; 1993; Lankshear and McLaren, 1993; McLaren and Lankshear, 1994; Giroux, 1993). Despite the fact that the word "homosexual" is no longer quarantined to medical or religious communities, there exists, apart from the important work of James T. Sears (1991; 1992), William G. Tierney (1993), and a few others, only a small number of criticalists who seriously address the plight of gay and lesbian students. Needed are more critical studies which locate the production of gender, sexuality, and identity within the context of the reproduction of social relations in capitalist society and the deformation of everyday life—what Lefebvre calls "the bureaucratic society of controlled consumption" (1990; Sunker; 1989).

While heterosexual teachers generally insist on ignoring the struggle of gay and lesbian students, they continue to consume images in popular culture that, while still largely condemnatory of homosexuality, are ostensibly more tolerant of gay sexual practices. Yet in the public schools, teachers rarely discuss homosexuality in any serious and informed manner with their students, and fail to provide them with a wide range of either critical literature or informed opinions on the subject. Some of the reasons are clear: a fear of dismissal for discussing a morally "taboo" topic; fear of reprisals from parents and religious leaders in the community, and so forth. Not to mention the teachers' own homophobic ideological moorings. A central question that I would like to pose is: How can teachers work together in the interests of developing a critical subjectivity among themselves and their students that can begin to rehabilitate the pathological development of homophobic discourses in current school policy and practice? Further, how can teachers and students develop a collective praxis that takes up in a politically charged and pedagogically progressive way the contradiction between the social relations of homosexuality and the social form of "alterity" (one's relationship to the "other")?

LANGUAGE, EXPERIENCE, AND IDENTITY

I want to turn for the moment to a crucial theoretical perspective that undergirds much of the constructionist approach adopted in recent years by proponents of critical pedagogy. This perspective could be useful in promoting a liberatory pedagogy that is profoundly antihomophobic. Briefly, this perspective holds that language and experience are nonidentical. Let me spend some time on this point, so that later I will be able to develop a position that links it with gay and lesbian identity.

Language is not stable. Similarly, identities are mobile and are structured around overdetermined equivalences. There is no normal language for making sense out of the world in general, or homosexual practices in particular. There is no fixed or neutral language against which one can judge the changing circumstances of utterances or their fluctuating instantiations (Bogue, 1989, Lankshear and McLaren, 1993; Giroux and McLaren, 1993). As Ronald Bogue points out, the purpose of language is to impose a certain moral order, and it is this practice which supersedes the transmission of information or the function of communication. Describing the position of Gilles Deleuze and Félix Guattari, Bogue argues that language constitutes the imposition of semiotic coordinates on the world of the child; further, such a language "categorizes the world, and in learning a language one must to some extent accept the codes—codes of privilege, power, domination, exclusion, and so on" (1989, p. 136).

Language transmits the moral order of indirect discourse that has already been put in place by the dominant social collectivities. All language acts are, therefore, "acts of power," in so far as they are linked to a "social obligation." Language is not something that is simply embedded in social relations and the concrete practices of individuals. It is decidedly more complex.

Slajov Žižek (1991) remarks that the way language relates to the totality of experience is already overdetermined by language itself, or, in Lacanian terms, language (the symbolic order) cannot be reduced to experience. In effect, the totality of language actually structures the horizon of our experience and the direction of our desiring. There is no passage from language to reality, no direct correspondence, no outside to ideology. The world is always ideological in the sense that we cannot remove ourselves to some transcendental platform outside of language in order to reflect upon our situatedness within language. The void that separates language from experience is what Žižek refers to as the "missing link of ideology" or the individual "subject." Hence, we can never find the "truth" of our perceptions, or

explain the origins of our experiences; all that we can do is find new contexts in which signifiers may be retroactively rewritten, reordered, or reex-
perienced. This is, I would argue, a way of explaining a central mission of
critical pedagogy.

We need to understand what Žižek means when he says that we always read
events "backwards" from the present, using new symbolic languages to give
past events new meaning. It means, in effect, that it is impossible to return to
an original or authentic experience that is not symbolically mediated or
overdetermined by language. For instance, a student's aversion to homosexuality can never be explained by understanding the psychocultural dynamics of his or her experience alone, but must also take into consideration the
way those experiences have been revisited or rewritten through particular
languages (the language of religious conservatism, political progressivism,
ideological fascism, biological sciences, or the particular language of citizenship used by teachers at school, and so on) that are used to mediate such
experiences.

The problem, according to Žižek, is that individuals often invent myths
which serve as structured fantasies that are retroactively employed to explain
their own origins through a fictional narrative that conceals its contingent
materiality or the fetish of its origin. What this means is that the external
contingent character of certain events must be repressed or transcoded in
order to maintain their level of self-reproduction. Žižek uses the example of
capitalism to explain this idea. He argues that in order to conceal capitalism's origins in expropriation, plunder, and violence, capitalism has produced the ideological myth of "primitive accumulation" to retroactively
explain its own genesis and to justify the "synchronous" functioning of current structures of exploitation: "the myth of the 'diligent saving worker' who
did not immediately consume his surplus but wisely reinvested it in production and thus gradually became a capitalist, owner of the means of production, able to give employment to other workers possessing nothing but
their ability to work" (1991, p. 107). According to Žižek, this ideological fantasy jumps into its own past in order to appear as its own cause. Thus, the
subject fills out the "missing link" of its own genesis through the narrative
structure of myth and a circular logic that "presupposes what it purports to
explain" (p. 107).

We need to make the contingency of myth visible by unmasking its narrative structure by means of which the synchronous system (the present)
retroactively organizes its own past. In this current historical juncture, the

dominant heterocentric culture retroactively organizes its own past through the ideological myth of heterosexuality (that is, that heterosexual relations are the only natural, civilized, and appropriate sexual relations). What is repressed in this myth is the idea that both heterosexuality and homosexuality are fictions: that heterosexuality has been retroactively written at the level of the political unconscious as *that which is violated by homosexual relations.* A sacerdotal status is accorded to the mythic origin of heterosexuality: that the only way to construct one's identity within the logic of civilized behavior is through a logocentric, heterocentric, and white, male perspective. This is an important observation and acknowledgment to make. Yet when we choose to resist the myth of the modernist Cartesian ego (whose structuring norm of sexual difference effectively demonizes homosexuality) by confronting it with its mythic origins, its constitutive outside, its relation to otherness, do we not simply recuperate the white, male, heterocentric voice in another, less obvious register? Do we not reinforce the very voice that nominates the resistance to its own colonizing effects? Perhaps this is inevitable, but at least such a form of resistance draws attention to the mythic and fictional nature of sexuality. Such a recognition can be a necessary (but not sufficient) step in developing a wider politics of liberation.

This idea needs to be addressed in more detail. For the purpose of this essay I merely want to stress the point that homosexuality and heterosexuality are social fictions constructed through the heterogeneous possibilities of discursive representations. That does not mean that the reflexive subject simply disappears, and is stripped of all historical agency and personal biography. Rather, it means that there exists neither a transcendental nor a biological grounding that incontestably makes heterosexuality more livable and pure when compared to homosexuality. Heterosexuality has meaning only in relation to other identities such as homosexuality. That is, heterosexuality and homosexuality have no "essence" of meaning, but rather, the terms are continually and culturally negotiated within diverse historical and social arenas and in terms of competing vectors of power. Within late patriarchal capitalism, both identities have been reduced to their binary oppositions through structures of linguistic exchange based on a seriality of antimonies: civilized/deviant; natural/unnatural; legal/illegal, and so on. Homosexuality is considered unlivable because it is constructed as the antithesis of what heterosexual communities consider "normal." It is based upon elements of identity expelled, and disavowed, and projected into the always already subordinate terms: gay, lesbian, or homosexual.

The key imperative for critical pedagogy is to interrogate the disparity between students' everyday experiences and relations and the inherited languages of white-supremacist, homophobic, and patriarchal capitalism. How is the dominant culture of schooling able to set the limit on how sexuality is defined and understood, and also able to make the boundaries of sexuality coterminous with those of citizenship? Why is there a lack of vocabularies in our schools for making sense critically of heterosexuality and homosexuality? The answer to these questions should become clearer as the essay progresses.

Jonathan Katz (1990) has argued that the current historical juncture of sexuality politics—or what he calls "the twentieth century heterosexual epoch"—began in the years 1892 to 1900, during which time U.S. doctors tentatively formulated the distinction between heterosexuality and homosexuality. This period also saw Krafft-Ebing break with the consensual, production-oriented view of heterosexuality as an "absolute procreative standard of normality," and move toward a consumerist view of heterosexuality as "other-sex attraction." Katz maintains that this important—perhaps even revolutionary—shift in emphasis provided the basis of understanding heterosexuality as a mode of pleasure.

This perspective was followed by a focus on "different-sex/same-sex eroticisms" and a discursive positioning of heterosexuality as the privileging norm—or "universal sanctifier" (1990, p. 28)—in an institutionalized move to "standardize masculinity and femininity, intelligence, and manufacturing" (p. 16) as well as regularize, naturalize, and police eroticism. Katz claims that, from 1900 to 1930, there occurred a distribution of the heterosexual mystique which he characterizes as a time during which "the tentative hetero hypothesis was stabilized, fixed, and widely distributed as the ruling sexual orthodoxy" (p. 16). It was not until the mid-1960s that heteroeroticism was distinguished from "a procreant urge linked inexorably with carnal lust" (p. 17). Katz's work questions the very heter/homo division itself.

THE HETEROSEX DICTATORSHIP

While, admittedly, heterosexuality and homosexuality existed before they were discursively defined as such, the privileging, modernist, ideological construction of heterosexuality and homosexuality has had an undeniably cruel effect on the social existence of gays and lesbians in general, and gay and lesbian students in particular, especially in terms of the way "the gay lifestyle" has been caricatured and demonized and the practices of heterosexuals have been glorified and sanctified, according to "society's particular organization of power and production" (1990, p. 30). According to Katz, heterosexuality must be understood in its historical specificity. He asserts that:

> women and men make their own sexual histories. But they do not produce their sex lives just as they please. They make their sexualities within a particular mode of organization given by the past and altered by their changing desire, their present power and activity, and their vision of a better world. That hypothesis suggests a number of good reasons for the immediate inauguration of research on a historically specific heterosexuality. (1990, p. 29)

Identities, both homosexual and heterosexual, are historically and culturally articulated. I would like to stress here that not all gay persons suffer oppression in the same way, since individuals are dynamically inserted into specific matrices of domination and subordination according to the axes of race, class, and gender. Other factors, such as geopolitical specificity, age, political affiliations, and so on, also play a part. We are not all gay or straight (or bisexual) in comparable ways. Katz warns against falling into the conceptual trap of viewing heterosexuality as monolithic or invariable, and urges that sexuality be understood as inextricably linked to race, class, gender, and modes of social organization. He is worth quoting at length on this issue:

> The common notion that biology determines the object of sexual desire, or that physiology and society together cause sexual orientation, are determinisms that deny the break existing between our bodies and situation and our desiring. Just as the biology of our hearing organs will never tell us why we take pleasure in Bach or delight in Dixieland, our female or male anatomies, hormones, and genes will never tell us why we yearn for women, men, both, other, or none. That is because desiring is a self-generated project of individuals within particular historical cultures. Heterosexual history can help us see the place of values and judgments in the construction of our own and others' pleasures, and to see how our erotic tastes—our aesthetics of the flesh—are socially institutionalized through the struggles of individuals and classes. (1990, p. 29)

A RADICAL MATERIALIST POLITICS OF SEXUALITY

Conservative approaches to sexuality politics overwhelmingly demonize sexual difference (difference from the heterosexual norm), whereas liberal per-

spectives stress tolerance for sexual differences in the sense that every identity is thought to possess an "essence" that exists beyond sexual practices. A
left-liberal sexuality politics, on the other hand, stresses the importance of
recognizing sexual difference in light of the contextual specificity of its production. That is, sexuality is to be understood as a form of significatory play
within particular communities (Anglo, African-American, and Asian communities, for instance). This form of sexuality politics is often approached
from the perspective of ludic postmodernist or poststructuralist theory,
which takes the form of an antitotalizing analytics (Morton, 1993) but which
de-emphasizes the constitutive and historical role played by social classes in
struggles over meaning.

   Donald Morton positions much of the progressive work on "queer theory"
in this category, especially the work of Eve Kosofsky Sedgwick, Teresa de
Lauretis, Alan Sinfield, and David Greenberg. Morton's argument, which
deserves serious attention, is that many of the exemplary texts of queer theory are "enabled precisely by [their] tendency to endorse and celebrate the
dominant academy's narrative of progressive change" (1993, p. 123). Morton
contrasts the position of ludic postmodernist approaches to queer theory—
whose office of theory is meant to disrupt chains of signification and semi-
otically unsettle dominant meaning structures—with that of critical cultural
studies or what he calls a resistance (post)modernism, a more Marxist-based
approach to social transformation which "investigates the way subjectivities
are reproduced and maintained in ideology through the operations of language and the political/social/economic structures of late capitalism"
(p. 135). From the perspective of a critical cultural studies or resistance
(post)modernist approach, ludic perspectives that shape much of the work
on queer theory currently celebrated in the progressive wings of the academy
are concerned primarily with the construction of "speaking subjects," and
are premised on a poststructuralist infatuation with subverting dominant
sign values and regimes of signification. The problem with the ludic perspective, contends Morton, is that it's concern with experience as the final
court of appeal for a politics of sexuality actually displaces the concern for
transforming society and the exploitative social relations of late patriarchal
capitalism with a bourgeois concern for textually deconstructing the concept of society. Morton is worth quoting on this issue:

   while ludic (post)modern theory demands the deessentialization, denatural-
   ization, and decentering of signs and representations in the name of per-

sonal libidinal liberation, resistance (post)modernism demands collective emancipation by the overthrow of existing exploitative and oppressive struc- tures and a rebuilding of the space of the public sphere along new lines of coherence. In other words, through "knowledge," not "experience," even if in the (post)modern moment "knowledge" is only a "knowledge-effect." (p. 138)

Morton fears (and rightly so) that ludic postmodernism presently has a stranglehold on the progressive discourse of queer theory, a hold that he largely attributes to "the complex historical formation of the social relations of production" (p. 142). He treats contemporary incarnations of queer the- ory as an ahistorical, postconceptual and atheoretical move that exalts expe- rience as the primary referent for understanding the construction of gender and sexuality. Experience is not decried by Morton, since, as a gay man, he understands that oppression is something fundamentally experienced. Yet he chooses to emphasize the importance of using theory to understand, interrogate, and transform experience in relation to the social totality. Morton writes: "I do believe that one *experiences* oppression as a gay per- son, as a woman, as an African-American, but one cannot *explain* that oppression on the level of experience—such an explanation will have to come from sustained theoretical engagements which are capable of con- structing emancipatory knowledges" (p. 142).

THE MOVE AWAY FROM BINARY OPPOSITIONS

One of the theoretical routes out of the binary thinking of the left's pre- dominately Hegelian tradition is a cautious move towards the thinking of Spinoza. This may seem an odd suggestion, and one that may be met with harsh criticism from many of my neo-Marxist colleagues. It is a move that one could see as early as Deleuze and Guattari's *Anti-Oedipus* (1972) and Althusser's *Essays in Self-Criticism* (1976). This theoretical direction (which, I need to emphasize, does not demand a dismissal of Hegel or the dialectic) has been evident in a number of contemporary works, including Pierre Macherey's *Hegel ou Spinoza* (1979), an essay by Etienne Balibar in *Rethinking Marxism* (1989), Antonio Negri's *The Savage Anomaly: The Power of Spinoza's Metaphysics and Politics* (1991), Deleuze's *Spinoza: Practical Philosophy* (1988), and in Norman O. Brown's *Apocalypse and/or Metamorphosis* (1991). This is not the time for a detailed discussion of Spinoza's thought, but is merely an attempt to point one possible way out of the binary thinking that has been inherited from the work of Descartes and that undergirds the work of contemporary Hegelians. As Michael Hardt summarizes so eloquently in his book, *Gilles Deleuze: An Apprenticeship in Philosophy* (1993), Hegelian ontology seeks an external support for its foundation, and finds it in negation. Deleuze draws upon the work of Spinoza to displace negation and affirm the concept of difference.

The materialist ontological position of Deleuze, following Spinoza and Bergson, does not locate being in the movement of oppositions, but rather in a politics of difference. Materiality is at the heart of the Spinozian imagination "in that it provides the possibility of reading the commonality and conflict in the encounters among bodies" (Hardt, 1993, p. 102). Here, reason is demystified and undermined as a given system of necessary truth. Hardt writes that: "In this context, contingency and necessity, imagination and reason are not exclusive and opposing couples, but rather they are plateaus linked together on a productive continuum by the process of constitution" (1993, p. 104). From a Spinozian perspective, the body is no longer subsumed within the order of the mind. Practical acts are not determined by theoretical reasons alone. Constitutive practices, in this view, have a relative autonomy. They are contingent, unforseeable, creative, and nonteleological.

The body and its relationship to power take on a new force in Spinoza's work and in Deleuze's appropriation of it. From this perspective, society does not exist outside an immanent field of forces. It is not constituted by some transcendental fiat. The key notion here is that "being is different in itself" (Hardt, p. 113). It is not defined by difference from another. A Spinozian view would suggest that homosexuality or heterosexuality need not be defined by their antagonism toward each other. They may be conceived simply as different assemblages of being that are not defined by their binary opposite. The politics that emerges from such a position has profound implications for a critical pedagogy that is antiracist, antisexist, and antihomophobic. Because it is a politics of affirming difference, critical pedagogy does not avoid critique, but it is able to push critique further—to its very limits—since it does not recuperate the essence of what it attacks by constructing an affirmation out of the supercession of the negation (as in dialectical logic). In Deleuze's ontology of ethics, being is conceptualized as "a hybrid structure constituted through joyful practice" (Hardt, p. 119). From this perspective, democratic society can be made more connected, less prone to deployments of reactionary power, and more connected to joyful social relationships and "powerful subjective assemblages" of being.

Norman O. Brown has recently remarked:

> Spinoza is the philosopher of the future because right at the beginning of modernity he saw that the Cartesian metaphysic would not work, and by systematic exposure of its internal self-contradictions he was able, in a supreme effort of intellectual abstraction, to arrive at the alternative. (1991, p. 123)

Spinoza undercuts the Cartesian notion of the self-contained, self-explanatory, self-subsistent, and self-determined individual which Brown describes as: "Individualism, pluralism, and lofty idealism on the subjective side; monism and materialism on the objective side: an irrevocable commitment to material development, opening up the infinite world of interacting energy in the physical universe and the infinite world of expanding desire in the human universe" (1991, pp. 123–124). It is an utterly bourgeois Cartesian position, notes Brown, to couple individualism and idealism on the subjective side with the commitment to materialism on the objective side.

Spinoza's perspective is radically monist, in that it suggests "the unity of the mind and the body in every individual and the unity of individuals with each other as parts of the whole" (p. 125). Spinoza's monism, if interpreted politically, "can be seen as setting the historical agenda for us today; to rectify the flaw in modernity; to arrive at one world; to reorganize the gigantic material processes of intercommunication released by modernity into a coherent unity; call it Love's Body" (p. 128).

When Spinoza talks about the social body, it is important to remember, as Brown notes, that the conception of unification at work here is not one that formulates members as functionally or organically differentiated or complimentary, but is more akin to Leibniz's identity of indiscernibles (p. 133). His idea of being is pre-Socratic whereas his philosophy of organism is post-Aristotelian, something we have no space to explore here. Suffice it to say that Spinoza's conception of intersubjectivity and community works against the logocentric conception of the body politic as based upon an "us" against "them" ideology—an ideology that is at the root of modern understandings of difference and that perpetuates the idea of homosexuality as being a "disease" that must be hacked away from the healthy tissues of civilized communities. A turn to Spinoza (and equally important, to Marx) could help us to liberate our conceptions of homosexuality from dualistic thinking that posits artificial boundaries between self and other.

GAY AND LESBIAN IDENTITY AND PRAXIS:
AN OPPOSITIONAL PEDAGOGY

In this section I will summarize in programmatic terms some of the positions presented in this paper. The purpose of this summary is to outline a series of initiatives in the construction of a critical pedagogy that is inclusive of gay and lesbian contributions to society and which, as part of its liberatory project, also examines the structured silences surrounding the oppression of gays and lesbians. Of serious concern here is developing a critical pedagogical approach that involves students in interrogating critically their own construction of sexual identity and in attempting to account for ways in which alternatives to their own identity are constructed through a politics of difference. The fundamental referent that guides such a curriculum is the struggle for social justice and the construction of a more radical democracy.

1. A central characteristic of the critical classroom is to develop a language of analysis and discussion that attempts to break down the intractable binarisms of homosexuality and heterosexuality which operate as part of the discourse of the oppressor. These binarisms are found not only in heterosexual identity politics, but in gay politics as well. For instance, in her recent article, "Making it Perfectly Queer," Lisa Duggan (1992) notes that the tendency of gay theorists to essentialize sexual identity as biological or psychological is fundamentally an Anglocentric and Eurocentric perspective. She writes that: "*Any* gay politics based on the primacy of sexual identity defined as unitary and 'essential' residing clearly, intelligibly and unalterably in the body or psyche, and fixing desire in a gendered direction, ultimately represents the view from the subject position of the '20th-century Western white gay male'" (1992, p. 18). Duggan also remarks that there should be an attempt to avoid the naturalization of the term "bisexual" by not casting it into terms that rigidly gender it.
2. Students need to see gender in a critical relation to desire. It is important, therefore, that gender and desire be understood as social and cultural constructions—as sites of historical specificity and struggle. This means introducing students to constructionist theories of sexual identity. According to Duggan:

Constructionist theories…recognize the (constrained) mobility of desire and support a critical relation to gender. They stake out a new stance of opposition, which many theorists now call "queer." This stance is constituted through its dissent from the hegemonic, structured relations and meanings of sexuality and gender, but its actual historical forms and positions are open, constantly subject to negotiation and renegotiation. (1992, p. 23)

3. Teachers need to reset the parameters of knowledge so that the perspectives of lesbian and gay students are given legitimacy in educational institutions, neighborhood communities, and at the level of state and federal bureaucracies. In a provocative and important essay, "Academic Knowledge and the Parameters of Knowledge," William G. Tierney (1993) develops an insightful case study of a university setting, in which gay and lesbian professors and students are shown to question the meaning of academic freedom within a repressive academic context in which "individuals are not able even to conceive of studying certain ideas such as lesbian and gay studies, which in turn makes academic freedom a concept that demands reanalysis and conceptual clarity from a postmodern perspective" (p. 149). If this is the case on most university campuses, and as a cultural worker in the university system I can attest that, for the most part, it is, then one can wonder what kinds of policies and practices prevail in most elementary, middle, and high school settings.

4. Teachers and students need to work collaboratively to identify the social and cultural processes that both shape and reproduce sexual identity formations in the school, community, and larger society.

5. Teachers and students should engage in a careful analysis of how institutional, organizational, and bureaucratic structures function to constrain and enable the process of sexual identity formation.

6. Teachers need to explore the ways in which sexual identity is informed both by social structures and human agency, and to consider how agency and structure constitute the dialectical weave of all identity. In this light, teachers need to pose and explore the following problem with their students: How is sexual identity inscribed and coded in lifeworld transactions (speech acts, communicative rituals, and routines) at the level of everyday school and classroom life?

7. Teachers and students need to establish a forum for dialogue whereby they can identify the strategies used to justify and arguments used to legitimize ethical, moral, and political positions on sexual identity. Tierney puts the issue as follows:

To come to terms with academic freedom, one must investigate the climate and culture in which a specific topic resides and ask a series of questions: How is knowledge conceived? Whose interests have been advanced by these forms of knowledge? How has what we defined as knowledge changed over time? How does the organization's culture promote or silence some individuals? How are some topics marginalized and others promoted? (1993, p. 158)

8. Teachers and students need to evaluate their own access, and that of other school and community members, to counterhegemonic discourses of sexual identity—those that do not depend on falling within the boundaries of an existing background consensus of taken-for-granted beliefs and normative discourses of authority.

9. Teachers need to raise the following question: What are the discourses of possibility and hope that exist in the school, community, and wider society that can be tapped in order to give students a better sense of how individual and collective struggle can and often does make a difference in the fight for social justice? As Tierney notes, "social constructionist interpretations far too often have the tendency to point out that change does not occur, but…it does" (p. 159). Further, how can students cauterize themselves against the degradation and violence of homophobic prejudice in order to carry forth a project of self and social transformation that is profoundly antiracist, antisexist, and antihomophobic?

10. Since sexual identity cannot, for the most part, remain tied to the tenure of theory, teachers need to explore how students can forge active alliances with progressive social movements and make a link between classroom practice and the public interest. Consequently, teachers and students need to explain ways in which coalitions can emerge that work across barriers of race, class, and gender.

I do not have the space to expand on these issues in relation to developing a curriculum and pedagogy of sexual identity. My purpose has therefore been more suggestive than explanatory. It constitutes a more modest goal of charting out, in a very broad sweep, some of what I feel to be the more significant theoretical insights and political issues that need to be raised, debated, and struggled over if schools are to participate in the construction of a more egalitarian social order with respect to a politics of sexual identity. Surely the question of sexual identity is a crucial area for schools to address critically in renewing their social contract with the public. Otherwise they simply become complicitous with the larger society in continuing the shameful legacy of constructing gay and lesbian identity as the antithesis of a democratic society. This can only lead to acts of "sexual cleansing" and sexual apartheid no less ominous than those which we continue to witness as part of our collective history. In fact, such acts already surround us, and we could see them more clearly if our moral conscience were not so terribly out of focus.

REFERENCES

Althusser, L. (1976). *Essays in Self-Criticism*. Grahame Lock, trans. London: New Left Books.

Balibar, E. (1989). "Spinoza, Anti-Orwell: The Fear of the Masses." *Rethinking Marxism, 2* (3), pp. 104–139.

Baudrillard, J. (1989). "The Anorexic Ruins." In *Looking Back on the End of the World*. D. Kamper and C. Wulf, eds. New York: Semiotext(e), pp. 29–45.

Bogue, R. (1989). *Deleuze and Guattari*. London and New York: Routledge.

Brown, N.O. (1991). *Apocalypse and/or metamorphosis*. Berkeley and Los Angeles: University of California Press.

Deleuze, G. (1988). *Spinoza: Practical Philosophy*. Robert Hurley, trans. San Francisco: City Lights Books.

Deleuze, G. and Guattari, F. (1972). *Anti-Oedipus*. Robert Hurley, Mark Seem, and Helen R. Lane, trans. Preface by Michel Foucault. New York: Viking.

Duggan, L. (1992). "Making it Perfectly Queer." *Socialist Review, 22* (1), pp. 11–31.

Freire, P. and Macedo, D. (1987). *Literacy: Reading the Word and the World*. South Hadley: Bergin and Garvey Publishers.

Giroux, H. (1993). *Border Crossings*. New York and London: Routledge.

———. and McLaren, P. (1989). *Critical Pedagogy, the State and cultural Struggle*. Albany, New York: State University of New York Press.

———. and McLaren, P. (1993). *Between Borders: Pedagogy and Politics in Cultural Studies*. London and New York: Routledge.

Hardt, M. (1993). *Gilles Deleuze: An Apprenticeship in Philosophy*.

Minneapolis and London: University of Minnesota Press.

Katz, J.N. (1990). "The Invention of Heterosexuality." *Socialist Review, 20*(1), p. 734.

Lankshear, C. and McLaren, P. (1993). *Critical Literacy: Politics, Praxis and the Postmodern.* Albany, NY: State University of New York Press.

Lefebvre, H. (1990). *Everyday Life in the Modern World.* Sacha Rabinovitch, trans. New Brunswick and London: Transaction Publishers.

Macherey, P. (1979). *Hegel ou Spinoza.* Paris: Maspero.

McLaren, P. (1989). *Life in Schools: An Introduction to Critical Pedagogy in the Foundations of Education.* White Plains, NY: Longman, Inc.

———. (1993). *Schooling as a Ritual Performance.* Second edition. London and New York: Routledge.

———. (forthcoming). *Radical Pedagogy: Oppositional Politics in a Postmodern Era.* London and New York: Routledge.

———. and Lankshear, C. (1994). *Politics of Liberation: Paths from Freire.* London and New York: Routledge.

Minkowitz, D. (1993). "Blind to the Rainbow: New York Media Strike Out on Curriculum Coverage." *Extra!, 6*(4), pp. 12–13.

Morton, D. (1993). "The Politics of Queer Theory in the (Post)modern Moment." *Genders, 17* (Fall), pp. 121–150.

Negri, A. (1991). *The Savage Anomaly: The Power of Spinoza's Metaphysics and Politics.* Minneapolis and London: University of Minnesota Press.

Sears, J.T. (1991). *Growing Up Gay in the South: Race, Gender and Journeys of the Spirit.* New York: Haworth.

———. (1992). *Sexuality and the curriculum.* New York: Teachers College Press.

Sunker, H. (1989). "Subjectivity and Social Work." *Education, 40,* Institut Für Wissenschaftliche Zusammenarbeit, Tubingen, Federal Republic of Germany, pp. 95–116.

Tierney, W.G. (1993). "Academic Freedom and the Parameters of Knowledge." *Harvard Educational Review, 63* (2), pp. 143–160.

Žižek, S. (1991). "The 'Missing Link' of Ideology." *Strategies, 6,* pp. 93–120.

11

Invisible No More

Addressing the Needs of Lesbian, Gay, and Bisexual Youth and Their Advocates

Karen M. Harbeck

I hope that the readings presented in this book, together with our related writings on the concerns of lesbian, gay, and bisexual (LGB) youth, will inspire and empower you to take action on their behalf. To be honest, many of you who are our heterosexual allies might be better able to afford the risks inherent in taking such action than are young students or your more vulnerable LGB colleagues. You can use your outstanding reputations in your schools, your tenure protections, your union clout, and your life experiences as an adult to educate your colleagues and sway their thinking in support of addressing LGB concerns. What you are doing is brave. I support you, and I want to prepare you for some potential consequences of your bravery. The concerns of LGB youth finally have people's attention. Now we need to do the additional very hard work of talking about these issues in a complex manner, providing services to youth, educating the entire educational community, and facilitating the process of attitudinal change.

CONCERN ONE: COMPLEX ISSUES WARRANT BROADER CONSIDERATIONS THAN JUST SUICIDE

The problems faced by LGB youth are real, troubling—and very diverse. It is true that we face a higher risk of suicidal thoughts, suicide attempts, and actual suicides. However, I believe that we also face a greater risk of being perfectionistic "A" students, National Merit Scholarship winners, earned-wealth millionaires, doctors, lawyers, artists, Olympic athletes, and over-achievers in all that we do. Like so many minority individuals, we can relate to that comment about "a woman having to be twice as good as a man to get half as far." Additionally, many of us have grown up with the feeling that our being LGB is bad, and that we must hide it. Therefore, we are perfect in *everything else* that we try to do, both because we fear that one imperfection will disclose another and because we think that we have so much to make up for because we have feelings of love for members of our same sex. Each of us responds to life, to puberty, to stress, and to hostility in very different ways, and I think that we do a disservice to everyone to so exclusively focus on one negative outcome—suicide.

Certainly, suicide prevention programs need to address the concerns of LGB youth. But every school program in the nation—and every research endeavor—should have its funding and viability evaluated in terms of its sensitivity to minority and women's concerns, including LGB issues and sexual harassment. We are everywhere, and invisibility is no longer a sufficient excuse for failure to educate and to provide services.

CONCERN TWO: AVOID TRADING ONE NEGATIVE STEREOTYPE FOR ANOTHER

With this extreme and sole focus on teen suicide we may be trading one negative stereotype for another. Young people who are exploring their sexual identities may conclude that suicide is the consequence of being LGB. Concerned parents today, listening to all of these dire messages about suicide, may pray even more fervently that their child not be LGB. We should remember and emphasize what is good about our lives, and champion that too. We are talking about loving another human being, and we must emphasize the positive aspects of that love, rather than solely emphasizing the extremely negative outcomes of society's oppression. Of course, talking positively about LGB lives is the very aspect of the discussion that is silenced by the demand that we not "advocate, solicit or promote" homosexuality in the schools. This restriction stifles honest communication. It permits our opposition to frame us in an ongoing discussion of our dysfunctional, dire disabilities and differences.

After nearly twenty years of lecturing and teaching about LGB concerns, it always amazes me that society, educators, pediatricians, and others know so little about our lives and the communities that we have established. We have softball leagues, church groups, newspapers, international travel events, dances, weddings, funerals, births, parenthood, publishing houses, literature, music, art, children, politics, Republicans, Democrats, cats—every imaginable interest, ability, and commitment—you name it. Our lives are not terrible. They are joyous, mundane, tragic and everything in between. And much of this has nothing to do with whether we are LGB; it has to do with being alive.

I know that dealing with the rejection of my family and with the struggles of everyday life as an out graduate student, attorney, and nontenured professor has engendered in me some of the personal characteristics of which I am most proud. *Adversity* molded my strength, my wisdom, my advocacy, and my vision of a better world. Many of the most incredible, courageous people that I look up to in life have transformed adversity into action and growth. Being LGB in our society provides a unique opportunity for *a whole continuum of responses*, ranging from joy and self-acceptance to suicide. We should model positive lives in order to move towards—and thereby hopefully transcend—the pain and isolation that lead to suicide and despair.

CONCERN THREE: ESTABLISH COLLECTIVE SUPPORT AND ADVOCACY

In advocating for the welfare of LGB youth, we should not lose sight of other related groups of individuals who need our support and advocacy. Our society still struggles with issues of race, national origin, religion, gender, physical and mentality ability bias, and sexual harassment. A great deal of coalition-building and cooperation is imperative in these areas. But even in the area of LGB concerns, our advocacy needs to include LGB parents, the children of LGB parents, other family members, our heterosexual allies, and LGB educators. The experience of persons in each of these populations is often one of isolation, vulnerability, and lack of collective support.

We must advocate to protect and support straight teachers who are willing to take the risk to address this important social and humanitarian issue in schools. Dr. James Sears provides a compelling look at what faculty colleagues think of the situation. After interviewing schoolteachers and counselors, Sears reports that they know that, because of their licensure and professional mandates, they have an ethical obligation to provide services for LGB youth. However, these same teachers and counselors are ignorant of our lives, minimally aware of alternative thinking to their traditionally engendered prejudices, and fearful that if they do take action, then their colleagues and employers will label them as homosexual too.

If it were not bad enough to find that our potential heterosexual allies are afraid to come out for us, data on identity management by lesbian physical education teachers is equally depressing. Although these teachers realize that the times are changing, and that they have numerous legal protections, they also are equally convinced that if they come out they will lose their jobs. They often distance themselves from LGB youth who might accidentally or intentionally "out" them at school if they were open or sympathetic. We lead such double lives that we are often unable to discuss both being LGB and at the same time being a teacher, counselor, or school administrator. We bifurcate our identities, and then we end up not feeling as if we truly belong in either world—or in any world. Although life is sometimes difficult, perhaps the cruelest measure is that we have internalized society's negative messages about who we are; thus, we inadvertently assist it in keeping us in our disesteemed place. People know that when they act in a courageous and embodied fashion, they feel better about themselves and the world that they live in. Teachers, administrators, and counselors should come out, if and when they can, and hopefully many individuals will be there to support them.

Another type of positive alliance that seems worth developing is the link between educators from different student age groups. Teachers from elementary, junior high school, high school, college, university, professional schools, and teacher training programs should work more closely together to form multilayered approaches to these educational and social concerns.

CONCERN FOUR: STRATEGICALLY PLAN FOR EFFECTIVE INTERVENTION
I advise colleagues to *strategically* plan their efforts to create safety in their schools for LGB youth. Sit down and work through the issues and arguments until you can present a positive, nondefensive, compassionate logic for your requests. Do your homework. Participate in good, old-fashioned consciousness raising and support groups, so that you feel empowered before taking

actions that are important to you. Develop a strategy for engaging hostile colleagues in an ongoing discussion of the issues, so that eventually some common and useful ground can be established. The process is one of ongoing education and communication, and this process is just as worthwhile as the ultimate outcomes that you are trying to achieve. In fact, my research suggests that, if actions are taken on our behalf without a full process of discussion and education, then those outcomes are vulnerable to the slightest change in personnel or circumstances, because people do not have a shared ownership or commitment to the mandate.

CONCERN FIVE: REQUIRE COURSES IN SCHOOL LAW

I truly believe that all school administrators and teachers should be required to take a school law course. Once they are familiar with the civil rights implications, the liability, and the employment rights concerns, I would hope that they would make fewer errors in judgment towards women and minority youth in our schools. And for your own protection, I urge you to become familiar with your own legal entitlements. For example, the National Education Association has provided free legal counsel since 1973 to any union member in any of the fifty states who has faced harassment or job loss on the basis of sexual orientation issues, whether or not you are in fact gay or lesbian. The American Federation of Teachers has done the same since 1974. If difficult circumstances arise as these issues heat up, know that you have support and allies with clout. In some communities, like San Francisco, for example, the most significant advocate for change in support of LGB concerns came from union demands for contractual protections.

CONCERN SIX: REVAMP ALL GRIEVANCE PROCEDURES

It is absolutely critical for state legislatures, departments of education, and local educational institutions to revamp their entire perspective on minority grievance processes. From my own personal experiences on the university level, as a school law consultant to local schools, and as someone hired to evaluate many institutions' procedures, I know that almost nothing is done to intervene in hostile or discriminatory situations until actual violence occurs. It would seem that the most effective thing to do would be to establish regions around a state, and then appoint ombudspersons for various grade levels—from elementary, junior high school, senior high, and college—so that people could reach the attention of the Department of Education when unfairness and discrimination are occurring in schools and colleges. It is my best professional assessment that almost all grievance processes in our educational systems are ineffective, including those designed to protect faculty members and administrators from the misbehavior of their colleagues. Perhaps if these new grievance procedures were combined with a massive educational campaign and an increased awareness of legal rights and obligations, we could eradicate much of the violence and pain that is occurring in our schools today.

CONCERN SEVEN: MAINTAIN A VISION OF YOUR GOALS AND PURPOSES

The struggle will not always be easy. The hardships of LGB persons have a long historical basis, and it will not change overnight. But the only way it *can* change is if those of us who can afford to take the risk take that risk— every time we need to—on behalf of those who have not yet found their own voices on this issue. My hope is that, if you are forewarned, you will not be caught off guard should outrageous things start to happen over this issue. I say this so that you retain your sense of humor—and your sense of purpose.

Throughout the months and years ahead, you will have countless opportunities to intervene in many ways on behalf of LGB concerns. Maybe you stop some gay jokes, or you modify a form that goes home to parents so that it is inclusive of diverse family structures. You may add LGB concerns to your classroom materials and lobby for library materials as well, or you may sponsor a Gay/Lesbian/Bisexual/Straight Alliance support group. Although there may be some voices of opposition and surprise, your efforts will have a positive impact, *even if it is not immediately apparent.*

I am reminded of one of my graduate students in teacher training who gave me a hard time because I spoke about LGB issues in my state-mandated minority studies course. A couple of years later, she wrote me a letter thanking me for taking the risk. Not only had she subsequently discovered that her brother was gay, but also that he was dying of AIDS. She left her new teaching position and spent six months nursing her brother until he died. She wrote me to thank me for helping her obtain the insight and courage to make that choice, so that she could have those very precious months with a brother with whom she had been inexplicably out of touch prior to her increased sensitivity. I tell this story to illustrate that when the going gets tough—and it will—the rewards or growth may not emerge instantaneously; they will, however, emerge somehow and somewhere in places that you and I can not even contemplate. Teachers know that simple truth.

Related to this point, I would like to share another experience that touched me deeply. I was asked to speak at the state department of corrections for juvenile offenders, young people incarcerated for criminal offenses and required to attend social issues classes as part of their rehabilitation. It may go down as the worst speaking engagement of my life. All of the prewritten questions were violent and sexually offensive, and the young people were so upset by our presence that they demanded that we all sit female, male, female, male all around the room so that none of them would have to sit near a homosexual who might make a pass at them. When I left the building I had the most overwhelming feelings of despair and wonder at why I subjected myself to these situations. I truly was convinced that in this instance, the effort had not been worth it, and the audience had been unreachable. A couple of years later I was lecturing at a state college, and after the speech was over, two young men with big smiles on their faces approached me and said, "Do you remember us, we were in the state corrections facility the day you spoke about being a lesbian." In front of all of their friends, each of them gave me a warm, intense hug, and said how much that speech meant to them, even though they did not know it at the time. Now when I go into hard situations, I think of them. No audience or situation is a lost cause in the long run, even if it seems impossible at first.

CONCERN EIGHT: MAKE USE OF SUCCESSFUL EXISTING INTERVENTION MODELS

Several intervention models for LGB youth are now in existence. I would urge all of our allies to keep in mind the dual intervention aspects of Project 10 (see the article by Virginia Uribe in this collection) and other successful program models. It is important to have support groups for those who wish to attend around LGB issues. But it is also important to educate the *entire* student population about these issues. Not only does this broader educational effort make schools safer for minority students, but also our research suggests that the general student body appreciates the increased information and intervention, that they become proud that they have friendships with their LGB peers, and that they are better prepared for life in our diverse society. They adjust. They grow, if given the guidance and the opportunity. And everybody benefits.

CONCERN NINE: AVOID SEXUALIZING THE DEBATE

We must not let the debate over LGB concerns be co-opted to focus only on sex. If I defined traditional marriage as merely legal permission for unrestrained sexual access, many would be offended at my narrow and pejorative perspective. Similarly, when others define my love and commitment as nothing more than sexual perversion, I am offended by their focus on my bedroom activities. Just as marriage embodies a complex, multifaceted relationship with each other, children, family members, and community, so does my relationship commitment.

Being a LGB person is a life, not a lifestyle. It is a choice, whether or not one believes in nature or nurture developmental origins. I choose to act on my feelings and express my personhood. And that choice and personal freedom is all the more precious to me because of society's long-held opposition to my feelings. If I do not assert responsibility for my actions, I am powerless. I can only beg of my oppressors to have pity on me, for after all, I cannot help what I am. I am proud of what I am. It is a positive, loving, and challenging life that I have chosen and made for myself.

Similarly, when I state my belief that LGB concerns should be raised at all grade levels, someone invariably says, "Good grief, she wants to teach first-graders about anal intercourse!" That is not the case, but first-graders might be taught that some children have two mommies or two daddies, and that two girls or boys can grow up and love each other. The research on sexual orientation development suggests that it is established by age five or six at the latest, even if it is not in the conscious awareness of the child. So talking about LGB concerns is not going to *cause* it, and it may be of tremendous comfort to young people struggling to express their uniqueness.

CONCERN TEN: ATTEND TO THE ORGANIZED POLITICAL OPPOSITION

We cannot be naïve about the forces converging to oppose change in educational concerns such as this one. The extreme conservative right has targeted school board elections across the country as the vulnerable key to local power. Thus the Ku Klux Klan, the John Birch Society, the Moral Majority, and other conservative groups have raised funds and targeted individuals to run for office on local school boards as if they were Joe or Jane Average Concerned Citizen. However, their political effort is financed and orchestrated by the extreme conservative right. Once elected, it is intended that these individuals come out of their own closets as advocates of right-wing concerns.

Whether we realize it or not, by raising LGB concerns in education, we are fighting in a larger battle over social change. We must organize under broader coalitions to combat this well-organized political machine. We must run for office, and we must speak our minds whenever possible, so that voices of reason may be heard over voices of hatred and bigotry. We must question the influences behind the voices of opposition. They would like to characterize those who are concerned about LGB issues as members of a political machine taking over the hearts and minds of our nation's children with extreme liberal perspectives. In reality, *they* are the political machine organizing "Operation Rescue" and "Operation Stealth" in subversive, and sometimes violent, attempts to impose their beliefs on the majority.

I am not saying that everyone who opposes LGB concerns in education is a right-wing member of the Klan. I *am* saying that the flames of this debate are being intentionally fueled by persons opposed to full participation for the African-Americans, Catholics, Jews, women, and homosexuals in our society. I am also saying that, from the evidence, it would appear that the conservative right is not solely a well-organized voice of opposition; it is also an intentional monger of violence and hatred in our society and in our schools.

Lesbian, gay, and bisexual concerns are a civil rights issue, a humanitarian concern, a question of fairness, equity, equal protection, and of valuing diversity and individual differences. They are a question of developing human potential and creativity, of making unique contributions, and of broadening our traditionally held views on gender roles, love, commitment, the family, and sexuality. Teachers struggle everyday to teach students calculus, or English literature, or American history. What, however, is the value of these subjects if your students are wounded by prejudice, suffer from low self-esteem and feelings of isolation, and are limited in their life opportunities by ignorance and discrimination based upon whom they choose to love?

REFERENCES

Sears, J. (1992). "Educators, Homosexuality and Homosexual Students: Are Personal Feelings Related to Professional Beliefs?" In *Coming Out of the Classroom Closet*. Karen M. Harbeck, ed. New York: Haworth Press.

12

Black-Gay or Gay-Black?

Choosing Identities and Identifying Choices

James T. Sears

> They say I do it, Ain't nobody caught me
> Sure got to prove it on me;
> Went out last night with a crowd of my friends,
> must've been women, 'cause I don't like no men
>
> —*Ma Rainey, "Prove it on Me Blues"* (Lieb, 1981, p. 124)

The image of today's "homosexual" has changed from the pre-Stonewall stereotype of limp-wristed, self-hating queers portrayed in films such as *The Boys in the Band*. Although contemporary films have helped to transform the homosexual image, from Albin (Michel Serrault) in *La Cage Aux Folles* to Andrew Beckett (Tom Hanks) in *Philadelphia*, the homosexual is still pictured as white. As educators, however, we must understand the complexities of growing up colored in a culture where "race matters," and gay where the homosexual has become the "new nigger" of the nineties.

This article details the life of one African-American, homosexual adolescent—Jacob—as he and several other black gay youth struggle for identity in a society fractured along fault lines of sexuality, race, class, and gender.[1] The life stories of these young men detail how various intersections make coming of age more difficult and complex than it is for their white counter-parts—straight or gay. Following this narrative and related discussion, I conclude with an overview of professional resources, and curriculum suggestions for educators who are seeking to better understand or integrate into their classrooms gay-related issues among adolescents of color, particularly African-Americans.

BECOMING A BLACK GAY MAN

Jacob lived on the western edge of the Carolina Low Country where cotton was once king and bottomlands wrap around small towns. "You would have to go elsewhere to enjoy any kind of recreation," he remembers. "Whether it's going to a decent movie or doing some nice shopping. It's a very quiet town. It's pretty much set in its ways." About one-half of the town's population is black, including Jacob. Though racial integration was instituted when he was in elementary school, the county maintains two elementary schools, two middle schools, and two high schools—one predominantly white and the other predominantly black.

Jacob's parents encouraged Jacob, the youngest in an old middle-class family of six, to explore his intellectual, social, and artistic talents. Since his brothers and sisters were of high school age at the time Jacob entered kindergarten, he found himself worried about being with other children his own age. Jacob remembers his first day in school:

I was always a mamma's child during that stage. I cried the first day. Then, I discovered that I was a people-person. I liked to be around people. Since I didn't have a lot of playmates prior to kindergarten, that was a whole new experience. After that first day, I had no problems.

During childhood, his parents supported him in his artistic interests: he took private piano and art lessons. Jacob was encouraged to develop his social and leadership skills: he organized neighborhood street carnivals, conducted parades on his street, and formed social clubs.

Jacob also excelled in school: "I was the teacher's pet. I thought it was great. I had no problems with it because, at first grade I looked at the situation and thought, 'I've got twelve years of this. I'm going to have to get along with these people.' I saw it as politics, even at the first grade." Jacob did not suffer at the hands of his classmates as the "teacher's pet." During the first and second grade, Jacob was a class leader, and had his "own little group" on the playground. He enjoyed school, respected his teachers, got along well with his classmates, and performed well above average academically.

At the beginning of Jacob's third grade year, racial integration began. Though he remained in what was the school district's all-black elementary school, some of his friends were transferred to the other school. A small proportion of whites, mostly working-class kids, were bused to his school. "I basically didn't look at them as being white kids," Jacob recalls. "It was just getting to know new students." Integration allowed Jacob the opportunity to make new friends. Celeste became a particularly good friend:

> I liked her because she was smart. I *was* the smartest kid on the block, then she comes. It was just fun to be around her. We were more mature than the other kids in the class. We used to play during recess. It didn't really dawn on me that she was white and I was black. Integration, though, was a big thing in my hometown. You would hear the adults talk about how much trouble there would be. I used to ask my mom if I could go over to visit Celeste. She would make excuses. Celeste would ask if she could come over to visit me and her parents would make up excuses.

By the time Jacob had entered fifth grade, he was actively involved in sports as well as schoolwork. In fifth grade, Jacob also had a new girlfriend. "I went through these little love letter stages: 'Do you like me?' It was the thing to do, so I wrote Rachel a letter and we dated for a while. We took two classes together. I walked her to school and carried her books."

As Jacob entered his last year in elementary school, he came to realize the meaning of being an African-American in a rural Southern town. On weekend nights, Jacob and some of his friends, along with many of the kids in the county, would go to their "hangout," the Star Crystal, the town's skating rink. One Saturday night in late spring, a black classmate got into a fight with a white girl. During the argument, the white girl's brother yelled out "Niggers!" Fighting broke out among blacks and whites. For several weeks it was the talk of the county.

About that same time, Jacob's sixth-grade teacher asked him to come by her classroom after school:

> Mrs. Green said, "Until last year, Jacob, Celeste had been doing much better than you. But you've made a big improvement. Big enough to be class valedictorian." She told me how important that was and how proud she was

because I was black. I asked, "Why should that make a difference?" In a nut-shell, she summed it up. "As far as being black, you have to do better. You have to give 120 percent over the white person." That stuck with me. When I got to junior high school, I had to make the top ten. In my hometown, there had never been a black person to make the top ten. From the day Mrs. Green talked to me, that was the goal I set for myself.

Not only was the meaning of being black impressed on Jacob's young mind, sixth grade was also the time of his sexual awakening. He recognized his strong attraction for guys at the age of ten. "I just felt more comfortable around guys. My best friend at the time, Rodney, we had a lot more to talk about, laugh about, joke about than I did with girls." He and Rodney never explored sex. The summer following his sixth-grade year, however, that changed, as Jacob was coaxed into engaging in sex with Lester, a high-school-aged neighbor. This began a nonemotional sexual relationship that contin-ued through Jacob's thirteenth birthday.

That fall, Jacob left his black-dominated elementary school for a predom-inantly white junior high school. "There was a lot more competition as far as grades in classes," Jacob noted. He was placed in the most advanced group. In most of these classes, he was the only African-American. He continued to earn good grades as well as engage in after-school activities.

He also continued to see Lester. "I would never call him and say, 'Let's have sex.' I would maybe go over and visit him knowing that there was nobody home. I knew that it would happen." As Jacob tried to cope with these emerging homosexual feelings and his occasional homosexual activities, his religious upbringing tugged at his insides:

I went to church every week, and I studied my Sunday school lesson. I used to tell myself that I knew that God would forgive me for my sins. Even though I knew I was doing them over and over. I would pray every night, "God, forgive me for my sins." It was like, you do whatever you want to do during the day, but at night don't worry about it because you're going to pray, and the Lord is going to forgive you.

Jacob did not label himself gay until he was sixteen; the central core of his identity, however, has always been color. "I'm proud of my black heritage," Jacob proclaims. "I wouldn't trade it for anything." During junior high school, Jacob continued to excel in academics. He became involved in student government and the drama club. At the end of his seventh-grade year, he was named to the "Superlatives" for being the most studious. "That's when people started looking at me as being a scholar. Throughout junior high and high school, I never made anything lower than an 'A'." Beginning in junior high school, Jacob felt under increased pressure:

> I knew at this point that my whole family thought I was the smartest person in the world. My parents got to the point where they didn't seem to even look at my report cards. They would just sign them because they knew I had made good grades. One time I switched report cards on them just to see if they would notice. My mom said, "Jacob! These aren't your grades. These can't be yours." So, I guess they paid some attention to them.

Three years later, Jacob completed the ninth grade having achieved his goal of making the academic top ten and graduating as class valedictorian. He had also become adept at hiding his sexual feelings from friends and family. As a high school student, Jacob continued to demonstrate superior academic and leadership skills. But the fact of his race also continued to weigh on him.

> It was still very much a racial situation in my high school. As far as being on top in academics or student government, I always had a strong sense of being black. I had to let it be known that I was not a "token." It meant a lot to be able to win as president in a class that was 70 percent white.

As an adolescent black male in the rural South the boundaries for Jacob's behavior were clearly circumscribed. Despite civil rights progress, being an African-American still exacts psychic and, at times, physical costs. Though he was elected class president, he felt his election was at least partly due to a sense of tokenism among students and faculty. Jacob's actions often were viewed by himself and others through a racial lens—a perspective, as the following school bus incident illustrates, which sometimes placed Jacob in physical peril:

> I drove a school bus during high school. We had a busing problem with the whites on a bus that went to a black school, and vice versa. I tried to be a very strict bus driver, but there were still fights on my bus. There was one particular incident in which a big white child got into a fight. I got him suspend-

ed off my bus. He had been in so much trouble that when he got suspended off my bus, he also got suspended from school for three days. His parents came to my bus and started to hassle and threaten me. I had to have police escorts for a week. Later the director of busing started coming down on the black bus drivers and being real unfair. I got elected to be spokesperson for the black drivers. I led a protest and we walked off our jobs. They didn't have buses for a whole day. There was chaos because nobody was there to drive all the black kids' buses. The administration was all over me saying, "You're class president. You can't do this." And, I was like, "No, but you see, I'm black...."

By virtue of Jacob's school-related activities and achievements, Jacob's effeminate mannerisms and lack of interest in girls were rarely questioned by friends or family. "It was like, 'He don't have time for girls. He's smart. He's doing his books.'" Jacob often played off this theme: "I knew there were a couple of girls interested in me. We would talk and I would play the intellectual role. It was like, 'I guess he really doesn't have time for me.' That's how I would psych them out." When his younger sister would ask about girlfriends during family dinner, he arrogantly replied, "I don't think there's a girl out there good enough for me. Besides, I don't have time. Look at my grades." Jacob's parents would back him up, saying "He doesn't have time for that, child. He's working on a scholarship for college."

During high school, Jacob did "hang together" with a peer group composed of a roughly equal mixture of boys and girls. This group included some "platonic girlfriends." Jacob remembers one with particular fondness: "We were real tight. We had our classes together, and we were in a lot of other things like honor society and going to parties and meetings. We just used to do things automatically together. I think that's what really kept all the people from asking." Nevertheless, a few adult neighbors suspected that Jacob might be gay because "I wasn't out getting dirty and playing football." Had he been pressed by his sister or an adult, he would have denied it, saying, "Are you crazy? I'm not gay!" Asked why his parents, who likely heard the neighbors' gossip, did not confront him on the matter, Jacob popped, "Maybe they were afraid of me saying, 'Yes'. I think that may have been why my parents never mentioned it to me."

Jacob privately proclaimed his sexual identity during his sophomore year, confessing to himself, "Well, you know you like to have sex with guys so that makes you a homosexual." He refused to place himself in the same category as those who were labeled "faggots" at his high school. There were about ten "hard-core faggots" in his school of fifteen hundred students. "In that little group, most of these white guys were open about it. They were very effeminate-acting. They openly said, 'Yeah I'm interested in guys. What are you going to say about it?'" Jacob would "pass for straight, and I really didn't associate with them. They were pretty much social outcasts." However, he was tuned into the news about gay life, and often thought about the problems confronting those who openly acknowledged their homosexuality. "I'd sit back and analyze situations that gay people were in," Jacob recollects, "like the people that struggled for gay rights or that got thrown in jail." Although he did not associate with the "faggot group" in high school, he empathized with the problems they were confronting. He felt their harassment was unjust. "I was reared that you don't judge a book by its cover, and you can't just say things about people." With his reputation for his willingness to stick up for others, few were surprised when Jacob finally called a friend down for such harassment. "One of my best friends used to make jokes about them and used to pick at them. I finally said, 'Have you ever been to bed with that person?' He couldn't say 'yes' and he wouldn't say 'no.' He just didn't say anything. So, I said, 'Then you can't talk.'"

Throughout adolescence, Jacob's primary concerns were issues associated with the color of his skin, not the gender of his sexual partner: "We did not get black history in my high school. I yearned for that. I went out and got it on my own. Most of the gay materials I read were pornographic materials or those little pamphlets you pick up at a club."

Jacob's identity as a black man and his commitment to academic excellence continued throughout his college years. His skin color, not his homosexual behavior, shaped his life's work and goals. In less than four years, Jacob completed college with honors, and found a job in state government. Declaring gay is less important for him than expanding the opportunities and influence of African-Americans, Jacob founded an organization, "Black Together," whose members regularly meet to share friendship and to work on social projects within the African-American community.

THE OLD AND NEW BLACK MIDDLE CLASS

The ancestors of the old black middle class were antebellum free artisans and gentry living in Southern port cities and northern commercial municipalities (Durant and Louden, 1986; Frazier, 1925; Landry, 1987). From the ashes and hopes of Reconstruction, Jim Crow laws undermined their economic autonomy while elevating their status within newly formed black communities (Frazier, 1939). The restrictive immigration laws and the industrialization of a post-World War I workforce spurred the growth of this middle class, which enjoyed its greatest pre-civil rights prosperity during the Harlem Renaissance of the twenties. The "new black middle class" emerged in the decades following the *Brown* decision. Writing in the mid-fifties, Frazier (1957) observed:

> The black bourgeoisie constantly boast of their pride in their identification as Negroes. But when one studies the attitude of this class in regard to the physical traits or the social characteristics of Negroes, it becomes clear that the black bourgeoisie do not really wish to be identified with Negroes. (pp. 215–216)

Jacob and his family are not members of the new black middle class. With his weekly piano lessons, exemplary academic performance, and passion for social leadership, Jacob reflects the values of the old, southern, black gentry. His biography, juxtaposed with that of Nathaniel's story, below, illustrates the contemporary boundary between the old black bourgeoisie and the new black middle class. Nathaniel's story also illuminates how community forces within the new black middle-class community can affect the identity of a black man with homosexual feelings.

Nathaniel's father is a commercial truck driver, and his mother is the head of nursing at a metropolitan hospital. Nathaniel has lived his eighteen years in upper-middle-class neighborhoods. He attended two of the nation's finest coeducational military academies from the first through the ninth grades. "I wanted to get out [of the academies] but my father wanted me [to stay] there. My father was basically scared of my mother who was the big breadwinner of the house. He couldn't take it so he took all of his anger out on us kids."

Nathaniel did reasonably well academically, though his first love was sports. "I was basically a quiet student who always worked and who did his best in doing what I had to do. But, I really love to run, just getting away, you know." By the time Nathaniel was in fifth grade, "I was noticing guys. Not knowing that I was gay—just curious about guys. I thought it was wrong and I kept wondering, 'Why am I attracted to men?'" At thirteen, he engaged in sex with another boy; a few months later Nathaniel had a steady girlfriend, Delta, with whom he also shared sexual intimacy. For the past five years, he and Delta have gone steady; for the past year and a half he has also been dating Hodding. Delta is black; Hodding is white. Noting "it's rougher being black and gay," Nathaniel claims that if homosexuality was more acceptable, "I probably would be strictly homosexual. When I got Delta, it was like a cover. I was having sex with a man, but for security I got a girlfriend and we've stuck together."

Finally, in tenth grade Nathaniel attended a public school. He was elated, "because I didn't have to wear a uniform and didn't have to carry myself as a military student anymore. I could let loose. I started wearing tight clothes. I really wanted to get an earring in the wrong ear, but I didn't want no one to know I was gay." As a high school senior in this predominantly white, upper-class school, Nathaniel seldom associates with other blacks. "I wanted to be like one of the preppies. I hang out with the jocks and the preps at school. My black friends sometimes give me a hard time because of the way I dress and the neighborhood I live in." Nathaniel also has confrontations with the "redneck-druggies." "They called us 'little pukes.' They are the hicks who hang out on the back porch, wear these rebel shirts, and run a four-wheel drive." Though occasionally harassed by them for his effeminate behavior, the jocks and preps stand behind him. "I guess they said, 'Gay guys don't wrestle. Gay guys don't have a girlfriend. Gay guys don't drive a '69 Chevelle.' So I must be okay."

In Nathaniel's suburban world, social class and family status are important considerations. His association with the preppies, disinterest in rap music and black history, and fondness for white men clearly distinguish Nathaniel from Jacob. In Jacob's rural county town, race was the important social marker. Both his inability to bring Celeste home after school and the fracas on that spring night at the Star Crystal illustrate the rural Southern boundary between his county's black and white citizens.

Unlike Nathaniel, however, Grant is part of the old black bourgeoisie. Grant's light skin is a historical reminder of the elasticity in sexual relations during the antebellum era, the special role of light-skinned servants in the operation of the Big House, and the premium placed on mulatto women and children by the old middle class. Shy, withdrawn, and bright, Grant changed schools in sixth grade, when the family moved to a mid-sized city. Unlike Nathaniel, he had difficulty adjusting to suburban white culture:

Most of the kids I went to school with were really wealthy. There was always a sense of inadequacy. I just didn't fit in. I didn't have the money. It was like the kids had bicycles and I didn't. I wanted one. When I finally got a bicycle, everyone was into mopeds. I was always late.

Grant lacked status at this school because of his parents' financial situation and his skin color. Grant's academic ability also proved to be a liability in this situation. One of three African-Americans in an accelerated class of twenty-nine students, Grant underscores the problems he faced in this new environment:

> It is really hard on black kids, especially if they are in accelerated classes. You get all of this negative feedback. It's done in a subtle way. I don't even think it's intentional. Whenever references are made to blacks, you can tell in the intonation of the teachers' voices—they tense up. Or, when you would go to the gymnasium for awards night, and everybody is mostly white, and a black comes up to the stage and gets an award—people start moving around in their chairs and you hear things. This is *still* the South. It's like being black is abnormal. Unless you're white, you're not normal. You would also get it from other blacks who were in the regular classes. They would always say that you were being "uppity" because you were in that class. They'd say you were trying to act like an "oreo." They'd shy away from you, and then the only people you have to associate with are whites. It was a vicious cycle.

Speaking of the "black community" or, for that matter, generalizing about any minority group diminishes differences among subgroups, and under-values the power of individuals to transcend those boundaries. Grant, a son of old middle-class parents, one a school teacher and the other a minister, was labeled an "oreo" by his more rowdy and less respectful black classmates. Jacob, dark-skinned, the product of an old middle-class background, and the recipient of academic honors, was not. Jacob's primary identity is black. He eagerly represented his fellow black coworkers in the bus walkout and his fellow students as the first black student body president. Nathaniel, a son of new upper-middle-class parents, is concerned with joining the right groups and wearing the most fashionable clothes. Projecting a bisexual image, he has little interest in African-American culture or his black heritage.

THE BLACK MIDDLE CLASS AND HOMOSEXUALITY

Race separated Jacob's personal and social worlds in the school community; homosexuality separated Jacob's private and public worlds in the African-American community. Though Jacob was successful in crossing the racial boundary in school, as evidenced by student elections and academic awards, he has been less successful in transcending the sexual boundary within his black community—particularly among the old black middle class.

Some observers of African-American communities have noted differences between poor and middle-class blacks' reactions toward homosexuality. For example, Cheryl Clarke (1983) writes:

> The poor and working class black community, historically more radical and realistic than the reformist and conservative black middle class and the atavistic, "Blacker-than-thou" (bourgeois) nationalist, has often tolerated an individual's lifestyle prerogatives, even when that lifestyle was disparaged by the prevailing culture. Though lesbians and gay men were exotic subjects of curiosity, they were accepted as part of the community (neighborhood)—or at least, there were no manifestos calling for their exclusion from the community. (p. 206)

This is underscored by John Soares (1979) who notes that middle-class black families "are so persistently monitoring their social standing that any family member departing from their peer group norm would experience a certain degree of ostracism. But, for what appears to be the majority of working class black people, gay lovers and steadies are accepted by or even into the family...." (p. 265). These observations may explain why none of the middle-class participants in my 1991 study have "come out" to their families, while all of the working class males have done so. As Irwin observes:

> When you're black in a black society and you're gay it's even harder. Blacks don't want it to be known because they don't want to mimic or imitate white people. They see it as a crutch and they don't want to have to deal with it. That's what they have been taught. They would do all sorts of things to deny that someone in their family is gay or that they're gay.

Referring to his black community, Malcolm declares:

> If they are going to see you with a man at all, they would rather see you with another black man. I think it goes back to racism and slavery. There was a time when whites owned blacks. If they think you're gay and you're with a white man, they think that he's your sugar daddy or you're a snow queen. If you happen to be a masculine type, then they think that the white is just using you to get that black stuff from a stud.

THE ENDANGERED BLACK MALE

The church and the family have been the bulwark of the African-American community as generation after generation have confronted challenges to the black spirit (Frazier, 1939; McAdoo, 1981). From the economic hardships during Reconstruction to the collapse of the Southern Depression economy and the social turmoil of the Civil Rights Movement, African-American family structures have evolved. Jacob's is the latest generation of a Southern black family that has survived and modestly prospered during the past nine generations.

During the past two generations, Jacob's two-parent family model has become more unusual, as the proportion of households headed by females has increased dramatically. Sociologist Robert Staples (1987) concludes that the decline of the nuclear black family is a reflection of the "greater sexual permissiveness, alternate family lifestyles, increased divorce rates, and reductions in the fertility rate" (p. 275). Lamenting this decline, he states:

> The basis of a stable family rests on the willingness and ability of men and women to marry, bear and rear children, and fulfill socially prescribed familial roles. In the case of women, those roles have traditionally been defined as the carrying out of domestic functions such as cooking and cleaning, giving birth to children and socializing them, and providing sexual gratification, companionship, and emotional support to their husbands. There is abundant evidence that black women are willing and able to fulfill those roles. Conversely, the roles of men in the family are more narrowly confined to that of economic provider and family leader. There are indications that a majority of black American males cannot implement those roles. (p. 278)

Staples cites homosexuality as one of the reasons for the black male's inability to fulfill his role. This "shortage of desirability of black males in the marriage pool," is augmented by "800,000 black men [who] are not available to heterosexual black women" (p. 281). The fact that many lesbians and gay men marry and have children or that they have contributed to black culture are subtleties lost upon crusaders for the African-American family—a fact not lost upon one writer for *Ebony* magazine:

> Individual homosexuals have been a part of the black race during our entire history on this continent. We have worked together, worshipped together, and together faced loneliness—all within the context of black family life—and

we have survived as the black Family to this very day. (Butts, 1981, p. 144)

The noted African-American poet Audre Lorde (1978) makes a similar point:

Instead of keeping our attentions focused upon the real enemies, enormous energy is being wasted in the black community today by both black men and heterosexual black women, in anti-lesbian hysteria.... [T]he unmarried aunt, childless or otherwise, whose home and resources were often a welcome haven for different members of the family, was a familiar figure in many of our childhoods. (p. 33)

For crusaders of the family, blurring sex roles or accepting homosexuality threatens family stability. This linkage between the integrity of the black family and African-American culture and the belief that transgressions of gender or sexual norms erode that integrity is at the heart of heterosexist and misogynist writings, ranging from *Soul on Ice* to "Black Woman" (Cleaver, 1968; Baraka, 1971) to gay bashing and Christian conservative documentaries such as *Gay Rights, Special Rights.*

BLACK AND GAY IDENTITIES
African-Americans like Jacob are often caught in the cross fire between allegiance to their racial heritage and to emerging gay communities:

Black lesbians and gays have often found themselves "caught in the middle" (so to speak) since the "two-ness" of identity (to use a term of W.E.B. DuBois) reflected in being both black and gay was not wholly approved in either the black or gay communities. To maintain comfortability in the black community, particularly in those places that cultivate black culture and black solidarity, many have felt a need to downplay their homosexuality.... And in order to maintain comfortability in the gay community, others have felt a need to downplay their blackness. (Tinney, 1986, pp. 72–73)

This need to downplay one's race or sexuality is reflected in differing biographies. As Jacob's life story portrays, despite accusations from some that he was "too white," blackness was the core of his identity. As a black adolescent, Jacob assumed a responsibility to his race: president of the junior class, leader of the bus boycott, class valedictorian. The allure of gay pornography was secondary to his interest in black studies. From that afternoon in Mrs. Green's classroom, to the bus boycott, to his first meeting of Black Together, Jacob's commitment and identification with his fellow blacks has been unswerving. Asked to choose between "being black and being gay," Jacob unhesitantly answered, "I'd choose to be black. I'm proud of my black heritage. I wouldn't trade it for anything."

Irwin also primarily identified himself as black. Commenting on the difficulty of being gay in the African-American community, he remarked:

> I'm black. I am going to remain black. I prefer being black although you have a disadvantage because of the color of your skin. You have to work harder, sleep less, and eat less to achieve and to be recognized. In my society, it's all right to see a white gay person. You would accept that as opposed to seeing a black gay person in a black society. The majority of black men are bullies. They don't want to be confronted with being gay. They call them "faggots" or "hunks." They won't say "sissy" because sissy sounds too pretty.

Unlike Jacob or Irwin, Nathaniel downplays what he (and popular culture) has constructed as his black identity. "I just don't get into breakdancing. I never did get into Fat Boys strings. I don't get into sprayed T-shirts. I don't like rap. I'm not a part of them." Similarly, Grant identifies himself less with skin color and more with homosexuality. "The ideal situation would be for me to be white and gay in the South," he discloses.

The differences in primary identity between Jacob, Nathaniel, and Irwin are imperfectly captured in the distinction made by some black scholars and observers between "gay-blacks" and "black-gays":

> Gay blacks are people who identity first as being gay and who usually live outside the closet in predominantly white gay communities.... Black gays, on the other hand, view our racial heritage as primary and frequently live "bisexual front lives" within black neighborhoods.... It would be wonderful if the two groups could meet, communicate, and share one another's strengths. Unfortunately, gay blacks are usually so mesmerized by and so assimilated into the white gay culture that black gays tend to write them off as hopelessly lost and confused. Black gays are often so strongly into our African-American identity that we would rather die than be honest enough with our homosexuality to deal with it openly. (Smith, 1986, pp. 226–227)

These observations are documented in a dissertation written by black clinical psychologist Julius Johnson (1981) and others (*e.g.* Icard, 1986; Loicano,
1989). During the late seventies, Johnson studied sixty black men whose primary identification rested with their skin color or sexuality. While both
groups viewed the larger African-American community as unsupportive, he
found black-gay men, such as Jacob, more likely to date other blacks and to
be less open about their homosexuality. Conversely gay-black men, like
Nathaniel, generally dated white men and became assimilated into the white
gay culture. Johnson also observed that "black gay men do not see their
covertness as being closeted." Homosexual blacks, like Jacob, who work within African-American communities to expand the social menu for blacks
often remain covert. The construction of their identities is integrally connected with their decision to become black and gay *or* gay and black.

Frantz Fanon (1967), the author of *Black Skin, White Masks*, wrote:
"Without a Negro past, without a Negro future, it was impossible for me to
live my Negrohood. Not yet white, no longer wholly black, I was damned"
(p. 138). Nathaniel, like the expatriate Fishbelly in Wright's *The Long Dream*,
seeks escape from his African-American identity, while Jacob, like Ralph
Kabnis in Toomer's *Cane*, struggles with the ambiguity of black identity in
the South.

Jacob has not lost his sense of black history, black community, or black
identity. The desirability of interracial dating for Nathaniel, however, is more
potent than establishing a primary identity as a black man. Each of these
adolescents-turned-men have redrawn their boundaries of identity differently. Constructed from their differing understandings about race, class, and
sexuality, these identities may, as Jean Toomer realized, ultimately result in a
fragmentation of self out of harmony with being. Losing one's identity within the homosexual community, as it is defined narrowly within the politically correct boundaries of the Castro or in the pages of *The Advocate*
magazine, is no more healthy than having one's identity defined within the
cultural contours of the old black bourgeoisie or by radical Afrocentrists. As
James Baldwin underscored, in his introduction to *Nobody Knows My Name*:

Nothing is more frightening than to be divested of a crutch. The question of
who I was was not solved because I had removed myself from the social forces
which menaced me.... The question of who I was had at last become a personal question, and the answer was found in me.... If I was still in need of
havens, my journey had been for nothing. Havens are high-priced. The price

exacted of the haven-dweller is that he contrives to delude himself....
(Baldwin, 1961, pp. 11–12)

Being "the other" nudges us outside the perceived normalcy of everyday
life to reflect upon our unexamined lives; it affords us the opportunity to
see things not as they appear to be, and the courage to peer into selves that
we wish we might not see. Being defined as the other, however, is different
from becoming the other. When we define ourselves through the mirror of
the dominant culture—be it Euro-American or heterosexual—we have
accepted others' definitions of identity and the social significance of being
colored or queer; in the process we our lose our identifiable self. The absence
of an identifiable self, like that of Joe Christmas in Faulkner's *Light in August*,
prevents one from taking this journey. Clinging to the crutch of our externally defined selves prevents us from asking the "personal question." This is
why exploring one's skin color and sexuality is so important, and *being* gay
or black is so fruitless. Gendered, racial, and sexual identities, as recent feminist and postmodernist scholars have detailed, are neither biological nor
universal. They are constructs necessary for social self-understanding
through peeling away the false masks of identity.

RESOURCES FOR EDUCATORS WORKING WITH GAY AND LESBIAN ADOLESCENTS OF COLOR

Into our everyday school world come adolescents—white, black, red, and
brown—with fractured identities and fragmented selves. As educators, we
have an ethical and social responsibility to meet their needs as human beings
in order for them to secure meaningful roles within our community. Persons
of color who are gay or lesbian face enormous challenges (as do those adults
who dare *educate* them). As educators, we *can* make an impact if we have
the knowledge and courage to do so.

COLORING THE RAINBOW CURRICULUM

It is of little value to gay adolescents of color to address homosexuality within the classroom if the curriculum pivots around the white experience. If we
wish to convey to young people the presence and value of diversity, then our
discussion about homosexuality must be multicultural and critical. In this
Rainbow Curriculum, we must highlight the various contributions of gay
Native Americans (see, for instance, Allen, 1983; 1986), Asian-Americans
(see Chung, Kim, and Lemeshewsky, 1987), Latinas/os (see Anzaldúa, 1990),

as well as African-Americans (see Shockley, 1984) and challenge the essentialist conceptions of race, gender, and sexuality.

Elsewhere, I have detailed the Eurocentrism of many sexuality curricula, and have argued that sexuality, including homosexuality, needs to be integrated throughout the curriculum (Sears, 1993; Sears, forthcoming). We desperately need a critically based, multicultural, sexuality curriculum. We need a curriculum that integrates sexuality in the arts and humanities as well as the natural and social sciences. Since this chapter focused on the experiences of several African-American adolescents, let me specify how we might integrate the African-American gay experience into the curriculum.

The arts and humanities have a rich sexual legacy. No unit on the Harlem Renaissance, for example, is satisfactory without a discussion of Langston Hughes, Alain Locke, Countee Cullen and the role that their homosexuality or bisexuality played in their lives and works (Garber, 1982; Reimonenq, 1993; Woods, 1993). Similarly, it is difficult to ignore homosexual artists in the African-American community (see Saint, 1991) represented in works such as *Giovanni's Room* and *Another Country* (Baldwin, 1956, 1962), *The Black Unicorn* and *Zami: A New Spelling of My Name* (Lorde (1978, 1982), or black gay culture captured in Isaac Julien's film *Looking for Langston*, Marlon Riggs' *Tongues Untied* and Jennie Livingstone's *Paris is Burning*, or the recently released documentary on a retired U.S. Army Sergeant's battle to stay in the military, *Sis: The Perry Watkins Story*. In contemporary novels written by African-American women, such as Alice Walker's *The Color Purple* (1982) and Toni Morrison's *Tar Baby* (1981), the complexities and contradictions of being black, female, and lesbian are portrayed. Also, there are the contributions of the early New Orleans' blues and ragtime black composer Tony Jackson, whose song "Pretty Baby" was written for his young man, and who was later "run out" of the city because of his homosexuality, and the legendary Bessie Smith, whose career began at Chattanooga's Ivory Theatre, nurtured through Ma Rainey (Sears, 1994).

In young adult books, there are also a number of novels that include lesbians and gays of color as the central characters, such as *Ruby* (Guy, 1977), a moving novel about a young West Indian's romance with her friend, Daphne; *The Dreyfus Affair* (Lefcourt, 1993), a story of the interracial love between a hard hitting shortstop and his second baseman; and *Coffee Will Make You Black* (Sinclair, 1994), the story of Stevie Stevenson becoming aware of her attraction to women. I should also mention one of the most noted science fiction writers, Samuel R. Delaney, whose works include *Tales of Neveryone* (1979) and *Return to Neveryone* (1994), and award winning writers Jewelle Gomez (1991), author of *The Gilda Stories*, about a black lesbian vampire, and Nikki Baker (1993), who wrote *Long Goodbyes*, the third in a series about an African-American lesbian detective.

In the social sciences, history and anthropology afford a variety of opportunities to discuss homosexuality and the African-American experience. For example, we should not ignore the contributions of leading civil rights figures such as Bayard Rustin, whose homosexuality cost him (and the movement) important leadership posts, or the inventive genius and educational leadership of George Washington Carver, who founded the Tuskegee Institute and later departed the Hampton Institute following a gay-baiting incident with DuBois. Here, I would recommend the new gay biography series, edited by the distinguished historian Martin Duberman, *Lives of Notable Gay Men and Lesbians*, which includes James Baldwin, Lorraine Hansberry, Audre Lorde, Bayard Rustin, and Bessie Smith.

In anthropology, we should also be willing to stress how different African cultures integrate various types of homoerotic and homosexual relations into their communities. In Lesotho in southern Africa, for example, there is an institutionalized friendship among adolescent girls and young women ("mummies and babies") that evidences a very close emotional and sometimes sexual relationship (Gay, 1986). Also in southern Africa, !Kung girls first engage in sexual play with other girls before participating in sexual activity with boys. In western Africa, one of the twelve marriages practiced by the Fon of Dahomey is that of "giving the goat to the buck" in which one woman marries another (Shostak, 1981). There are also the women of Azande who reside in polygamous households, undergoing a ritual that creates strong bonds (Evans-Prichard, 1970); and a study has been published on the influence of Kwaanza and Native American culture on lesbian unions (Butler, 1990). Finally, in eastern Africa, the Swahili Muslims of Mobasa (Herskovits, 1967), while observing sharply defined gender roles, accept lesbianism. A similar pattern of various homosexual behavior is found for males, such as that among Hutu and Tutsi youth in the old kingdom of Rwanda (Junod, 1927). All of these examples clearly illuminate the human capacity to define and construct a variety of sexual and gendered patterns.

Homosexuality may be silenced in the classroom, but it is not absent from the arts and humanities or natural and social sciences. Educators truly committed to multicultural education must challenge students' sexual essential-ism and xenophobia while rejecting their schools' Eurocentrism and homophobia.

PROFESSIONAL RESOURCES

A great variety of prose and scholarship regarding homosexuals and people of color has appeared during the past fifteen years. It ranges from anecdotal essays in *Haciendo Caras—Making Face, Making Soul* (Anzaldúa, 1990) and *Brother to Brother: New Writings by Black Gay Men* (Hemphill, 1991) to *Pieces of My Heart*, a lesbian of color anthology (Silvera, 1991) and the writings of Indigenous North American women in *Colour of Resistance* (Fife, 1993). There is also the poetry of a Cherokee lesbian, *Simple Songs* (Sears, 1990) and an African-American, *Living as a Lesbian* (Clarke, 1986), as well as novels written by gay American minorities, such as *Cultural Revolution* (Wong, 1993). Scholarly works include those on Native Americans, *Spirit and the Flesh* (Williams, 1986) and *Gay Spirit* (Roscoe, 1987), Latinas/os, *Compañeras* (Ramos, 1987) and *Chicana Lesbians* (Trujillo, 1991) as well as those focusing on indigenous cultures such as China (Hinsch, 1990), Central and South America (Murray, 1987), and the South Pacific (Herdt, 1984). These and other works form the essential reading list for any educator who wishes to understand the complex intersections of race and homosexuality, particularly among those cultural minority groups most commonly found in public schools.[2]

NOTES

Portions of this chapter are substantially revised excerpts from *Growing Up Gay in the South* (Sears, 1991).

1. Due to space limitations, I have restricted myself to gay, black males. Lesbianism, after all, is the most blatant challenge to the black male. Lesbian feminist writer Ann Shockley (1984) declares, "the independent woman-identified woman, the black lesbian, was a threat. Not only was she a threat to the projection of black male macho, but a *sexual* threat too—the utmost danger to the black male's institutionally designated role as 'king of the lovers.'" (p. 269).

2. Within African-American studies, a booklist would certainly include:

Beam, 1986; Clarke, 1986; Cornell, 1983; Hemphill, 1991; Moraga and Anzaldúa, 1981; Roberts, 1981; Smith, 1986. I also recommend several recent anthologies that include essays by and about lesbians and gay men of color: Garber, 1994; McNaron, Anzaldúa, Arguelles and Kennedy, 1993; Nelson, 1993. Educators should also be aware of support groups for lesbians and gay persons of color such as the National Coalition for Black Lesbians and Gay Men (Box 19248, Washington, DC 20036) and periodicals such as *BLK* (Box 83912, Los Angeles, 90083), a monthly magazine featuring news and essays on issues of interest to Black gays. There is also the annual national black gay and lesbian conference and institutes, sponsored by the Black Gay and Lesbian Leadership Forum (Box 29812, Los Angeles, 90027).

REFERENCES

Allen, P. (1983). *The Woman Who Owned the Shadows*. San Francisco, CA: Spinsters/Aunt Lute Foundation.

———. (1986). *The Sacred Hoop*. Boston, MA: Beacon.

Anzaldúa, G., ed. (1990). *Haciendo Caras—Making Face, Making Soul*. San Francisco, CA: Aunt Lute Foundation.

Baker, N. (1993). *Long Goodbyes*. Tallahassee, FL: Naiad Press.

Baldwin, J. (1956). *Giovanni's Room*. New York: Dial Press.

———. (1961). *Nobody Knows My Name*. New York: Dial Press.

———. (1962). *Another country*. New York: Dial Press.

Baraka, A. (1971). *Raise Race Rays Raze*. New York: Random House.

Beam, J., ed. (1986). *In the Life: A Black Gay Anthology*. Boston, MA: Alyson.

Butler, B. (1990). *Ceremonies of the Heart*. Seattle, WA: Seal Press.

Butts, J. (1981). "Is Homosexuality a Threat to the Black Family?" *Ebony*, April (pp. 138–140, 142–144).

Chung, C., Kim, A., and Lemeshewsky, A., eds. (1987). *Between the Lines: An Anthology by Pacific/Asian Lesbians*. Santa Cruz, CA: Dancing Bird.

Clarke, C. (1983). "The Failure to Transform: Homophobia in the Black Community." In *Home Girls: A Black Feminist Anthology*. B. Smith, ed. New York: Kitchen Table/Women of Color Press.

———. (1986). *Living as a Lesbian*. Ithaca, NY: Firebrand.

Cleaver, E. (1968). *Soul On Ice*. New York: McGraw Hill.

Cornell, A. (1983). *Black Lesbian in White America*. Tallahassee, FL: Naiad Press.

Delaney, S. (1979) *Tales of Neveryone*. New York: Bantam.

———. (1994) *Return to Neveryone*. Middletown, CT: Wesleyan University Press.

Duberman, M., ed. (1994). *Lives of Natable Gay Men and Lesbians*. New York: Chelsea House.

Durant, T. and Louden, J. (1986). "The Black Middle Class in America." *Phylon, 47* (4), pp. 253–263.

Evans-Prichard, E.E. (1970). "Sexual Inversion among the Azande." *American Anthropologist, 72* (6), pp. 1428–1434.

Fanon, F. (1967). *Black Skin, White Masks*. New York: Grove.

Faulkner, W. ((1932). *Light in August*. New York: Modern Library.

Fife, C. (1993). *Colour of Resistance*. Toronto: Sister Vision Woman of Colour Press.

Frazier, E.F. (1925). "Durham: Capital of the Black Middle Class." In *The New Negro*. A. Locke, ed. New York: Boni.

———. (1939). *The Negro Family in the United States*. Chicago, IL: University of Chicago Press.

———. (1957). *Black Bourgeoisie*. New York: Free Press.

Garber, E. (1982, May 13). "Tain't Nobody's Business." *Advocate, 342*, pp. 39–43, 53.

Garber, L., ed. (1994). *Tilting the Tower*. New York: Routledge.

Gay, J. (1986). "Mummies and Babies and Friends and Lovers in Lesotho." *Journal of Homosexuality, 5* (3), pp. 97–116.

Gomez, J. (1991). *The Gilda Stories*. Ithaca, NY: Firebrand.

Guy, R. (1977). *Ruby*. New York: Viking.

Hemphill, E., ed. (1991). *Brother to Brother: New Writings by Black Gay Men*. Boston, MA: Alyson.

Herdt, G. (1984). *Ritualized Homosexuality in Melanesia*. Berkeley: University of California Press.

Herskovits, M. (1967). *Dahomey*. Evanston, IL: Northwestern University Press.

Hinsch, B. (1990). *Passions of the Cut Sleeve: A History of the Male Homosexual Tradition in China*. Berkeley: University of California Press.

Icard, L. (1986). "Black Gay Men and Conflicting Social Identities." *Journal of Social Work and Human Sexuality, 4* (1/2), pp. 83–93.

Johnson, J. (1981). *Influence of Assimilation on the Psychosocial Adjustment of Black Homosexual Men*. Unpublished doctoral dissertation, California School of Professional Psychology, Berkeley, CA. *Dissertation Abstracts*

International 42,11, 4620B.

Junod, H. (1927). *Life of a South African Tribe*. London: Macmillan.

Landry, B. (1987). *The New Black Middle Class*. Berkeley: University of California Press.

Lefcourt, P. (1993). *The Dreyfus Affair*. New York: Random House.

Lieb, S. (1981). *Mother of the Blues: A Study of Ma Rainey*. Amherst, MA: University of Massachusetts Press.

Loicano, D. (1989). "Gay Identity Issues Among Black Americans." *Journal of Counseling and Development, 68*, pp. 21–25.

Lorde, A. (1978). *The Black Unicorn*. New York: Norton.

———. (1982). *Zami: A New Spelling of My Name*. Freedom, CA: Crossing Press.

McAdoo, J., ed. (1981). *Black Families*. Beverly Hills, CA: Sage.

McNaron, A., Anzaldúa, G., Arguelles, L., and Kennedy, E., eds. (1993). "Theorizing Lesbian Experience." *Signs 18* (4).

Moraga, C. and Anzaldúa, G., eds. (1981). *This Bridge Called My Back: Writings by Radical Women of Color*. New York: Kitchen Table/Women of Color Press.

Morrison, T. (1981). *Tar Baby*. New York: Random House.

Murray, S., ed. (1987). *Male Homosexuality in Central and South America*. New York: Gay Academic Union.

Nelson, E. (1993). *Critical Essays: Gay and Lesbian Writers of Color*. New York: Haworth Press.

Ramos, J., ed. (1994). *Compañeras: Latina Lesbians*. New York: Routledge.

Reimonenq, A. (1993). "Countee Cullen's Uranian 'Soul Windows.'" *Journal of Homosexuality, 26* (2/3), pp. 143–165.

Roberts, J. (1981). *Black Lesbians*. Tallahassee, FL: Naiad Press.

Roscoe, W. (1987). *Gay Spirit*. New York: St. Martin's Press.

Saint, A., ed. (1991). *The Road Before Us: 100 Gay Black Poets*. New York: Galiens.

Sears, J. (1991). *Growing Up Gay in the South: Race, Gender, and Journeys of the Spirit*. New York: Haworth Press.

———. (1993). "The Impact of Culture and Ideology on the Construction of Gender and Sexual Identities: Developing a Critically-Based Sexuality Curriculum." In J. Sears, ed. *Sexuality and the Curriculum: Policies and Practices of Sexuality Education*, (pp. 139–156). New York: Teachers College Press.

———. (1994). *Generations: An Oral History of Lesbian and Gay Southern*

Life. Unpublished manuscript.

———. (Forthcoming). *Teaching Sex in America: Communities, Cultures, and Identities.* San Francisco, CA: Jossey-Bass.

Sears, V. (1990). *Simple Songs.* Ithaca, NY: Firebrand.

Shockley, A. (1984). "The Black Lesbian in American Literature." In *Women-Identified Women.* T. Darty and S. Potter, eds. Palo Alto, CA: Mayfield.

Shostak, M. (1981). *The Life and Worlds of a !Kung Woman.* Cambridge, MA: Harvard University Press.

Silvera, M., ed. (1991). *Pieces of My Heart.* Toronto: Sister Vision Woman of Colour Press.

Sinclair, A. (1994). *Coffee Will Make You Black.* New York: Hyperion.

Soares, J. (1979). "Black and Gay." In *Gay Men.* M. Levine, ed. New York: Harper and Row.

Smith, B., ed. (1986). *Home Girls: A Black Feminist Anthology.* New York: Kitchen Table/Women of Color Press.

Staples, R. (1987). "Social Structure and Black Family Life." *Journal of Black Studies, 17* (3), pp. 267–286.

Tinney, J. (1986). "Why a Gay Black Church?" In *In the Life: A Black Gay Anthology.* J. Beam, ed. Boston, MA: Alyson.

Toomer, J. (1923). *Cane.* New York: Harper and Row.

Trujillo, C., ed. (1991). *Chicana Lesbians.* Berkeley, CA: Third Woman.

Walker, A. (1982). *The Color Purple.* New York: Harcourt Brace and Jovanovich.

Williams, W. (1986). *Spirit and the Flesh.* Boston, MA: Beacon Press.

Woods, G. (1993). "Gay Re-Reading of the Harlem Renaissance Poets." *Journal of Homosexuality, 26* (2/3), pp. 127–142.

Wong, N. (1993). *Cultural Revolution.* New York: Persea Books.

Wright, R. (1958). *The Long Dream.* Garden City, NY: Doubleday.

13

African-American Gay Youth
One Form of Manhood

Kenneth P. Monteiro and Vincent Fuqua

CAFE: 3 A.M.
Detectives from the vice squad
with weary sadistic eyes
spotting fairies
Degenerates
some folks say.
But God, Nature,
or somebody
made them that way.

—*Langston Hughes*

Culturally, the African-American gay man is a descendant of Africans living in a culture dominated by descendants of Europeans; racially, black[1] in a white-dominated society; and homosexual in a heterosexually dominated society. African-American gay men are treated as marginalized people within the margins of society. To be African, black, male and gay in America is to challenge the basic assumptions of society simply by existing. The question is, what can we learn from this challenge?

This investigation focuses on the African-American experience because the breadth of experiences represented by "people of color" is too immense. People of color are descendants of ethnic groups which represent eighty percent of the population of the world. Attempting to discuss the majority of the world in one chapter would beg trivialization. This article will also not attempt to capture the issues related to transgenderism and transsexualism. These topics are often associated with homosexual desires, but they can also occur independent of them, and they deserve adequate investigation in their own right. Finally, we limit our discussion to young men, because there are enough differences between the basic issues of African-American, male, homosexual desires and lesbian desires to warrant a separate discussion (see Hall, 1991, and Mays and Cochran, 1991 for discussions of African-American lesbian experiences).

Acknowledging the virtual absence of empirical research on African-American male sexuality (see also, Cochran and Mays; 1991: Peterson, 1992), care must be taken to distinguish between data sources which demonstrate the existence of particular homosexual experiences, for instance, case study, single observation, or convenience sample studies, and sources which can reliably establish typicality, for instance, large scale random-sample studies. In the case of African-American gay men, there are virtually no studies which could claim reliable data concerning typicality. The lack of data offers both a challenge and an opportunity. Critical to the discovery of good answers is a set of good questions considered using appropriate methods. Therefore, this investigation will focus as much on redefining the theoretical questions which should shape new research as it will on reviewing the limited empirical research relevant to this topic. Data concerning African-American, male, same sex desires will be drawn broadly from empirical research, literary reference, documentary accounts, professional observations by the authors and one clinical consultant to this report, and two structured interviews of young (twenty- and twenty-three-year-old) African-American, gay men.

DEFINING TERMS

Traditionally, social scientists have attempted to precisely differentiate between the sexual actions, tendencies, and psychological identities of individuals. In particular, researchers commonly distinguish between homosexual behavior, orientation, and identity. Savin-Williams (1990) offers a set of definitions which are consistent with others in the field. Homosexual behavior is seen as the performance of the actual sexual experiences or acts committed by an individual with a member of the same biological sex. *Homosexual behavior* may only occur once, or may occur frequently in the person's life. Savin-Williams defines *homosexual orientation* as "a preponderance of sexual or erotic feelings, thoughts, fantasies, and/or behaviors desired with members of the same sex." Here, the individual's sexual feelings or behaviors associated with male partners must be more frequent than those associated with women or other sexual partners. "Sexual identity by contrast represents a consistent, enduring self-recognition of the meanings that sexual orientation and sexual behavior have for one's self" (Savin-Williams, 1990). This definition might imply, erroneously, that the only meanings one could ascribe to sexual behavior would involve self-identity. Not all meaningful behaviors are perceived as central to the definition of self. We would add to this definition, then, that *male homosexual identity* occurs when a person designates his sexuality as central to his definition of self. It is this last concept, homosexual identity, which most closely approximates the common definition of "gay."

Such apparent clarity of definitions may be slightly misleading. As noted by others (for example, Greenberg, 1988), the specific emotions, thoughts, or behaviors that different cultures or individuals might consider homosexual may vary significantly. Situational, personal, and cultural context may also contribute to the meaning of behaviors. For example, the social stereotype reinforced by European-American social science research on male gender roles (Lewis, 1975) suggests that, for (European-American) men, public displays of emotion and nurturance—particularly towards other men in the form of touching or embracing—are clearly unmanly. These behaviors may be seen by some as signs of homosexual tendencies. Whatever degree of truth is reflected in this stereotype, it seems to be highly context-bound. It has been observed that African-American males often express public emotionality, nurturance, and intimacy with other men, and that European-American males may be more likely to express affection to men in private or all-male settings. Nowhere is this context effect more evident than in all-male sports competitions. One former high school coach (J. Daniel, 1993, personal communication) observed that his African-American male athletes tended to be more emotionally expressive in their individual athletic performance and in their public displays of affection and enthusiasm with other athletes. These public displays are believed to be part of the reason for the NFL's recent creation of an "excessive celebration" penalty. In contrast, he noted that, in private or all-male settings (for instance, locker rooms, practice games without spectators), his European-American males were more likely to become involved in highly animated and affectionate "horseplay." These are natural homo-affectionate expressions, expressions of same-gender liking or loving, but they are not necessarily or even typically homosexual. Both the occurrence and interpretation of the male-male expressions of affection appear to be linked to personal, cultural, and situational context.

Deciding which forms of homo-affectionate expressions are indications of homosexual behaviors, orientations, or identities is difficult to define independent of context. To continue with a sports metaphor, let us say that heterosexuality is analogous to baseball and that homosexuality is analogous to football. For some actions, such as swinging a bat or tackling, it would be easy to say which was a football behavior and which was not, but what would one say about running? Jerry Rice is a professional football player and an excellent runner, who may also play baseball. We might feel fairly confident saying that he had a football orientation because most of his athletic experience involved football, despite the fact that this need not logically be true. What about Bo Jackson and Dion Sanders? They both play a great deal of professional baseball *and* football. Are they biathletic? Should they identify as baseball players, football players, neither, both? We will not attempt to resolve these apparent ambiguities. Attempting to objectively categorize subjective experience often leads to the creation of fuzzy categories (Medin and Ross, 1992), categories which have a basic structure but which do not have clear either/or boundaries. Thus, we understand—but reject—the academic and political reasoning for attempting to unambiguously distinguish hetero and homosexual behaviors, orientations, and identities. For this investigation, however, we will use the terms *gay* and *homosexual* to refer to young men who engage in or desire homosexual acts, whether or not they may exhibit other sexual desires or actions.

The implications for focusing on the homosexual experiences of African-American men are neither trivial nor obvious. Despite romantic images of the American melting pot, the majority of African-American boys develop into manhood in African-American communities fairly separated from European-American men (Ploski and Williams, 1983). It is reasonable to hypothesize that their same-sex desires are primarily born within this African-American context. Admittedly, they are influenced by European-Americans and, since African-American social scientists are few, the experiences of African-American young men are more often studied and judged from a European-American perspective. Yet there can be no automatic presumption of similarity or difference between the experiences of African- and European-American men. Such an assumption would mistakenly define the African-American experience as simply a variant or distortion of the European-American experience. We will attempt to refocus the discussion in order to address the African-American, male, homosexual experience as *one of the variations of growing up African in America.*

BASIC DIFFERENCES IN EUROPEAN- AND AFRICAN-AMERICAN EPISTEMOLOGIES

Cultures are not monolithic, and neither are the research paradigms that they spawn. Yet the cultural epistemology—the ethos—of a people does shape the nature of their academic, philosophical, and scientific debate. It influences virtually all works, and usually determines which will hold sway in the academy. Though individual philosophical theories and empirical models may vary from the cultural core assumptions, they will continue to be influenced by the cultural *Zeitgeist*, and will be drawn to conform to the prevailing paradigm. Philosophically and operationally, European-centered models of social science tend to be dominated by Cartesian notions of reductionism, empiricism, and dualism. For reasons of politics, religion, and science, most modern, European-American, social and psychological theories tend to embrace Descartes's dualism, rejecting the monist and wholist approach espoused by his contemporary, Spinoza, and others (Murphy and Kovac, 1972). This is a critical difference between European- and African-centered approaches to human behavior. Modern European-centered theories emphasize the difference or opposition of concepts and things. Most particularly, they separate the physical from the spiritual nature of humanity, offering the former to science and relegating the latter to religion. Most such theories are predicated on the following assumptions:

1. People can be divided into physiological, psychological, or social parts, and the study of these separated parts will remain accurate representations of these parts as they exist within the whole. This legitimizes studying homosexuality as separate from other components of a young man's development, presuming that the meaning of his sexuality is independent of his other personal characteristics.
2. Similarly, people and the subdivisions of a person can be studied outside their normal context, presuming that their decontextualized meaning will be the same as their meaning in context. The sexuality of young gay men can be studied independent of the situational or cultural context in which they develop.
3. The divisions or categories made for scientific study can and should be defined as mutually exclusive sets, accentuating contrasting character-

istics and minimizing similarities. Thus an object is defined as being X and, by necessity, not Y. To be masculine is seen as necessarily not feminine; to be straight is necessarily not gay.

4. The totality of human experience is explainable by that which can be empirically observed and measured. The only factors which are legitimate in the study of human experience are those which can be observed directly or indirectly by one of the physical senses and can be shown to exist in the material world. There is no place for the study of the spiritual aspects of human experience in social science. The definition of spirit in this context is not restricted to the religious connotation of soul; it refers to a person's mind, feeling or animating principles which are distinct from or transcend their physical existence (Oxford American Dictionary). In its broadest context, it refers to the animating abstract principles underlying any physical entity, human or nonhuman. Thus, European-American social science assumes that the nature and meaning of being gay is only a scientific question, and can be examined separate from a person's values, beliefs, and their relationship to a spiritual base.

African-centered theorists (for instance, Amen, 1990; Asante, 1980) do not deny that people can choose to study elements of experience, that divisions or distinctions can be made, that objects can be removed from their original context for study, or that the physical aspects of existence are important. To the contrary, the very existence of the physical universe "depends on their being differences and opposition. It (the universe) guarantees them" (Amen, 1990). They argue, however, that the meanings of these elements are best understood in their relationship with other physical elements and their spiritual/abstract origins, where the spiritual origin of all objects in the world is a unitary entity embodying all elements and principles necessary to produce the variety of observed experience. African-centered epistemology accepts as nonparadoxical the assertion that all things are simultaneously the same and different. Similarity or difference depends on the level of analysis. The more abstract/spiritual the analysis is, the more likely one is to find universal communality. The more materially based and empirical the analysis is, the more one will observe the differentiation. For example, this perspective should see all sexuality as being derived from the same spiritual/abstract elements and principles. Observed differentiation is a function of how these sexual elements and principles are arranged in context with other elements of the person's experiences. These notions of spirit and simultaneous one-ness and different-ness may appear overly esoteric, alien, and even not use-ful to many European-centered social scientists. However, they are so critical to understanding the African-American experience that they deserve greater consideration before proceeding.

To better illustrate the African-centered approach to describing social expe-rience, and to fully appreciate the implications of these differences in views, it may be helpful to use particular aspects of the European-American theo-retical approach to the study of language as partial analogies to the elements embodied in the African-centered approach to the study of human experi-ence. Major European-American theories of language accept the notion that the language one speaks is built on a small, finite set of sounds and symbols whose combination is governed by a set of abstract rules (Anderson, 1990). In its most radical form, the same finite set of symbols and rules is consid-ered to be universal to all human languages (Chomsky, 1965). This finite set of common elements and rules is generative. That is, it is able to produce an almost infinite number of well-formed and understandable utterances. A native speaker differentiates well-formed utterances from ill-formed utter-ances not simply because she or he has heard an identical one before, but because the new utterance conforms to the underlying principles, the spirit, of the language. For example, English uses twenty-six letters with implicit rules concerning which letters should follow which. If we were to invent a new word that we wanted to be accepted into English, we would have better luck with "wible" than we would with "wxble." Both are new, but one violates the spirit or abstract principles of the language. Further, we could expect that the various possible meanings of "wible" could change as it is used in a number of contexts, very much like the word "bad" changes meaning from when a principal says it about a student's disruptive behavior to when a stu-dent uses it to describe a friend's fashionable jacket.

Following these principles, an African-American-centered approach to understanding male-male affection and sexual desire must examine both the variety of naturally occurring manifestations of affectionate and sexual behavior (both heterosexual and homosexual), examine their relationships to the practical and spiritual elements and rules underlying the behaviors, and address their meaning in the current context in which they are found. The well-formedness, health, or "normalcy" of the sexual expression is not defined by whether the physical form of the expression conforms to some previous model of well-formedness. It is judged by its ability, in context, to assist in bringing a balanced or harmonious relationship among the various physical, affective, cognitive, and spiritual components of the individual within his social and cultural context. The inclusiveness of a study which satisfied all of these constraints is admittedly beyond the scope of any single investigation. However, we will attempt to lay a groundwork for the types of studies which, together, might satisfy these requirements.

IMPLICATIONS OF EPISTEMOLOGY ON THEORIES OF SOCIAL-SEXUAL DEVELOPMENT

This rather simple contrast between European- and African-American epistemologies presents different challenges to European- and African-American theories of social development, particularly as they relate to homosexuality. The most common European-American theories of social development, described in mainstream texts, agree that the young male is exposed to personal and social conflicts, the appropriate resolution of which will lead to health and the inappropriate resolution of which will result in dysfunction (see Sarafino and Armstrong, 1986; Feldman, 1989, for discussions of social development). The most common African-American theories about the development of ethnic identity tend to concur that social and personal challenges partly drive development (for instance, Cross, 1991; Cross, 1979; Cross, Parham, and Helms, 1991; White, 1984). The European centered theories tend, however, to ignore—or consider in isolation—any spiritual aspects to this development. Akbar and other African-American theorists (for instance, Akbar, 1989; Hayles, 1991, Nobles, 1991) argue that the development of a healthy sense of self demands that the individual develop and integrate his thoughts, feelings, and behaviors within the context of his community and his spiritual values. Health is measured by the harmony or disharmony among the elements (Akbar, 1989).

African-American models of psychosocial experience reflect the mixed cultural and academic heritage of their originators. Elements of both European- and African-American thought can be found in different degrees within the various theories. One may detect elements of Freudian (for instance, Cress Welsing, 1991), behaviorist (Hayes, 1991), social learning (Banks, Ward, McQuater and Debritto, 1991) or social cognitive (Spencer, 1985) approaches in the writing of a variety of African-American social scientists. Vestiges of apparently European-American-centered thinking may remain for dysfunctional reasons of tradition or training (Woodson, 1933); however, the existence of such features *per se* should not necessarily constitute a problem for

African-American-centered theories (Boykin, 1979). The existence of cor-
responding elements within both African-American and European-
American-centered theories is not necessarily contradictory since, from an
African-American-centered perspective, being African-American-centered
is not defined as the opposite of being European. In addition, given the
heavy reliance of classical European thought on ancient African philosophy,
theology, and science (Drake, 1987; Ben-Jochanon, 1970; Mbiti, 1970), cor-
responding elements may be vestiges of ancient African scholarship which
have survived in European scholarship. Consistent with most academic
endeavors, the ongoing challenge for African-American-centered theorists
is to separate the theoretical elements which are consistent with the basic
theoretical approach from those which are not, whether the origins of the
elements appear to be African or European.

It is not surprising, then, that a number of theories of African-American
development concerning social and racial identity formation (for example,
Cross, 1991; Cross, Parham, and Helms, 1991; White, 1984) contain structures which include specific stages, behaviors, or social outcomes like their
European-American-centered counterparts. The most prominent African-
American-centered models, however, continue to diverge from European-
American-centered models by reasserting that spirituality is a crucial part
of development. They further claim that normalcy and health are defined
as a function of the integrity and harmony among the spiritual, physical,
and sociocontextual elements of a person's life (Akbar, 1991, Amen, 1990;
Nobles, 1991). This might imply a history of greater openness to the possible
naturalness of certain homosexual behavior as a part of African-American
culture. Instead, we find an apparent paradox. The African-American community appears passionately opposed to public expressions of homosexual
behavior, while it is cognizant and tacitly tolerant of private homosexual
experience (Poussaint, 1990; Strickland, 1993, personal communication).
The complimentary observation has been made that, though the public gay
movement is most prominent in European and European-American societies, homosexuals are also more likely to be actively oppressed in those same
cultures (Greenberg, 1988).

ETHNIC IDENTITY AND THE DUAL REALITIES OF AFRICAN-AMERICAN HOMOSEXUAL MEN

The dual existence of European-American and African-American-centered
approaches in the African-American academic community is mirrored in

the dual cultural experiences in the everyday lives of African-Americans. The typical African-American boy is torn by sometimes antagonistic social values concerning his developing manhood. It has been long recognized that men of African descent, growing up in a variety of European-dominated societies, may experience a fragmentation of their sense of ethnic identity (Fanon, 1967). Speaking specifically about the American experience, DuBois (1903) observed that "...one ever feels his two-ness...two warring ideals in one dark body." DuBois speaks eloquently about a significant social challenge posed to the African-American male. There is great social pressure to emulate models of European-American male social development, to submit as servant or slave to European-American men, or to develop a sense of manhood that is independent of those foisted upon him by a European, male dominated society (see Akbar, 1989; DuBois, 1903; Fanon, 1967; Woodson, 1933; or Wright, 1974, for more detailed discussions). The African-American homosexual male is not exempt from this socialization process.

The European model of adult manhood, as mentioned earlier, appears to value being aggressive, independent, dominant, self-confident, nonconforming to groups, pragmatic, emotionally self-controlled, good with objects, and an initiator of sexual activity. Women are seen as the opposite of men: passive, dependent, nurturant, self-deprecating, conforming, having a facilitating attitude, emotionally expressive, good with people, and sexually receptive (Kagan, as summarized by Lewis, 1975). The young European-American boy is socialized to emulate masculinity and eschew femininity as described above. The African-American model of adult manhood, as described by a number of authors (for instance, Kunjufu, 1985), includes some elements common to both European masculinity and femininity, excludes some elements of both, and includes values promoted by neither European gender role. On a spiritual level, the young boy is assumed to be born with the spirit of male and female. Masculinity differentiates itself from femininity in the style and form that it takes, not in its basic nature (Lewis, 1975).

Young African-American men and women are often encouraged to balance strength with gentleness, independence with interdependence, and emotional control with emotional expressiveness; either the male or the female can be the sexual initiator or receiver. These complimentary characteristics of African-American masculinity tend to confuse European-American observers of the African-American experience. Racist caricatures by European-Americans have exaggerated both the hypermacho, sexually crazed images of the African-American male, as well as the nurturant, emotional, "feminine" males (see Bogle, 1974). One landmark social science study reflects the same confusion about the broader African-American definition of masculinity. Moynihan's observations of the simultaneously assertive and nurturant characteristics of African-American men (reprinted in part in Staples, 1978) led him to believe that these men were emasculated, and he referred to their families as a "tangle of pathology."

The African-American male, then, is offered two basic models of masculinity—European-American and African-American. The first demands denying one's culture and risking rejection by both groups as a "wannabe" white man. Because he can never be a true European, he may feel subordinate to real Europeans. In the second, the young man comes to value his African-American culture and understand his relationship to race and racism as a black man. He may still be devalued, however, by a white, male-dominated society.

One theoretical model (Cross, 1991, 1979; Cross, et al., 1991) describes ethnic identity formation as a five stage process that is employed by African-Americans to deal with this conflict. It hypothesizes an initial stage where in individuals attempt to deny their Africanness (culture) and their blackness (social race), revering that which is white and denigrating that which is black. It then suggests several stages—initiated by some experience with racism—wherein the individual is prompted to learn more about his culture and about his relationship to racism. He values (possibly in an exaggerated form) that which is African/black and indiscriminately rages at anything European/white. The model also includes a final stage in which the individual confidently accepts his culture and race and opposes actual expressions of racism or oppression. At the same time, he no longer finds a need to denigrate all that is European/white simply because it exists. There is general empirical support for this model (see Cross, 1979), and some validation concerning this model of racial identity formation in African-American lesbians (see Hall, 1991) also exists.

In our interviews, both of our respondents expressed some elements that relate to the model. Respondent A spoke about knowing little about his culture or about race and racism until his teens. After several racist experiences, he began to reevaluate himself and to study his culture. Visibly angry, he stated that he was "pissed, really pissed" that the educational system and society in general had denied him opportunities to study his culture.

Respondent B stated that his family had always taught him about his Africanness and that he always remembered such with pride. He did, however, also mention an anger at experiencing European-American "role-models" who denigrated his ethnicity. The anger that each respondent expressed, both toward experiences of overt racism and toward the feeling of having their culture hidden from them by American educators, is reminiscent of the anger or rage described by other authors investigating African-American male social development (for instance, Grier and Cobb, 1968). Both said they currently described themselves as proud, African-American, gay men, though Respondent A said that he had only recently come to that point in his development.

Dr. Strickland (1993, personal communication) reported that his African-American gay clients are from three large urban centers which have significant African-American communities, and that all of his clients defined themselves as African-American, Afro-American, or black, expressing strong pride in their heritage. Unlike his European-American clients, these clients expressed ethnicity as an important defining aspect of their existence, and the majority stated that their ethnicity was more central to their identity than was their sexuality. All of his European-American clients stated that their sexuality was more central to their self-identity than was their ethnicity.

Several writers have captured this process of young, African-American, gay men wrestling with race and culture. Shepard (1986) writes poignantly about not being white and questioning the value of being black; his main character is a gay "black man who deeply fears most...other black men...(and is) also afraid of white men...their power...both sexual and social." Nero (1991) speaks of addressing a black aesthetic from the perspective of an African-American gay perspective. Simmons (1991) presents one of the few public challenges to the prevailing views of the African-American community toward homosexuality while at the same time promoting the importance of an African-centered epistemology. He presents a model of development which demands throwing out what he sees as the bathwater—homo-antagonistic beliefs and actions—while keeping the baby, African-centered values.

Whether emulation of European-American manhood is either a desirable or achievable goal for some African-American men, it will not be the primary focus of this discussion of African-American homosexuality. If full integration and homogenization of the African-American male into the European-American experience is possible, and if some young African-

American men choose such a path, then European-American approaches to gender and sexuality will suffice in guiding that discussion. Given the differences in epistemology, social science theory, and life experience pointed out above, we argue that most, if not all, African-American men who experience homosexual desires and acts will do so as *African*-Americans. Thus, we will focus on how the African-American gay youth challenge the prevailing notions of becoming a man within the African-American context.

HOMOSEXUALITY AND THE AFRICAN-AMERICAN COMMUNITY

There is a long-held and pervasive public view of a number of African-American social scientists that homosexual desires and actions are either nonexistent in African and African-American societies or, when they occur, they are simply contaminates of European societies or by-products of oppression. Such writers point to the homosexual activities which occur in prison or which involve rape, prostitution, or relationships with white men as examples of African-American homosexuality that has been created by oppressive conditions or submission to European-Americans. Some confuse homosexuality with cross-gender behavior, effeminacy, or weakness (for example, Cress Welsing, 1991). Some (for example, Hare and Hare, 1984; Kunjufu, 1985) hypothesize that homosexuality is the product of a conspiracy perpetrated by white female schoolteachers; another the product of "prison breeding" (Asante, 1980). Some simply define it as sinful, that is, out of harmony with ones spirit or natural origins (for instance, Amen, 1990). It is also clear that many African-American clergy and civic leaders are among the most vocal opponents of gay civil rights (Poussaint, 1990). Madhubuti (1990) reflects the general lack of public acceptance of African-American male homosexuality within many black empowerment or liberation movements.

There are notable public exceptions to the above. There are, of course, the writings of known African-American gay and lesbian activists, such as James Baldwin, Samuel Delaney, Audre Lorde, and Bruce Nugent. Along with many less-famous clergy who advocate respect for gays and lesbians, Reverend Jesse Jackson made explicit during his political campaigns that he supported civil rights for gays and lesbians. A more dramatic example is the obscure yet powerful debate within the black empowerment movement highlighted by the response of Huey Newton, prominent Black Panther leader, to a list of twelve demands published in 1970 in the *Berkeley Tribe* under the title of "Third World Gay Revolution: What We Want." Newton's extensive response reflected his thesis that "(w)hatever...personal opinions and...insecurities about homosexuality...we should try to unite with them in a revolutionary fashion...We must gain security in ourselves and therefore have respect and feelings for all oppressed people." It was reported that, despite Newton's prominence at that time, the Black press ignored this public letter (Lane, 1991). Public statements against homosexuality, yet private tolerance, are both part of the African-American experience (Poussaint, 1990), and understanding both in context will give direction to our study of the development and expression of same-sex desires in young African-American males.

Contrary to common mythology, homosexual experience in African and African-American societies dates back to antiquity, and—though homosexuality represents only a relatively small portion of the broader African homo-affective experience—homosexual acts appear to have been present throughout recorded history. Despite the difficulties in translation and interpretation when determining reference to statistically rare and culturally varied behaviors that might signal homosexuality (see Greenberg, 1988), there are references to homosexual behavior in ancient Kemet (Egypt), among the Amugawe in Kenya, the Kwayama/Bantu in Angola, Sudan, Ethiopia, Nubia, Ghana, Zimbabwe, Senegal, and Uganda, and in other regions of Africa. In contrast to the stereotype of European male-male behaviors, African and African-American homosexual behavior has occurred in a social context wherein men (heterosexual or homosexual) share a rich tradition of homo-affective experience, as illustrated in the opening anecdote concerning the affectionate behavior of athletes. Strong affiliative and loving bonds are encouraged in a wide range of African and African-American communities. The manhood rituals of ancient Kemet (Egypt), West Africa rites of passage (see Nobles, 1991), and African-American manhood rituals (see Kunjufu, 1985) all value training males to be emotionally expressive. "Bundling," or groups of men sleeping in physical contact, is common in some West African communities (Greenberg, 1988). Virtually the only actions which seem to be definitively "homosexual" in an African/African-American context are actions specifically *intended* to excite another man into sexual arousal.

In fact, some would claim that the specific devalued behaviors have more to do with whether one takes an active ("masculine") or passive ("feminine") role in the sexual encounter, reflecting the interrelationship of gender-role issues and sexuality. In Beam's interview (1986) of a young African-American gay man living in a small Alabama town, the young man explains that the majority of local African-American men who engage in homosexual acts self-describe as straight or heterosexual. Sexual activity with other men is not seen as unmanly, as long as it is not discussed publicly and is not called homosexual. Simmons (1991) examines Amiri Baraka's (LeRoi Jones's) autobiographical torment about his homosexual desires as he reflects on what it means to be a young African-American man. Coincidentally, this attitude—which more devalues perceived submissiveness or passiveness than male-male sexuality (see Greenberg, 1988)—is echoed in an ancient Egyptian myth, concerning the sons of Osiris, Horus and Seth, which dates back to the reign of Rameses (1160 BC).

Cass (1990) presents a stage model of homosexual identity formation which is similar to that proposed by others. She describes six stages of development. The first two stages involve confusion over what being gay is, and whether it is possible that the individual could conceivably be gay. The third and fourth stage involve accepting homosexuality as an identity. The fifth stage involves anger and confrontation with those who do not accept homosexuality, as well as an isolation into gay settings and avoiding nongay settings. In the sixth stage, the individual is seen as integrating his gay identity into his definition of self as one, but not all, of the parts of the self. Disclosure of one's sexuality becomes almost automatic. The latter point refers to the importance of the coming-out process; this seems central to the writing of many gay and lesbian European-American writers (see Eichberg, 1990). One study of African-American lesbians found little congruence between the elements of this model and the reports of the women who were interviewed (Hall, 1991). There was particular divergence on the importance of "coming out" as public disclosure of sexuality. These women emphasized personal self-awareness and shared awareness with those close to them, but they were much less likely to define public disclosure as a necessary part of a strong self-identity. There are no comparable studies with young men.

The two young men whom we interviewed explained the discovery of their sexuality in the following way. Both said that they were aware of their attraction to other boys at a very young age, though they did not define these feelings as homosexual. They even had sexual experiences with other boys, but they continued to define themselves as heterosexual well into their late teens, while continuing to have experiences with girls and boys. These early encounters with boys often occurred in the context of "horseplay." Heterosexual youth report the school as the most common contact point for meeting and initiating relationships (Westney, Jenkins, Dobbs-Butts, and

Williams, 1991). Though there are no comparable data on gay youth, given the amount of time and social activity centered on school campuses, it is likely that this may be true for them as well. One of the young men reported that boys in high school develop code words and slang to signal that they might consider homosexual advances. They may even establish locations where they are most likely to meet.

Dr. Strickland (1993, personal communication) reported that the majority of his African-American gay clients refer to their behaviors as gay or bisexual. During the earlier stages of therapy, the teenagers tend to prefer the term gay, while the older clients prefer bisexual. This may be either a cross-generation issue or an issue of self-acceptance. The older clients are more likely to use the term gay in the posttreatment phase of their experience. Dr. Strickland also reports that they rarely use the term homosexual as a self-descriptor. His clients reported that, as youth their tendency was to have experiences with peers or older young men. His reports corroborate other findings that these experiences are often linked to extensions of typical male-male horseplay.

It is difficult to determine what percentage of any population engages in homosexual behavior because of the secrecy which surrounds it. For European-Americans the estimates are as high as twenty-five percent of adult males having ever had some homosexual experience (Savin-Williams, 1990) to as low as two percent of them identifying as exclusively homosexual. These figures are imprecise for European-Americans, and they are even less informative for African-Americans. Further, the sexual experiences of African-American men appear more labile. In a CDC study of gay/bisexual men with AIDS, fifteen percent of the European-American men reported having sex with women while thirty-three percent of the African-American men reported recently engaging in sex with women (reported in American Red Cross, 1989). These findings are consistent with findings (Bell and Weinberg, 1978) that African-American men were more likely than European-American men to label themselves as bisexual (thirty percent versus thirteen percent) and are also consistent with a national study of homosexual and bisexual AIDS patients (reported in Cochran and Mays, 1991) which indicated that African-American gay men were more likely to report having had sex with women in the past year than European-American gay men (twenty-two percent versus fourteen percent). In a study in progress concerning African-American men with AIDS, almost sixty percent of the gay/bisexual subjects who have been tested to date reported having had sex with women, and virtually the same percentage of gay/bisexual males report having children as do heterosexual males (Monteiro, 1993 personal communication).

Since most of these studies included data from both younger and older men, their generalizability to the young gay experience is difficult. It is reasonable, however, to hypothesize that: (1) a certain percentage of young, African-American, gay, and straight men have early experiences with other young men and young women; (2) these experiences may occur earlier for some than others; and (3) with age, some will become predominantly gay, some predominantly straight, while others will continue to enjoy sex with both men and women throughout their adulthood. What is not known is the distribution of these behaviors, the processes underlying them and the social, personal, cultural, and spiritual meaning of them.

Sexual identity and racial identity do not develop in isolation. Since the former tends to be most publicly supported in the gay, white, male community and the latter in the heterosexual black community, it should be predictable that these young men may often feel deeply conflicted by the apparent contradictions presented by their developing identities. Delaney and Beam (1986) address the twin dualities of ethnicity and sexuality as follows: "As a black man, (he) tended to straddle two worlds: white and black. As a gay man, (he) straddled them too: straight and gay." Some of these young men may come to give priority to their ethnic identity (black gays) and others to their sexual identity (gay blacks) (see also, Cochran and Mays, 1991, Johnson, 1982; Peterson, 1992, for more detailed discussions). The priority of identity may relate to the degree to which the individuals feel a part of the African-American or gay communities and indicate preferences for their patterns of socialization. Dr. Strickland (1993, personal communication) reported that, because his clients were from urban areas with high percentages of African-American men, most of them identified as African-American first and gay second, with only a minority reporting the reverse. He did note that those who identified first as African-American tended to be most secure about ethnicity and least secure about their sexuality. Conversely, those who identified as gay first appeared to have a more secure sense of their sexuality while remaining most conflicted about their ethnicity.

Some have indicated that young African-American men may have greater exposure to sexual experiences with European-Americans than with African-Americans (for example, Bell and Weinberg, 1978), or they may have greater opportunity to explore their homosexuality within the European-American gay community because its social venues are more public (see Peterson, 1992). This judgment may be incorrect. Given the racism in the European-American gay community (see Demarco, 1983; Icard, 1985; Smith, C.M., 1986; Smith, M.J., 1983) and the privacy surrounding gay interactions in the African-American community (Smith, C.M., 1986), many European-Americans and African-Americans socialize separately. In addition, much of African-American gay social life is often constructed to overlap with or blend into the African-American heterosexual social life. These two factors make it difficult to assess what is typical for the young African-American gay male, particularly if the entry point into the African-American gay community is through the European-American gay community. For example, the convenience sample used by Bell and Weinberg (1978) oversampled African-Americans in bars, baths, and through social networks. Since they did not mention targeting predominantly African-American bars or African-American social networks, there is concern that they may have over-sampled African-Americans who more frequently socialize in or near the European-American gay community. Many African-American bars and businesses are not listed in the European-American gay directories, and a number of African-American gay social groups—some in existence for over thirty years with members in cities across the country—are virtually unknown to most European-Americans and to many African-Americans who socialize primarily in European-American gay environments.

SOCIAL ADJUSTMENT: THE INTERACTION OF RACE AND SEXUALITY

The stresses and strains of racism and homo-antagonism (negative feelings, beliefs or actions towards homosexuals, including but not limited to homo-phobia) do affect the development of African-American gay men. There are a set of related stereotypes that would suggest that because of racism, African-Americans must be disproportionately dysfunctional and, because of homo-antagonism, gays and lesbians must also be disproportionately dys-functional. Given these stereotypes, the assumption might be made that African-American gay men must be, by their very nature, seriously dysfunc-tional. Interestingly, these stereotypes are reflected in two parallel sets of research literature on race and sexuality concerning mental health. In addi-tion to the literature which defines blacks or gays as organically abnormal, there exists an additional parallel set of literatures: one argues that being black and oppressed should produce, in a fairly automatic way, self-hatred which will result in lowered self-esteem and poor mental health (see

Baldwin, Brown, and Hopkins 1991 for review); the other argues that, like-wise, being gay and oppressed should produce self-hatred, lowered self-esteem and poor mental health (see Savin-Williams, 1990 for review). Neither hypothesis receives much support.

In an extensive review and critique of the black self-hatred literature, Baldwin et al. (1991) find these studies rife with methodological flaws. They also lack consistent evidence for a generalized self-hatred. This is not to say that some individuals may not experience self-hatred based on race. It argues that, as a group, African-Americans are not inherently self-hating. Similarly, Savin-Williams (1990) reports a review of over three dozen studies of the self-esteem and self-concept of lesbians and gays. He finds approximately an equal number of studies reporting higher self esteem for gays and lesbians and studies reporting higher levels for heterosexuals. Most studies report no differences. Though the studies about gays and lesbians did not report separate findings for African-American gay men, they suggest that assuming that oppression and hatred by others *automatically* leads to self hatred is simplistic at best. In the case of race, Baldwin et al. (1991) argued that the self-hatred hypothesis is simply an extension of a racist philosophy which assumes that the self-worth of blacks must be determined by the value assigned by whites. By extension, it could be argued that the gay self-hatred hypothesis reflects a homo-antagonistic model which presumes that the self-worth of gays and lesbians is determined by the value assigned to them by heterosexuals.

The existing data would suggest that a person's particular culture, race, and sexuality do not directly determine health or dysfunction; however, they do serve as part of the context in which health or dysfunction develop. Though race or sexuality *per se* may not determine mental health, social adjustment to issues of race and sexuality may be crucial in the development of the young African-American male. For example, race and sexuality do appear to be related to some risk behaviors, such as drug use and unsafe sex, suggesting that racial and sexual psychosocial conflict may be related to higher levels of psychological and physical distress. Though he does not imply that there is necessarily a causal relationship, Dr. Strickland (1993, personal communication) reports that—in the context of expressing anger at a variety of people in their lives who do not understand the importance of their sexuality—many of his clients displayed serious denial regarding their sexual responsibilities. They reported "a prevailing wish to cast caution to the wind in regard to placing themselves at risk for HIV infection."

Adolescents and young adults are challenged by learning healthy habits, attitudes, and social patterns concerning drug use and sexual behavior. Though over ninety percent of high school seniors report using alcohol, fifty to sixty percent report using marijuana, and about six percent report cocaine use (Johnston, Bachman, and O'Malley, 1982), most young adults do not become addicts. This latter point—the fact that most do not become addicted—is difficult to remember in the context of the dramatic tragedies which can occur when addiction does occur. Though the African-American community as a whole may not consume more alcohol in general than does the European-American community (Ploski and Williams, 1983), it does report the greatest number of addictions and addiction-related diseases (Staples, 1991). The gay community also reports serious alcohol abuse problems (Icard and Traunstein, 1987). Addiction and abuse are often related to social isolation or other social adjustment problems. It would be important to find out whether the degree to which African-American youth achieve integration of their racial and sexual identities relates to drug and alcohol abuse.

Adolescence and young adulthood are times of sexual exploration and, at times, confusion. As reported elsewhere (see Savin-Williams, 1990 for a review), the percentage of adolescent boys who admit to being gay can be lower than one percent, but the number who report homosexual behaviors can be as high as twenty-five percent. African-American youth generally report earlier sexual experiences than European-American youth (Zimbardo, 1992), and African-American gay/bisexual adults appear to demonstrate greater variability in their sexual behavior—being more likely, even when gay, to also have heterosexual contact. With these unique characteristics, understanding the complexity of the sexual experiences of young African-American males is critical, particularly in the context of the current AIDS epidemic.

AIDS transmission in the African-American community is not identical to that in the European-American community. An African-American male is three times as likely to contract HIV as a European-American male. Only five percent of the European-American cases are by intravenous drug use (IDU) while eighty-one percent are by homosexual contact. In the African-American community, thirty-four percent of the transmissions are reported as IDU related, forty-five percent are primarily related to male to male homosexual behavior, and eight percent are related to the combination of homosexual behavior and IDU use (Center for Disease Control, February, 1989). The majority of the cases for African-American females involve IDU use or sex with an IDU user or bisexual partner, while the majority of

African-American children with AIDS are born to infected mothers. It is clear, then, that the African-American community is more socially connected in ways that open routes for the HIV virus to cross arbitrary social boundaries concerning sexual identity than is the European-American community (Monteiro, 1991). In addition, recent research has demonstrated that African-American gay men are very likely to engage in high risk sexual behaviors and that bisexual and gay men were more likely to engage in high-risk behaviors, with secondary partners—people other than their spouses or lovers (reported in Peterson, 1992). Understanding African-American sexual behavior, then, is critical to understanding African-American, male, health behavior and the health of the African-American community in general.

Educators are well aware of the numerous reasons that schools have become the focal points for discussions of adolescent and young adult social adjustment. Clearly, school based programs that promote mental and physical health are critical to the development of our young, African-American, gay males. Of more direct concern to educators is the growing base of evidence that social and affective adjustment may have as much to do with scholastic performance and persistence in school as does academic preparation. Feelings of self-worth (see Covington, 1984) and student anxieties (see Hill, 1984) are major determinants of school success. These effects are as pronounced once students reach college. Research has begun to demonstrate that the psychosocial factors that influence the retention of African-American college students are not identical to those that influence European-Americans. One set of studies demonstrated that noncognitive social factors, such as self-confidence and community service, predict student grade point averages for African-American college students as well as or better than Scholastic Aptitude Test (SAT) scores. Moreover, the willingness of African-Americans to persist at college is strongly related to self confidence, social support, community service, and understanding racism, but it is not strongly related to SAT scores (Tracey and Sedlacek, 1987). These findings underscore the importance of understanding how racial and sexual identity formation relates to the social and affective dimensions of adjustment and achievement.

REDEFINING THE QUESTIONS

It is clear that there is inadequate data to completely describe the homosexual experiences of African-American men or the various meanings of these experiences across men, situations, and their life-span development. We do appear, however, to have enough knowledge to assess the limitations of the current professional commentary on the experience. This investigation has attempted to demonstrate that:

1. African-American male homosexuality exists, and that it is an integral part of the African and African-American experience;
2. Development of a meaningful understanding of one's race, culture, and sexuality are all critical aspects of the developing self-concept of young, African-American, gay men;
3. Neither race nor homosexuality *per se* appear to directly determine health or dysfunction, though they do serve as a context which influences the nature and interpretation of health and dysfunction;
4. African-American homosexuality is a real and important part of the African-American community, which can be addressed within an African-American-centered approach to social development;
5. Our understanding of the behaviors of African-American men concerning ethnic and sexual identity formation is integral to our understanding of the general African-American community; and,
6. There is reason to believe that the adjustment of young, African-American, gay males to the dual challenges of racial and sexual identity may contribute to their individual health and achievement, and by extension to that of the general community.

Despite what has been demonstrated to be known, any definitive statements about the nature, development, typicality, or implications of African-American homosexualities is premature. This poverty of research on African-American gay men offers a wealth of possibilities for every form of academic research. Though researchers from other theoretical perspectives may choose to study African-American gay youth, African-American-centered researchers must be willing to lead in examining the subtle and intricate patterns of male homosexualities as they manifest themselves within African-American communities.

Informal observation and speculation are always critical components in the thinking process, academic or nonacademic. These speculations inform and guide the other analytic and synthetic approaches to gaining knowledge. There is, however, a clear need to extend beyond the information garnered by informal observation and speculation. Comprehensive descriptive studies are essential to determine the varieties of African and African-American male homosexualities. These should include historical as well as contemporaneous investigations. There must be a reliance on both text- and oral-based inquiries. These studies must also investigate the cognitive, affective, and spiritual meanings ascribed to the observable homosexual acts by those studied. These descriptive studies will begin to clarify the debate over what is or is not part of the sexual experience of African-American youth.

Large-scale correlational and experimental studies will be useful in informing us about the relationship between race, culture, sexuality, and other psychosocial factors. It will be important to understand the relationship between race, culture, homosexuality, and issues regarding adolescent and young adult socialization. Studies might include investigations of the varieties of gay intimate and social relationships, the family patterns of African-American gay men, and the social and personal achievement patterns of these men. Cognitive studies might attempt to model the ways in which these men mentally represent their racial, cultural, and sexual identities, and they might explore how these representations influence their social perceptions and behaviors. Studies of African-American gay men with children—and those without—might clarify the desires of these men for fatherhood and the patterns of fatherhood that they express. Studies of the other adult social roles held by African-American gay men would clarify the variety of social patterns that are likely to be a part of the future development of young African-American males.

Admittedly, these empirical descriptions will inform us about "what is" but not "what ought to be." In an African-American-centered approach to social science, social science researchers cannot divorce themselves from the spiritual, moral, and value-based aspects of their studies (Clark, 1979). The African-American-centered approach rejects the Cartesian dualism that the spirituality of humanity belongs to religion and the animal qualities to science. But African-American-centered approaches do not give precedence to any one religion, or religious official in this debate, for spirituality is not the sole domain of religion and the African origins of models of spirituality predate the current major religions (Ben-Jochanon, 1970). Further, though organized religions offer important texts, traditions, and methods for exploring spiritual and moral study, they do not singularly or collectively constitute the only methods or sources of spiritual inquiry. This also implies the complimentary argument that the worldly is not exempt from religious or spiritual scrutiny. Science is not the sole guardian of the physical aspects of humanity. Theologians and clergy must continue to be challenged to test the applications of their spiritual/abstract principles to current real-world situations. An African-American-centered approach to spirituality demands that the abstract elements, principles, and processes which constitute human nature be applied in real context. This approach is shared by other African-American theologically based approaches to the study of race (for instance, West, 1992) or women's issues (Cannon, 1988). This form of ethical and spiritual debate "starts with experience instead of with theories of values and norms" (Cannon, 1988), insuring that theory serves to explain reality, rather than bending reality to support theory. Specifically, there must be detailed studies of the particular manifestations of homosexual expression and the degree to which their expressions, in context, demonstrate a basic integrity among the various elements of the individual—thoughts, feelings, behaviors, values, and relationship to community.

From the perspective of educators, these basic studies should allow us to institute better educational and mental health programs which would support the healthy development of young, African-American, gay men. In a community that agrees that its men are endangered (Kunjufu, 1985), we must remedy both the dangers which are truly external to our community as well as those which are self-generated. In order to do so, we must know more about the true nature of the strengths and weaknesses in our young, African-American, gay men as they relate to the strengths and weakness of our community as a whole.

NOTES

The authors would like to thank Dr. D. Philip McGee for his insightful critique of an earlier draft of this manuscript. They would also like to thank Dr. Stanley Strickland for sharing his clinical observations gained from over twelve years of practice. Additionally, we would like to thank the two young men who were willing to be interviewed for this study.

1. *African-American* is a term which emphasizes the cultural origin of these men while *black* emphasizes their social race and their relationship to racism, particularly white supremacy. Both terms are academically appropriate and refer to basically the same group of people, but

they emphasize different aspects of the individual's experience. We will use *African-American* except where it is intended to emphasize racial experience.

REFERENCES

Akbar, N. (1989). *Chains and Images of Psychological Slavery*. Trenton, NJ: New Mind Productions.

———. (1991). "Mental Disorders Among African-Americans." In *Black Psychology*. Third edition. R.L. Jones, ed. Berkeley, CA: Cobb and Henry.

Amen, R.U.N. (1990). *Metu Neter*. Volume I. Bronx, NY: Khamit Corp.

American Red Cross (1989). *HIV/AIDS Education: Instructor's Manual*.

Anderson, J. (1990). *Cognitive Psychology and its Implications*. New York: Freeman and Company.

Asante, M.K. (1980). *Afrocentricity: The Theory of Social Change*. Buffalo, NY: Amulefi.

Baldwin, J.A., Brown, R., and Hopkins, R. (1991). "The Black Self-Hatred Paradigm Revisited: An Africentric Analysis." In *Black Psychology*. Third edition. R.L. Jones, ed. Berkeley, CA: Cobb and Henry.

Banks, W.C., Ward, W.E., McQuater, G.V., and Debritto, A.M. (1991). "Are Blacks External: On the Status of Locus of Control in Black Populations." In *Black Psychology*. Third edition. R.L. Jones, ed. Berkeley, CA: Cobb and Henry.

Beam, J. (1986). "Emmett's Story: Russell County, Alabama." In *In the Life: A Black Gay Anthology*. J. Beam, ed. Boston: Alyson Publications

Bell, A.P. and Weinberg, M.S. (1978). *Homosexualities: A Study of Diversity Among Men and Women*. New York: Simon and Schuster.

Ben-Jochanon, Y. (1970). *African Origin of the Major "Western Religions."* New York: AlekebuLan Books.

Bogle, D. (1974). *Toms, Coons, Mullatoes, Mammies and Bucks*. New York: Bantam Books.

Boykin, W. (1979). "Black Psychology and the Research Process: Keeping the Baby but Throwing Out the Bath Water." In *Research Directions of Black Psychologists*. A.W. Boykin, A.J. Franklin, and J.F. Yates, eds. New York: Russell Sage Foundation.

Cannon, K. G. (1988). *Black Womanist Ethics*. Atlanta, GA: Scholars Press.

Cass, V. C. (1990). "The Implications of Homosexual Identity Formation for the Kinsey Model and Scale of Sexual Preference." In *Homosexuality/*

Heterosexuality: Concepts of Sexual Orientation. D.P. McWhirter, S.A. Sanders and J.M. Reinisch, eds. New York: Oxford University.

Center for Disease Control (February, 1989). *HIV/AIDS Surveillance.* Atlanta, GA.

Chomsky, N. (1965). *Aspects of the Theory of Syntax.* Cambridge, MA: MIT Press.

Clark (X), C. (1979). "Black Studies or the Study of Black People." In *Black Psychology.* First edition. R. Jones, ed. New York: Harper and Row.

Cochran, S.D. and Mays, V.M. (1991). "Sociocultural Facets of the Black Gay Male Experience." In *The Black Family.* Fourth edition. R. Staples, ed. Belmont, CA: Wadsworth Publishing.

Covington, M. V. (1984). "The Motive of Self-Worth." In *Research on Motivation in Education.* Volume I. R. Ames and C. Ames, eds. San Francisco: Academic Press.

Cress Welsing, F. (1991). *The Isis (Yssis) Papers: The Keys to the Colors.* Chicago: Third World Press.

Cross, W.E. (1979). "The Negro to Black Conversion Experience: An Empirical Analysis." In *Research Directions of Black Psychologists.* A.W. Boykin, A.J. Franklin, and J.F. Yates, eds. New York: Russell Sage Foundation.

———. (1991). *Shades of Black Diversity in African-American Identity.* Philadelphia: Temple University Press.

———. Parham, T.A., and Helms, J.E. (1991). "The Stages of Black Identity Development: Nigrescence Models." In *Black Psychology.* Third edition. R.L. Jones, ed. Berkeley, CA: Cobb and Henry.

Delany, S.R. and Beam, J. (1986). "The Possibilities of Possibilities." In *In the Life: A Black Gay Anthology.* J. Beam, ed. Boston: Alyson Publications

Demarco, J. (1983). "Gay Racism." In *Black Men/White Men.* M.J. Smith, ed. San Francisco: Gay Sunshine Press.

Drake, S.C. (1987). *Black Folk Here and There.* Volume I. Los Angeles: Center for AfroAmerican Studies, UCLA.

Dubois, W.E.B. (1903, reprinted 1990). *The Souls of Black Folk.* New York: Vintage Books.

Eichberg, R. (1990). *Coming Out: An Act of Love.* New York: A Dutton Book.

Fanon, F. (1967). *Black Skin, White Masks.* New York: Grove Press.

Feldman, R.S. (1989). *Adjustment: Applying Psychology in a Complex World.* San Francisco: McGraw-Hill.

Greenberg, D.F. (1988). *The Construction of Homosexuality.* Chicago: The

University of Chicago Press.

Grier, W.H. and Cobb, P.M. (1968). *Black Rage*. New York: Basic Books.

Hall, D. (1991). *Black Lesbian Identity Formation and Community Involvement*. Unpublished masters thesis, San Francisco State University, San Francisco, CA.

Hare, N. and Hare, J. (1984). *The Endangered Black Family*. San Francisco: Black Think Tank.

Hayes, W.A. (1991). "Radical Black Behaviorism." In *Black Psychology*. Third edition. R.L. Jones, ed. Berkeley, CA: Cobb and Henry.

Hayles, V. R. (1991). "African-American Strengths: A Survey of Empirical Findings." In *Black Psychology*. Third edition. R.L. Jones, ed. Berkeley, CA: Cobb and Henry.

Hill, K.T. (1984). "Debilitating Motivation and Testing: A Major Educational Problem—Possible Solutions and Policy Applications." In *Research on Motivation in Education*. Volume I. R. Ames and C. Ames, eds. San Francisco: Academic Press.

Icard, L. (1985). "Black Gay Men and Conflicting Social Identities: Sexual Orientation Versus Racial Identity." *Journal of Social Work and Human Sexuality, 4*, pp. 83–93.

———. and Traunstein, D.M. (1987). "Black, Gay, Alcoholic Men: Their Character and Treatment." *Social Casework, 68*, pp. 267–272.

Johnson, J. (1982). *Influence of Assimilation on the Psychosocial Adjustment of Black Homosexual Men*. Unpublished dissertation. California School of Professional Psychology, Berkeley, CA.

Johnston, L.D., Bachman, J.G. and O'Malley, P.M. (1982). *Student Drug Use in America 1975–1981*. Washington, DC: U.S. Government Printing Office.

Kunjufu, J. (1985). *Countering the Conspiracy to Destroy Black Boys*. Chicago: African-American Images.

Lane, A.J. (March, 1991). "Newton's Law: Historic Black Panther Letter Tries for Coalition with Black Lesbian and Gay Men." *BLK*, pp. 11–15.

Lewis, D.K. (1975). "The Black Family: Socialization and Sex Roles." *Phylon, 36*, pp. 221–237.

Madhubuti, H. (1990). *Black Men: Obsolete, Single, Dangerous?* Chicago: Third World Press.

Mays, V.M. and Cochran, S.D. (1991). "The Black Women's Relationship Project: A National Survey of Black Lesbians." In *The Black Family*. Fourth edition. R. Staples, ed. Belmont, CA: Wadsworth Publishing.

Mbiti, J.S. (1970). *African Religions and Philosophies*. Garden City, NY:

Anchor Press.

Medin, D.L. and Ross, B.H. (1992). *Cognitive Psychology.* New York: Harcourt, Brace and Jovanovich.

Monteiro, K.P. (1991). *A Framework for AIDS Services for Black Gay/Bisexual Men.* San Francisco: Bayview Hunter's Point Foundation.

Moynihan, D.P. (1978). "The Tangle of Pathology." In *The Black Family: Essays and Studies.* Second edition. R. Staples, ed. Belmont, CA: Wadsworth.

Murphy, G. and Kovac, J.K. (1972). *Historical Introduction to Modern Psychology.* Third edition. San Francisco: Harcourt, Brace and Jovanovich.

Nero, C.I. (1991). "Toward a Black Gay Aesthetic: Signifying in Contemporary Black Gay Literature." In *Brother to Brother: New Writings by Black Gay Men.* E. Hemphill and J. Beam, eds. Boston: Alyson Publications.

Nobles, W.W. (1991). "African Philosophy: Foundations for Black Psychology." In *Black Psychology.* R.L. Jones, ed. Berkeley, CA: Cobb and Henry.

Peterson, J.L. (1992). "Black Men and Their Same-Sex Desires and Behaviors." In *Gay Culture in America.* Gilbert Herdt, ed. Boston: Beacon Press.

Ploski, H.A. and Williams, J. (1983). *The Afro-American.* Fourth edition. New York: John Wiley and Sons.

Poussaint, A.F. (1990). "An Honest Look at Black Gays and Lesbians." *Ebony,* September, pp. 124–126 and 130–131.

Sarafino, E.P. and Armstrong, J.W. (1986). *Child and Adolescent Development.* San Francisco: West Publishing.

Savin-Williams, R.C. (1990). *Gay and Lesbian Youth: Expressions of Identity.* New York: Hemisphere Publishing.

Shepard, R. (1986). "On Not Being White." In *In the Life: A Black Gay Anthology.* J. Beam, ed. Boston: Alyson Publications.

Simmons, R. (1991). "Some Thoughts on the Challenges Facing Black Gay Intellectuals." *In the Life: A Black Gay Anthology.* J. Beam, ed. Boston: Alyson Publications.

Smith, C.M. (1986). "Bruce Nugent: Bohemian of the Harlem Renaissance." In *In the Life: A Black Gay Anthology.* J. Beam, ed. Boston: Alyson Publications.

Smith, M.J. (1983). "No Blacks: Racism in the Gay Press." In *Black Men/White Men.* M.J. Smith, ed. San Francisco: Gay Sunshine Press.

Spencer M.B. (1985). "Cultural Cognition and Social Cognition as Identity Correlates of Black Children's Personal-Social Development." In *Beginnings: The Social and Affective Development of Black Children*. M.B. Spencer, G.K. Brookins, and W.R. Allen, eds. Hillsdale, NJ: Lawrence Erlbaum Associates.

Staples, R. (1991). "Substance Abuse and the Black Family in Crisis: An Overview." In *The Black Family*. Fourth Edition. R. Staples, ed. Belmont, CA: Wadsworth Publishing.

Tracey, T.J. and Sedlacek, W.E. (1987). "Prediction of College Graduation Using Noncognitive Variables by Race." *Measurement and Evaluation in Counseling and Development, 19*, pp. 177–184.

West, C. (1992). *Race Matters*. Boston: Beacon Press.

Westney, O.E., Jenkins, R.R., Dobbs-Butts, J., and Williams, I. (1991). "Sexual Development and Behavior in Black Preadolescents." In *The Black Family*. Fourth edition. R. Staples, ed. Belmont, CA: Wadsworth Publishing.

White, J.L. (1984). *The Psychology of Blacks: An Afro-American Perspective*. Englewood Cliffs, NJ: Prentice Hall.

Woodson, C.G. (1933, 1969). *The Miseducation of the Negro*. Washington, DC: Associated Publishers.

Wright, B. (1974). "The Psychopathic Racial Personality." *Black Books Bulletin, 2* (2), pp. 25–31.

Zimbardo, P.G. (1992). *Psychology and Life*. New York: HarperCollins.

14

The Politics of Adolescent Sexual Identity and Queer Responses

Glorianne M. Leck

When you think about sex, are your thoughts primarily about procreation? Is sex more often about recreation? Is sex about power and/or pleasure? What is the subject of Madonna's *Erotica*? What is the message of Rogers and Hammerstein's *I'm Just A Girl Who Can't Say No!*? What is the attitude of Wrecks-N-Effects' *Rump Shaking*?

As adolescents enter their daily struggle with their own feelings and the meaning of their sexuality, they must negotiate within the political and cultural discussion at this historical moment. As citizens and educators, we cannot afford to turn or be turned away from an open exploration of the political grounding of ideas and definitions of human sexuality. Schools are a public forum and we must protect them as "public."

In her excellent study of *Justice and the Politics of Difference*, Iris Young

(1990) reminds us that: "The primary meaning of public is what is open and accessible. Indeed in open and accessible public spaces and forums, one should expect to encounter and hear from those who are different, whose social perspectives, experience and affiliations are different" (pp. 119–120).

When an early school law of the Massachusetts Bay Colony (The Olde Deluder Satan Act) attempted to guarantee children the right to go to school to study the text (in that case, a Bible) for themselves, it was assumed that children needed to protect themselves from the influences of a deluded parent or pastor—or from the Olde Deluder Satan himself. This law represented a community insight into the dignity of the soul of each child, as well as the need for a child's own exploration of controversy and biblical interpretation. Since that time, however, the U.S. government—even while making claims for and funding some aspects of public education—has been moving more and more toward protecting the parochialism of parents. The government appears to cater to the demands of religious special interest groups as they attempt to dictate what can be presented in public schools. The recognition of children's need for protection from their parents' parochialism has been all but lost. Intellectual explorations have been discouraged in schools; neutralized information and so-called basic skills have become the focus of schooling. The individual's quest for meaning and identity have been rendered extracurricular.

The allowing of parochial schooling, the talk now of voucher systems, the school board actions in which parents' protests can cause the removal of superintendents—all of these reveal the extent to which we as a nation have lost sight of basic democratic goals and of the need for our children to learn responsibility for their own thoughts and actions.[1] We are currently encountering certain parochial pressure groups who are fighting against the public schools' distribution of information about the cause—and devices for the possible prevention—of the spread of sexually transmitted diseases. Their pressure is intended to force schools to teach and perpetuate the naïve notion that sex is primarily a "reproductive" act. That sex-as-reproduction message usually insists that heterosexuality is "normal" or "natural," and that same-gender/sex affections and oral and anal sex are opposed to what is normal. In this context, homosexuality can be portrayed at best as a "naturally abnormal" biological state, or at worst as a behavior of sinful choice.

The pressure groups who seem to control our schools and other public discussions of human sexuality operate from a notion that sexuality is and should be strictly a sacred reproductive function of the human body. In this particular philosophical view, there is an appearance of essentialist/scientific objectivity about social function as biologically driven. Such an interpretation of meaning sidesteps the rich and troublesome terrain of socialization, culture, and power as it is played out through sexual relations, patriarchal values, and economic self-interest. The very notion that there could or should be a biology based sexual morality, or that there is any one "right" way to believe, is as much an issue as is the idea of a single definition of, or emphasis on, sexuality. Both should be part of the public discussion. In the absence of public open discourse, young people who are struggling with their own sexual feelings and identity are vulnerable to private influences. The home and the church are private influences, and may be either healthy and caring, or abusive and violent, or they may be simply silent on the topic. What options do we offer?[2] What protection do we provide for young people who are struggling with sexual issues, especially as they relate to abuse of power?

Who wants sexuality to be considered only in terms of its reproductive consequences? In this time more than any other, sexual activity is not necessarily reproductive in all of its lived and felt meanings. Sexuality is a social and historical construction of meanings. It can be entirely a private and consensual pleasure-making activity. Sometimes sexuality can be constructed as dramatic and political, and certainly sexual activity can and does interface with such social constructs as romance and violence.

Dominant political forces may be perceived to have an investment in the clear expression of order and responsibility that is related to the economics of child support. However, what claim can a society make over the consensual nonreproductive sexual behaviors of its adult members? We are citizens in a nation-state founded upon and defending the very notion of individual's having the right to pursue their life, liberty, and happiness. We must pause to ask ourselves: "Why would a controlling power group deny the sensual, playful, erotic, and creative aspects of sexuality, and define it only in terms of its reproductive features?"

I suspect that few of the most traditionally married heterosexual couples who merge for parenting limit their sexual behavior to the sole purpose of reproducing themselves. In fact, it appears that because they are "married"— and, by implication promising to be economically and socially responsible for the consequences of their reproductive activities—they are granted the full latitude of sexual erotic play. The freedom to be sexual, in its fullest sense, is extended to married heterosexual couples as a "special right."[3] The extension of this same marriage privilege is revealed in the distribution of health care benefits: a company or school district will pay four thousand dollars in benefits for a married employee and only two thousand dollars in benefits for an unmarried employee. In recent history, people have been institutionally rewarded for marrying and having children.

While this is neither the time or place, it would be appropriate for us to think carefully about who makes those rules and extends those privileges, and why. Under what historical and economic circumstances were these privileges developed? This too should be part of the public discussion in our schools. Studying government, economic, and military history always appears to be put before the social studies discussion of social history.

Schools are clearly a part of the social and political history which is strongly steeped in a set of social policies meant to control reproduction through economic and sexual privilege. Here we need to look at the sometimes scandalous history of federal and state government's involvement—or reluctance to get involved—in research that is related to birth control, pregnancy termination, and sexually transmitted diseases, as well as diseases that affect particular ethnic, racial, or gender groups—other than employed working men.

The power of religious institutions as conveyors of "morality" has been just such a significant and featured part of our schooling history. The notion of one "morality" is an impediment. It makes it difficult to field open and pluralistic public discussion about the sexual identity conflicts for today's young people as well as their teachers and parents.

Students of the 1990s are being told on the one hand to abstain from sex and limit their reproduction, and on the other hand to loosen up and enjoy their sexuality. Those interest groups who are clinging to traditional values continue to promote the idea that sex is a procreative behavior, and it should be limited to the context of a lifetime marriage. The popular culture, on the other hand, shouts out the joys and freedoms of nonreproductive sexual play and performance.

The most traditional social constructions of the meaning of sex do not include sexuality as a part of the individual's right to the pursuit of happiness. It appears that the traditional essentialist idea of sex-as-reproduction is in serious trouble in a time when the presence of birth control and the same old (although more graphic) "sex is the most important thing in your life" messages pervade the popular culture. Having "good" sex, having an attractive sexual partner, and being chosen as an attractive sexual partner are not new messages. I am not even sure that these messages are more prevalent than they were in their earlier, more subtle forms.

Among other things, the presence of birth control and the abundance of sexually stimulating popular culture seem to have moved the age of sexual achievement among the working and middle classes to a younger age than in the 1930s, forties, and fifties. Sexual preoccupation among adolescents is no longer—if it ever was—subtle. Imagine if we did not have the scares of genital herpes and AIDS. What would we do then about adolescent (and adult) sexual activity? Imagine the decreased significance of gender and biology, when sexuality is viewed primarily as recreation rather than procreation. Imagine the difference in economic lifestyle, when one can couple without a commitment to having, raising, and providing for a child. Imagine how economics and access to alternate forms of adoption would allow same-sex (or -gender) couples to choose to parent together and still have their preferred erotic partner who shares their sexual orientation.

In these questions, and the reality that they reflect, we can see the traditional assumptions underlying a biology-as-destiny view being opened up to challenge. One need look only as far as the developing public spectacles. Our popular culture is rich with a variety of rigidly heterosexual, reactionary homosensual, flexible bisexual, cross-gender, transgender and gender-bender players. In these stagings, we see "fixed sexual identities" as well as the challenge of "changing sexual identity" performances. As the ambiguities of gender and the meaning of sexuality take center stage, performance of gender and sexuality becomes and represents a way of resisting the traditional definitions of sex as exclusively a reproductive activity. To display one's gender or sexual "queerness" is to resist the modernist/industrialist/scientist ideas that identity has to be fixed and that sex has to be reproductive.

In popular culture—especially in musical entertainment, film and theatre—gender and sexuality are seen in transforming portrayals of traditional, creative, and/or reactive constructions of human sexuality and gender. In the stage light, such expressions as being lesbian, gay, or transgender may be shown as either a "naturally abnormal" identity behavior or as a "lifestyle experiment." To show either heterosexuality or homosexuality as a "fixed identity" is to portray sexuality as a biological matter that is related to what is traditionally viewed as a "fixed" reproductive identity. To demonstrate oneself as "queer" is to challenge the concept of a fixed or an essential (consistent and/or final) sex or gender identity. In a discussion about lesbian and gay politics and queer theory, the editors of *Radical America* (Volume 24, No. 4) asked: "What are we to make of the pervasive interest in "cross dressing"? Has "cross dressing" replaced "coming out"—does "performing your-self" catch some of the desire for mobility, the fear of standing still, of being pinned down, found out, left out, or fixed, that "coming out" (discovering, revealing, expressing your "true self") cannot?" (p. 9).

A significant number of us who were previously identified as lesbian or gay now identify ourselves as "queer." "Queer" represents a more mobile, growing, and transforming concept of who we are or who we may become. It is likely that many of us from earlier generations, who are "lesbian"- or "gay"- identified, are so because we came to believe that we had no other options within the ideological oppression which stems from compulsory, heterosexual, reproductive, social restraints. We were labeled as different from heterosexuals. We became their opposites. Our difference was essen-tialized, scorned, and called perverted. We were given—and we took on—a "sexual identification" which was created in relation to heterosexuality as the prescribed sexual identification. In language that referred to us in terms of our biology, we were called "homosexuals." As we historically resisted being seen as sick and abnormal, our social life circumstances have created room for even greater creativity. It has been expressed in "lifestyle" and "sexstyle" issues.

We claimed language that referred to *the lack* of cumbersome sexual repro-ductive obligations in our sexual expressions, and we called ourselves "gay." In language expressing the gender differences between men and women in patriarchy, women have looked to our historical roots, and we identified ourselves as "lesbians." Now we encounter the construct of "queer." Queers may be seen as those people in the margins—even of gay *and* lesbian (oppo-sitionally designed) lifestyles—who resist being identified by a particular sexual orientation.

If all of lifestyle in a heterosexist society appears to be designed around the economics of reproduction and production, then imagine the creative space for those of us who would create instead of procreate. That in itself calls for a lifestyle that is designed around celebrating "variety and pleasure." You will see young people expressing those values in their costume, body languages, and their resistance to the expected sexual behaviors. Queer-identified young people are going to have needs and expectations that are different from those that are associated with gay, lesbian, and bisexual youth.

It does not take great imagination to know that binary definitions have served to limit the social and intellectual exploration of sexual boundaries and their social meanings. This dominance of binary definitions and related dualistic thinking has discouraged us from being "queer." It is important for us as teachers as well as for those of us who are queer to understand the power of reclaiming the meaning of the concept of queer. Queer is not fixed, not traditional, and not bound to a final identity. In the current vogue of queer theory, the boundaries of sexuality may be explored without the constraints of binary opposition, or without the constraints of the idea that identity is unchanging and means the same thing in all contexts.

As young people become more attuned to the influences of the postmodernists' efforts to deconstruct dualistic (both traditional and modern) notions and the related constraints of the idea of "fixed sexual identity," we are going to see more challenges to that old limited conception of sex as biology and reproduction. I wish to suggest, therefore, that the reader learn much more about queer theory and the freedom that one gains and the responsibility that one must take on when sexuality is explored rather than uncovered or defined.

Recently our attention was called to a talk-show-type phenomenon called "Lesbians Until Graduation" (LUG). Some young college-aged women are electing to explore and express their sexuality in same-gender relationships which allow them to have joyful sex without the risks of heterosexual reproductive liaisons. This arrangement takes care of their felt need to become sexually active, and it allows them to avoid some of the risks—including pregnancy, disease and non-consensual sex—of sex with men who are also experimenting with their sexuality.[4] This choice of what appears to be a bisexual-type lifestyle is not to be confused with lesbianism. It is experienced as nonchoice, and is grounded in sexual orientation. The LUGs wait to decide about their commitment to reproductivity until after they have established their economic stability and after they have explored their own sexual pleasures.

Thanks to the breakthrough made by feminists, the sexual liberationists (including queer theorists) will necessarily be deconstructing the "biology as destiny" issue in modernist as well as in traditional Western cultural, political, and economic values. As popular-culture artists, academics, and adolescents challenge and explore the boundaries of limitation that are constructed by modernist notions of fixed sexual identity, we are more likely to see dialogue about and expressions of sexuality that are "in your face" as sensual, erotic, and phantasmagoric.

Reflect for a moment on the language of disrespect used by youth in the 1940s, the fifties, the sixties, and now in the nineties. The words "fuck," "suck," "dickhead," etc., are all around our halls, and are interspersed into daily slang. The referent of the language is very different from the earlier curses of "hell," or "damn," or "oh, shit!" For adults who are in authority positions to deny the more direct sexual references of language, or to try to repress or isolate this language of sexuality, violence, and power, seems to me to be setting up an even greater division between public discourse and private acts. I am not suggesting that the language ought to be invited as always "appropriate"; I am simply suggesting that its meaning and its presence need to be addressed directly—and not simply with another "thou shalt not!" The language tells us of the discourse level, as well as the need for public discussion of the significance of the feelings to which it refers. Violent, aggressive language may be better discussed than repressed. What do young people know about the options and alternatives to violence in their social sexual relations? Who is discussing that with them?

Struggling for acceptance and identity seems to or can be a process of risking and performing ranges of possible behaviors. Finding out how certain roles feel, how certain words sound, and how people respond to an act or one's language is an important part of social exploration. A common contemporary violent outburst is now likely to include calling someone a "faggot." This language tells us something about the potential for gay-bashing, as well as something about the safety issue for lesbian and gay youth in our schools. Can we afford to allow it to go unchallenged, not discussed? Who suffers from this undiscussed violence? Who benefits from this kind of intimidation? What does the silence teach, if not complicity?

For lesbian- and gay-identified youth, the important struggle—just as for an individual identified as heterosexual—is likely to continue to be the struggle for self-respect and acceptance. The plethora of negative judgments that are made by parents, teachers, peers, and religious communities is of great significance. Negative reactions by one's parents, teachers, and peer group are all too significant in our sense of self-worth. The interaction between the youthful explorer of sexual values and the gatekeepers of the traditional rewards is a dynamic part of a whole system that is designed to define and maintain the definitions of sex, eroticism, and gender. We need to review our part in, and the consequences of, all of this.

Most adolescents are likely to find themselves located in a sexual and gender culture that is more often than not hostile to same-sex or same-gender erotic play, preference, or orientation. In that much of the social and institutional activity of the U.S. high school is designed for, includes, and promotes heterosexual rituals, we are likely to see definite resistance to lesbian, gay, bisexual, and queer displays and/or explorations. It is quite predictable that traditional thinkers—in order to make even stronger the community's emphasis on acts and procedures of heterosexism that oppress queer-, lesbian-, gay-, and bisexual-identified adolescents—will monitor the rules and curriculum in order to try to retain heterosexual privilege and ultimate control over the school's social environment. And just as that heterosexist system was developed to enforce a hierarchy and a definition of normalcy that becomes synonymous with the heterosexual notion of sex as a reproductive act, so we can see heterosexuals reacting to defend their rights to special erotic privileges because they themselves have married and reproduced.

Young, openly queer adolescents will remain the greater oddity and the fighters for sexual freedom in most schools. Unfortunately, it may become the case that lesbian and gay adolescents will become even more oppressed, for the old "turn your head, shake your head, but tolerate it if they aren't blatant" attitude could be transformed into outright witch-hunts and hostile verbal harangues. These would be committed by those who continue to be defensive and resistant in their claims to having the one and only definition of "morality."

For those young people who are exploring bisexual and erotic experimentation, "queer" may be a much more appropriate category for both their own and for our understanding of their behavior. We cannot know—and they may not know—whether or not the behavior is experimental or is authentically felt as a need and an orientation to their sexuality. Attempts to solidify or force sexual identity will more likely than not have negative consequences.

Because we tend to restrain sexual social behavior, we do little to publicly discuss, and thus encourage, the individual's efforts to create boundaries or understandings about violent and nonconsensual sexual impositions, such as incest, pedophilia, torture, and rape. The media teases people with sexual "deviance," markets the horrors of sexual abuse through power, and flashes exotic possibilities for sexual play, all in the same medium and manner. Without avenues for discourse among ourselves at all levels of society, we will deprive the public of the discussion of meanings of and the junctures of power, oppression, and consent within human sexual interactions. When the interpretations of variant sexual activity are privatized, and no public dialogue is allowed—especially in the high schools—then the meanings will tend to be controlled by the existing powers and prejudices of the leaders in the peer groups. One need only look at some of the recent cases of gang rapes by athletes, fraternity brothers, neighborhood gangs, and so on, to get a sense of the presence of a vacuum of discourse in schools, as well as in churches and families.

In the absence of information, prejudice is fostered and conveyed. This is the sort of prejudice that operates when heterosexual reactionaries lump sexual behaviors such as pedophilia into gay lifestyle, deliberately ignoring the fact that pedophilia is not a same-gender or same-sex attraction. Pedophilia is specifically about adult sexual power over children. The children and the adults may be male or female, and the adult may have a gender or sexual preference, or it may simply be an issue of the availability of children. What does a young man who believes he might be gay think when he hears this constant association of gay men with pedophilia?

If we do not have open dialogue about sexual orientation, erotic preference, and gender stereotypes, we will continue to live on our individual knees in a kind of social vulnerability. The efforts to oppress the public discourse about human sexuality will continue by the usual means of economic penalty and negative social judgments. The question is: Do we as educators and citizens see the consequences of this ideology, and will we resist it?

NOTES

1. It seems important to remind ourselves of the unique way in which our "government-sanctioned" American culture treats fully sexually functioning adults as a special category called "teenagers." In many other cultures, puberty is the beginning of adulthood. Move to another perspective and look at the frustration that we generate in a fully sexually developed being when we try to use fear and age rules to delay their entry into sexual play for as much as ten or more years. To prohibit them from even discussing—in public, government-controlled places—the feelings and risks of sexuality is quite incredible.

2. In interviews with young gay men, we learned about the problem of not having open dialogue about gay life options. We consistently heard stories about how, in the absence of information, they turned to the streets and to what they heard from prejudiced heterosexuals about "the gay life." So they went to cruising spots, gay bars, and pornography shops

to seduce older gay men who could take them out and show them the life. Each reported his regret of the high-risk behaviors in which he had become involved in order to learn from the streets and alleys. What other options had we given them? Were there centers where they could meet other gay men and discuss and learn about their health care, their sex mate options, etc.? Could they discuss it with some gay teachers or even with a high school guidance counselor? They said, "No!" There were no options open to them. We must all remember that lesbian and gay young people are most often raised in households where the heterosexual lifestyle is required, and it is not usually safe to discuss homosexuality with parents and guardians. Gay and lesbian youth have to find their families-of-kind. That option is not frequently guided by general human service agencies, and certainly it is not attended to in most school environments.

3. In recent attacks against efforts by lesbian, gay, and bisexual people to get "equal protection" ordinances, the antigay agenda has been calling this political behavior the seeking of special rights. In this twist of rhetoric, the defenders of heterosexual privilege and their own special rights reverse the facts to make it appear that lesbian, gay, and bisexual people (who have lost jobs, housing, custody of children, and often even the freedom of association and safety in public places) are asking for more privileges than others have. An analysis of special privilege leads quickly to our understanding that special rights are usually granted by people in power to themselves and "their own kind."

4. This is a solution more available to females than males because lesbian activity is generally still trivialized as a "phase" or an immature sexual behavior. One can "recover" socially from a female same-sex liaison with greater acceptance than one can from having been in a male-with-male extended sexual partnership. This is a consequence of the continued presence of patriarchal value, which sees male behavior as much more significant than female behavior. Females are generally viewed as at a level between children and men, and therefore, we are more often forgiven for our "immature" and "unreasoned" choices. Please note this is not an advantage if one is seeking recognition, credibility, or identity as a whole and equal human being.

It should also be noted that lesbians are believed, at this point in time, to have the lowest risk for the transfer of HIV. This is also appealing to some young women who wish to enjoy their sexuality with reduced health risks. Men, on the other hand, have a high risk for the transfer of HIV in their sexual activities. This serves as a deterrent to same-sex experimentation between bisexual men. In each case we are talking about the privilege of sexual choosing for sexual experimentation. We are not talking about sexual orientation, which constitutes an entirely different set of factors in human sexual behavior.

REFERENCES

Young, I.M. (1990). *Justice and the Politics of Difference*. Princeton, NJ: Princeton University Press.

Radical America. (1990). Editorial introduction to special issue on "Becoming a Spectacle: Lesbian and Gay Politics and Culture." *Radical America, 24* (4).

IV

THE DEVELOPMENT OF SAFE SPACES FOR LESBIAN, GAY, AND BISEXUAL TEENAGERS

15

Project 10

A School-Based Outreach to Gay and Lesbian Youth

Virginia Uribe

This decade is emerging as the "gay nineties" because of the increased visibility of gay and lesbian issues in the media and in the public consciousness. As one of the major institutions in society, the educational system is facing one of its most pressing challenges—the acknowledgment of gay and lesbian youth as a significant part of the total school population. Because their existence is less visible than other minorities, youthful homosexuals are often ignored. Crossing every boundary of race, religion and class, they have sat through years of public school education in which their identities have been overlooked, denied, or abused. They have been quiet due to their own fear and sense of isolation, as well as the failure of their parents and of adult gay men and women to be their advocates. The result has been the creation of a group of youngsters within our schools who are at significantly high risk of dropping out of school.

In 1989 the United States Department of Health and Human Services issued a report on teen suicide which contained the startling finding that as many as twenty to thirty percent of all teenage suicides may be linked to conflict over homosexuality (Gibson, 1989). This information alone should prompt educators to examine existing attitudes toward homosexuality, the effect of these attitudes on both the gay and nongay population, and how such attitudes are contrary to the public school's mission of teaching all children to respect individual diversity.

Negative biases have often been espoused by critical persons within the homosexual child's educational milieu. These include school principals, teachers, coaches, counselors, and peers (Bidwell, 1988; DeCecco, 1984). In varying degrees, these negative attitudes are by-products of the conscious and unconscious fears and reactions that have come to be known as homophobia—the irrational fear of homosexuals or the subject of homosexuality.

PROJECT 10—A MODEL SCHOOL PROGRAM

Project 10, named for the often-cited and occasionally disputed Kinsey report estimate that ten percent of the population is homosexual, began in 1984 as a way of addressing the underserved needs of gay and lesbian students in the Los Angeles Unified School District (LAUSD). A model program was developed by this writer, a counselor at Fairfax High School, one of the fifty-two senior high schools in the LAUSD. The focus of the model is education, reduction of verbal and physical abuse, suicide prevention, and dissemination of accurate AIDS information. The method by which the model is carried out is workshops for teachers, counselors, and other support personnel, as well as support groups set up on each senior high school campus for students who are dealing with sexual orientation issues. The goal of the support groups is to improve self-esteem and provide affirmation for students who are suffering the effects of stigmatization and discrimination based on sexual orientation.

Project 10 support groups average ten to twelve students at any given time. All races and family backgrounds are represented. About sixty-five percent of the students are males. Usually there is one male and one female who serve as cofacilitators. Some of the facilitators are gay or lesbian; most are not. All the facilitators operate on a volunteer basis. Students are informed of the existence of Project 10 groups through signs in the counselor's office, word of mouth, and referrals by counselors or teachers. Participation is completely voluntary. Absolute confidentiality of groups is maintained, and no one is permitted in the group except the participants and the facilitators.

The labels *gay* and *lesbian* are generic. Actually the groups have many students who identify as bisexual, transgender, or unsure. It is not the philosophy of the program to impose labels, rather it is to provide a "safe space" for these young people to talk freely. We ask that all adults be trained through workshops before they agree to be facilitators, and they must be nonjudgmental with regard to sexual orientation.

The support groups make up the heart of the project program. Most students in these groups have social, family, or personal problems that affect their academic work. In addition to dealing with issues of sexual orientation, the counselors/facilitators provide counseling with issues such as staying off drugs and alcohol, avoiding high-risk sexual behavior, getting jobs, staying in school, and going to college. When appropriate, facilitators suggest outside agencies that may be able to provide additional services. Most of the support groups meet once a week—sometimes after school, sometimes during the lunch hour, and sometimes during the school day.

Testimonials from the students themselves indicate that the support groups are valuable and empowering. Their success is also measured in terms of improved attendance and academic performance, improved relationships with primary family members, and by the number of males who agree to attend AIDS education programs sponsored by local human service organizations.

A small number of critics, mostly from organized groups, have faulted the Project 10 program. They claim that it is a recruitment program, that it promotes homosexuality, and that homosexuality is a subject that should not be dealt with in school. Opponents stage periodic demonstrations at the Los Angeles Board of Education.

The Project 10 model of education and school-site support groups has been sought out by educators throughout the United States and Canada. As is evident, it is a fluid model, adaptable to individual school and district needs. In its most ideal form, the Project 10 model consists of:

1. A district resource center;
2. A paid coordinator for the program;
3. Ongoing workshops to train counselors, teachers and other staff members on issues of institutional homophobia and the special needs of gay and lesbian youth;
4. Development of trained, on-site school teams to whom students can

5. Assistance to librarians in developing lists of fiction and nonfiction materials on gay/lesbian subjects;
6. Enforcement of nondiscrimination clauses, antislur resolutions, and codes of behavior with regard to name-calling;
7. Advocacy for lesbian and gay student rights through commissions, task forces, PTAs, and community outreach programs; and
8. Networking with community agencies, parents, educational organizations, and teachers' unions.

WHAT ABOUT PARENTS?

Without question, the disclosure of homosexuality by a gay or lesbian child is a traumatic event for any parent. Family relationships are a major concern for the adolescent, and a great deal of anxiety is often associated with whether or not to "come out" to parents, and if so, how it should be done. There is no formula for this process, and the ways in which children disclose are as varied as the individuals themselves. The fear of rejection or disapproval is ever-present. For some young people the threat of expulsion from the home is very real. In many instances, exposure is forced; parents discover their child's homosexuality by accident, and the young person is pressed into revealing the fact prior to adequate preparation.

The strategy of deception which characterizes the development of lesbian and gay socialization distorts almost all relationships, including family relationships. The adolescent may attempt to develop or maintain and create an increasing sense of isolation. The adolescent realizes that his or her membership in the family is based on a lie. Even in their homes, the youngsters are forced to act a role. Distancing becomes a mechanism of survival for lesbian and gay adolescents with the fear that their parents will discover their secret.

Ineffective communication, poor self-esteem, and unresolved grief and anger often complicate "coming out." Frequently, misinformation about homosexuality, religious beliefs, and homophobia can have a negative influence in the disclosure process. Educators should understand that when a child "comes out," the parent must also "come out," and yield all their heterosexual expectations for that child. This process can be very difficult, and it can take months or years. Parents typically pass through stages of denial and anger. Some reach a grudging acceptance of things they cannot change. Others educate themselves and begin to accept their children with the

unconditional love that they so desperately need. One group that is extremely helpful for parents going through this process is Parents and Friends of
Lesbians and Gays (P-FLAG) which has over two hundred chapters in the
United States and Canada. Educators should familiarize themselves with
their local chapters and make use of their services.

GAY AND LESBIAN TEENS OF COLOR

The various cultures and races reflected in the United States are also reflected in the lesbian and gay population. Such adolescents face the prospect of
living their lives within three rigidly defined and strongly independent communities: the lesbian and gay community, their ethnic or racial community,
and the society at large. Each community fulfills basic needs which often
would be imperiled if such communities were to be visibly integrated. A
common result is the constant effort to maintain a manner of living that
keeps the three communities separate. This is a process that leads to
increased isolation, depression, and anger, centered around the fear of being
separated from all support systems, including the family.

Discrimination on the basis of sexual orientation is often compounded by
economic disadvantage. A person of color, or a woman of any color, is more
easily subjected to discriminatory policies. Further, unemployment rates are
higher among some minority groups, adding the burden of poverty, drug
abuse, and alcohol to the quality of interaction among lesbian and gay persons of color.

Negative stereotyping and the practice of discrimination against lesbians
and gays make the ethnic gay man or lesbian the least desirable combination for acceptance and assimilation. A hierarchy—suggesting preferences
for whites over Latins, over blacks, over Asians, over American Indians or
any combination of these except for whites—defines and complicates the
level and intensity of discrimination. This endless downward spiral continues when one introduces other variables such as gender, sex-role behavior,
physical disabilities, shades of skin color, age, religious affiliation, and other
variables. As with parent issues, school personnel need to recognize the special issues that exist among minority lesbians and gays, and they should
familiarize themselves with any community resources that may exist.

SETTING UP A GAY-FRIENDLY CURRICULUM

When we talk about a "gay-friendly" curriculum, it is important to define
what we mean. A special course in gay and lesbian studies probably will not

happen in the near future in a high school setting. What we can try to do, however, is to encourage teachers to include gay and lesbian topics in their individual classes whenever relevant and appropriate. For example, there are many occasions in a health education class when the subject of homosexuality will arise; the same is true in history, psychology, political science and art classes. In almost any class where there is a great deal of interaction, gay and lesbian topics will come up if the students feel that it is safe to discuss them. In this open class setting, however, there are two problems. First, many teachers feel awkward, or ill-prepared to discuss homosexuality. It should be kept in mind that a lot of clinical knowledge is not necessary—most of the issues are concerned with attitudes. Second, some people feel that if they discuss homosexuality in anything but negative terms, they will be accused of "condoning" or "promoting" it. This assertion should be placed in the irrational category to which it belongs. Gay and lesbian topics are in the newspapers, magazines, on radio, TV dramas, talk shows, and news programs. In short, they are everywhere. Students on the verge of adulthood have a right to seek information about current social issues, and to develop critical skills that are based on scientific evidence and social justice rather than on myth and ignorance.

Related to curriculum is the question of setting up a gay-oriented club on a high school campus. This is different from a support group although both could exist on a campus. At Fairfax High School in Los Angeles, a group of gay and nongay students chartered a club called the Harvey Milk Club. The purpose of the club was educational. The club had a constitution that followed the format of all other school clubs, and membership in it was open to anyone. Unlike the support groups, the setting was not confidential, and the issues discussed were societal rather than personal. Films were shown, and various speakers addressed the group. The club was involved in school activities such as the Club Fair, and from time to time they held fund-raisers. The administration was somewhat skittish about the club; they sought advice from the district lawyers who could find no reason for the Harvey Milk Club not to exist. It was not, however, entirely a rosy picture. Many students did not want to come near a club that was identified as gay or lesbian, even if it was open to everyone. When the main organizers graduated, the club stopped functioning. More recently, a coalition of private schools on the East Coast has formed a Gay/Straight Alliance which exists successfully in several schools (Hetrick-Martin Institute, 1993). (See Warren Blumenfeld's article in this collection.)

TIPS FOR SCHOOL ADMINISTRATORS

In the current climate, administrators will at some time probably have to face a variety of gay- and lesbian-related situations. Examples include: teachers and students coming out of the closet; discussions of gay and lesbian issues in classrooms; teachers or students wanting to put up a display or a poster around gay and lesbian issues; counselors/teachers putting up hotline numbers, including those of gay and lesbian community centers; requests for speakers representing the gay and lesbian community; protests against ROTC programs or military recruiters on campus; instances of harassment against gay/lesbian teachers; same-sex couples wanting to go to the prom; and lesbian or gay parents.

   The following suggestions have been drawn from real-life scenarios and may be helpful. First, administrators should have a firm policy of nondiscrimination at their school site. Harassment against gay and lesbian teachers or students should not be tolerated, whether it be between students, students and teachers, or among teachers themselves. Second, disclosing one's sexual orientation is an option that teachers and students have if they choose to exercise it. Administrators should respect this option, and protect both staff and students from a hostile environment to the extent that they can. Third, court cases have generally upheld the right of same-sex couples to attend school dances, as long as their behavior is not disruptive. The conventional wisdom is "don't make a big issue out of it." Fourth, discussing gay and lesbian issues in a classroom is not the same thing as having a lesson on sex or reproduction. Teachers should be careful that the classroom discussion does not lapse into sexually explicit conversation. Finally, if a parent complaint should arise, ask them to put the complaint in writing, specifically stating their objections and the reasons for them. The administrator can then, calmly but firmly, review the complaint in light of the suggestions mentioned above.

CONCLUSION

Gay and lesbian students are perhaps the most underserved students in the entire educational system. Prejudice and discrimination often interfere with their personal and academic development. Suicide rates are alarmingly high in this group; this alone should prompt educators to examine existing attitudes toward homosexuality and the destructive effects that being stigmatized has on gay and lesbian youth. Supportive resources are meager. Therefore it is very important that faculty and staff workshops be instituted, so that accurate information can begin to replace the myth and ignorance that surround the subject of homosexuality. The Project 10 model, developed in the Los Angeles Unified School District, is a model that can be replicated by any school or school district. Above all, educators must commit themselves to the idea that the mission of public education is to serve *all* children, and that some children *are* gay and lesbian. To exclude these children, either by indifference or discrimination, is to perpetuate a system that is scientifically unsound and morally unjust.

REFERENCES

Bidwell, R. (1988). "The Gay and Lesbian Teen: A Case of Denied Adolescence." *Journal of Pediatric Health Care, 2* (1), 3–8.

DeCecco, J.P. (1984). *Bashers, Baiters, and Bigots: Homophobia in American Society.* New York: Harrington Park Press.

Gibson, P. (1989). "Gay Male and Lesbian Youth Suicide." In U.S. Department of Health and Human Services, *Report of the Secretary's Task Force on Youth Suicide.* Washington, DC: U.S. Government Printing Office.

Hetrick-Martin Institute (1993). *You Are Not Alone. National Lesbian, Gay, and Bisexual Youth Organization Directory, Spring 1993.* New York: Author.

16

"Gay/Straight" Alliances
Transforming Pain to Pride

Warren J. Blumenfeld

Rachel Mazor is a seventeen-year-old junior at Brookline High School, situated a few miles west of Boston. Last year, while serving on that school's student Judicial Council, she voted with the majority to reprimand a student brought before the council on charges of hurling homophobic insults at another student at the school. Earlier, two of her classmates had confided to her that they are gay. They had also expressed deep concern about the overt and subtle forms of homophobia they experience at the school, and the detrimental impact this has on themselves and on other students struggling to come to terms with their sexuality. After learning about the formation of "gay/straight alliance" groups at other area high schools, Rachel, who defines herself as heterosexual, and her two friends talked with Ellen Abdow, a Judicial Council faculty advisor, who agreed to help them form a similar group.

Peter Atlas, a math teacher at Concord Carlisle Regional High School (CCRHS)—located in proximity to the historic "shot heard 'round the world" in colonial days, activated another revolution of sorts when he disclosed his sexual orientation in an article published last fall on National Coming Out Day (October 11) in the *Voice*, a CCRHS campus newspaper. His motivations for taking this action were twofold: first, he did it for the students. "It was an attempt to alleviate some of the fear, shame, loneliness, and despair of kids in the high school today that I also felt as a closeted teen," he told me. And second, he did it for himself and other staff members. "It takes much more energy to be closeted than it does to be out," he continued. "All of the energy I used in worrying that I would say the wrong thing is now freed up for other things. I think I'm a much more effective teacher now on many levels."

Shortly after his disclosure, four students asked Atlas if he would help them organize a gay/straight alliance group at the school. Today, the group exists as "Spectrum: CCRHS Lesbian, Gay, Bisexual, and Straight Alliance" with five faculty members serving as advisors. One other staff member has since "come out," and now a parallel gay/straight *faculty* group ("CCRHS Committee on Gay and Lesbian Youth") meets once a month with upwards of twenty-five members in attendance, including two student liaisons from Spectrum, faculty from each of the academic disciplines, the vice principal, a librarian, a school nurse, and guidance counselors.

Thus, Brookline High School and Concord Carlisle Regional High School joined an ever-increasing list of "Gay/Straight Alliances" in public and independent private schools throughout the Northeast and in many other parts of the country. These alliance groups are steadily becoming important pieces in an overall strategy to ensure that schools fulfill their mandate of providing the best education possible in a safe and welcoming environment for students of all sexual identities.

A brief sampling of high school campuses reveals a variety of names for these groups. Like Brookline High School, some use "Gay/Straight Alliance" in their title—for example, Belmont High School Gay/Straight Alliance, Newton North High School Gay/Straight Alliance. Others choose more distinctive terms, such as Spectrum (signifying the full range of sexual orientations) at CCRHS and Project 10 East at Cambridge Rindge and Latin High School. Some unique names at private schools include Northfield Mount Herman School Homo-Bi-Hetero Society, GASP! (Gay and Straight People) at Milton Academy, and LeSGaB (Lesbian, Straight, Gay, and Bisexual) at

Noble and Greenough School.

In addition to the gay/straight alliances and parallel faculty groups, some schools provide support groups specifically for students who self-define as "lesbian," "gay," "bisexual" (hereafter referred to as "LBG") or who are in the process of "questioning" their sexual identity.

More than fifty students showed up for the Gay/Straight Alliance meeting at Brookline High School the day I was invited to attend. A student standing next to me said, with a lilt in her voice: "This is one of the biggest meetings we've ever had." Meetings at Brookline High School are held on Wednesdays during the school year, from 2:30 P.M. until about 4:00 P.M., though some have gone as late as 5:30. To create as safe an environment as possible, the founders drew up a list of "Rules for Participation," which are clearly posted in the room. The first rule states that meetings and discussions are confidential—names of group members and anything said at meetings are to remain within the confines of that space. Rule Two asserts that students, teachers, and staff participate as equal members, with no one having a greater voice or privilege than any other. And the final rule maintains that members are in no way obligated to declare or define their sexual identification, nor are any assumptions to be made regarding members' sexual orientation.

Next to the rules are posted the group's goals, which include, first, "to promote acceptance, support, and celebration of all sexual orientations, and discussions about homophobia," and second, "to provide a safe place for Brookline High School students and staff to talk about sexuality and anti-homophobia programs in the community."

The agenda of the group changes each week, depending on the needs of the participants, but Rachel emphasizes that they attempt to strike a balance between the political work of raising consciousness and reducing homophobia at the school, and dealing with the more personal or emotional issues of the members. The day I attended, one of the facilitators began the meeting with a popular "icebreaker" called "Common Ground." In this exercise, participants form a closed circle and the facilitator calls out, for example, "I am wearing the color green," or "I feel happy today," whereupon members for whom the statement is true enter the middle of the circle. Following this game, members gathered to discuss a recent homophobic attack on a student in the nearby town of Fitchburg.

Other group activities include discussions on predetermined themes, led either by the members or by invited outside speakers. Sometimes meetings are organized around watching a movie or listening to a radio show on issues dealing with sexual orientation. One meeting was spent writing letters to congressional representatives in support of lifting the military ban on lesbian and gay people. Rachel was pleasantly surprised to receive a personalized letter back from Barney Frank, her representative. Members have also made signs and posted them around campus in an attempt to educate and increase LBG visibility. One sign read: "Someone You Know Is Gay," and another listed famous LBG historical figures. Members also have had a T-shirt printed, announcing: "Love and Let Love, GSA" over a pink triangle—a symbol of LBG pride and solidarity. Sometimes teachers invite members to lead discussions on issues related to sexual orientation for their classes.

Like gay/straight alliance groups at other area high schools, activities at Concord Carlisle Regional High School's Spectrum vary. Some meetings are set aside for discussions on a topic that a student at a previous meeting volunteers to research during the week and lead at the meeting. Past discussions have centered around the questions: "Why are lesbians called 'lesbians' instead of 'gay'?" "What was the Stonewall riot?" and others. One week during lunchtime, members circulated a petition in support of a federal civil rights bill protecting people against discrimination on the basis of sexual orientation. They received over six hundred signatures in a school of 850. Also, responding to a request by a parent to attend a Spectrum meeting, the group sponsored an open house attended by a number of members' parents, most of whom were very supportive. Discussions at the open house centered around the screening of the video "Gay Youth." Other activities have also included an end-of-the-year party and a dance. Spectrum meetings are held on Thursday evenings from 6:00–8:00 P.M., and a staff member usually supplies the pizza. Stephanie (a pseudonym), a student cofounder of Spectrum, is generally pleased at the response, but is aware that some stumbling blocks remain. "I am sure there are a lot of kids who want to come," she said, "but feel they can't because they are scared to—afraid their friends will spread rumors—or because they are so unsure of themselves and can't bring themselves to go."

THE PAIN

As a diversity workshop facilitator, I receive phone calls from a variety of individuals, inviting me to conduct sessions for schools, businesses, and community and religious organizations around issues of sexual orientation, race, and gender. Recently a high school teacher called to ask for help in defusing what she termed, "a very uncomfortable situation." As it turns out, students were taunting a young man in one of her classes whom they perceived to be gay. Though she has led discussions on the topic of prejudice, shown films, had students read novels with positive gay and lesbian characters, and finally, made it known to students that name-calling and other forms of harassment have no place at the school, she wanted me to lead an in-service workshop to sensitize the faculty and also to talk to the students in order to personalize the issue, thereby making it less threatening, less of a "them" versus "us" dichotomy. We discussed possible options for reducing prejudice at the school (including the formation of a gay/straight alliance group), and I thanked her for her sensitivity and willingness to tackle this difficult issue. I promised to meet with her to design a workshop, and we decided on a time to get together.

As soon as I had placed the phone receiver onto its pedestal, I found myself staring into space. As I did, a flood of memories washed over me. I visualized this student, this young man—the focus of harassment, isolated from peers—as myself in a time long past. However, I often find it difficult to believe that those awful school years ended for me so long ago.

I have come to realize that, though much progress has been made over the years, conditions remain very difficult for LBG, transgender, and "questioning" students today, because school is still not a very "gay" place to be. Though other essays in this book discuss in great depth the difficulties young people experience in a homophobic school (as well as general societal) environment, I would like at least to highlight certain aspects of this environment to reveal the context in which many gay/straight alliance groups emerge.

> I remember in fifth grade, we had this thing called the "fag test." What would happen is that a kid would go up to another kid and scratch him on the hand as hard as he could, and if it made a scar, or if it bled, that meant he was a fag. (A seventeen-year-old student, in Blumenfeld, 1992, p. 95)

Adolescence can be a difficult time for most young people. However, for heterosexuals in particular, social and educational structures are usually in place to support their emerging sexual identity. Through the process of socialization, their feelings are validated and mirrored by their peers, and by supportive adult role models including parents, teachers, and positive media portrayals. The situation is often quite different for young people experiencing strong same-sex attractions. Though the origins of sexual orientation are not completely understood, orientation is generally believed to be established during early childhood, probably before the age of five (Bidwell, 1988). Though some young people do come to terms fairly early with their LBG or transgender identity, and have little difficulty gaining the support they need, enormous peer pressure to conform, coupled with the social stigma surrounding homosexuality and bisexuality and lack of support systems, causes many young people to turn inward. Seeing and hearing demeaning stereotypes and myths about homosexuals and bisexuals, derogatory epithets from peers and family members, negative and misleading media portrayals, little information presented in the schools—or worse yet, absolutely nothing at all—their initial sense of being somehow different often turns into either self-denial of these feelings or self-hatred, resulting in isolation and withdrawal in order to keep their "hidden shame" a secret from everyone.

Young people who are merely perceived as gay, lesbian, bisexual, or transgender, as well as those who are actually "out," are often the target of verbal or physical abuse from peers and even family members. According to the U.S. Department of Justice: "The most frequent victims of hate violence today are blacks, Hispanics, Southeast Asians, Jews, and gays and lesbians. *Homosexuals are probably the most frequent victims*" (Finn and McNeil, 1987). A National Gay and Lesbian Task Force survey of over two thousand gay and lesbian people found that ninety percent have experienced some form of victimization on account of their perceived or actual sexual orientation. More than one in ten has been threatened directly with violence. Victimization was reported to have occurred at home, in schools, and at other community sites (National Gay and Lesbian Task Force, 1984). Forty-five percent of the males and twenty-five percent of the females have been harassed or attacked in high school or junior high school because they were perceived as lesbian or gay. Approximately thirty-three percent of the two thousand respondents were assaulted verbally, while more than one in fifteen were physically abused by members of their own family. These figures were substantially higher for young people who are open about their sexual orientation while still living at home.

Randy Driscoll, a senior at Wareham High School in Massachusetts, knew he was gay when he entered high school. Though he kept his feelings tightly wrapped inside, he was often the target of attack. "Freshman year of high school is already hard enough," he said, "but the big seniors pushing you around because the rumor is you're the 'faggot' made it ten times worse....

I was spit on, pushed, and ridiculed. My school life was hell" (Governor's Commission On Gay and Lesbian Youth, 1992).

Thus the vicious cycle begins. With this abuse often comes poor self-esteem and fear, which frequently lead to poor school performance, chronic truancy, and in many cases, dropping out of school altogether. Others compulsively bury themselves in their school work or other activities. All this seriously impedes their emotional and intellectual development placing them at greater risk for general dysfunction (Remafedi, 1985). As conflicts arise over issues of sexual orientation, young people often turn to substances to reduce the pain and anxiety. One study found that fifty-eight percent of young gay males interviewed could be classified as having a substance abuse disorder as defined in the Diagnostic and Statistical Manual III (Ziebold, 1979).

According to Beth Winship, syndicated teen advice newspaper columnist: "Some of the saddest, most hopeless letters I receive are from gay teens. At their age, when sexuality is of paramount importance, doubts about 'inappropriate gender behavior' are excruciating and sometimes the teens are even suicidal. A high price indeed" (Winship, 1992).

Evidence on teen suicide confirms her perceptions. A report commissioned by the U.S. Department of Health and Human Services on the incidence of youth suicide found that most of the suicide attempts committed by LBGs occur during their youth, and that they are two to three times more likely to attempt suicide than are their heterosexual counterparts (Gibson, 1989). Other studies found that nearly all LBG suicides occur between the ages of sixteen and twenty-one (Pollak, 1985) and the earlier a young person is aware of same-sex attractions, the greater the problems they face and the more likely they are to develop suicidal feelings and behaviors.

Sharon Bergman, an eighteen-year-old student at Concord Academy—a private school in a wealthy suburb of Boston—looked back through her diaries beginning at age ten, when peers continually called her "dyke," "lezzie," and "queer," and she counted the times she seriously contemplated ending her life. "Eighteen separate occasions have brought me to hold a shining razor against my wrists, or to empty out a hundred aspirin and count them over and over trying to think of reasons not to swallow them," she said, "or to peer out my third-floor dormitory window and try and calculate how I would need to jump to most effectively dash my brains out on the fire escape below" (Governors Commission on Gay and Lesbian Youth, 1992). Fortunately, Sharon sought help before it was too late. "I never slashed," she continued. "I never swallowed. I never jumped. I was much luckier than some people."

Bobby Griffith was not so fortunate. Lacking support from family and friends, and being denied valid information in high school for his emerging sexual identity, a few days into his twentieth year, Bobby did a back flip over a highway overpass in the path of a truck and semi-trailer, and was killed instantly. Bobby too kept a diary. At age sixteen, he wrote:

> I can't let anyone find out that I'm not straight. It would be so humiliating. My friends would hate me, I just know it. They might even want to beat me up. And my family? I've overheard them lots of times talking about gay people. They've said they hate gays, and even God hates gays, too. It really scares me now, when I hear my family talk that way, because now, they are talking about me.... Sometimes I feel like disappearing from the face of this earth. (Miller, 1992)

What makes Sharon's story different is the options available to her. "Each time [I wanted to kill myself] I was able to call someone from the Concord Academy Gay/Straight Alliance," recalls Sharon, "or someone who I'd come out to through the strength and support I received there—each time I cried to the sympathetic ear on the other end of the phone or at the end of the dormitory hall. If not for the support that I found…at a homo-affirmative high school, I would be dead today."

THE PRIDE

"A homo-affirmative high school," would have seemed unattainable only a few years ago. It is something, though, that is closer to reality for students and staff alike, propelled, in large measure, by the courageous people involved in the high school gay/straight alliance movement.

"Five years ago, if you would have said, 'Peter, in five years you are going to come out…and you are going to be a faculty advisor of a gay/straight alliance in your high school, which gets thirty students to come every week,' I would have said, 'I don't even imagine that. That's not even part of my imagery of the future.'" But this is precisely Peter Atlas's reality. Though a few students and parents voiced concern over his public declaration and the formation of Spectrum (one student's parents forbade her from attending the group), the overwhelming response was positive. In fact, a number of parents, students, other teachers, and even a principal of a middle school in a neighboring town sent letters of encouragement.

Excerpts include, from a father: "My son showed me the recent copy of the school newspaper with your letter to the editor. I wanted to write and support your courageous statement. You will undoubtedly pay a price for your honesty, yet others would pay a price for your silence, and that price could be fatal...." From a mother of a female student: "...I do want to say that I am very impressed by your courage and your honesty, qualities that I have always worked to impress in my children and you are an excellent person for them to know. Hopefully my son will get to know you when he reaches CCRHS...." From a CCRHS female student: "...I just wanted to thank you for writing the letter to the *Voice*. Although I'm not a homosexual, I think the letter was very encouraging to those of us who are. I also think it was very educating to the heterosexuals in the school...." From a principal: "...I wanted you to know how much I admired your willingness to speak up on this important civil rights issue. Your presence as a teacher with courage will be a positive experience for your students and your colleagues as well."

And, down the road from CCRHS, support was also forthcoming for Devin Beringer, a seventeen-year-old bisexual senior at Concord Academy, as he was coming to terms with his emerging sexual identification: "Coming out was not the traumatic experience that it is for many other gay and lesbian teens," he said. "At Concord [Academy] there was no verbal abuse since calling someone a 'faggot' or 'dyke' is a hate crime and equivalent to a racial slur. I lost a couple of friends along the way, but there was no real negative response."

The same is true for Jessica Byers, a student leader in Project 10 East, which includes the equivalent of a gay/straight alliance at Cambridge Rindge and Latin High School—a racially, ethnically, and economically diverse campus situated across the Charles River from Boston. Initially, the group was intended primarily to support gay, lesbian, and bisexual students, but Jessica proposed opening it to anyone wanting to discuss issues around sexual orientation, and more people began attending meetings. She volunteered to staff a table announcing the group at Freshmen Club Day at the beginning of the year, where between ten and fifteen people signed up, and on National Coming Out Day, she and others handed out pink triangle buttons, which were then worn by hundreds of members of the CRLHS community, creating a virtual pink sea, symbolizing support and solidarity.

Jessica is also a member of the Governor's Commission on Gay and Lesbian Youth—an advisory body created by executive order in February

1992 by Massachusetts Governor William F. Weld in response to the growing epidemic of LBG youth suicides. The commission has since released a series of reports, which suggest ways to make schools and communities safer for this at-risk population.

Jessica graduated from CRLHS this past June, and looking back over the year, she is encouraged by the strides taken by the group and proud of her own accomplishments, one being following through on her decision to take another female student to her senior prom. "I had really wanted to do it for a long time," she said, "and if I didn't do it, I would really regret it." She was inspired by the support she received from her group and her family, and by the story of Aaron Fricke (1981), a courageous high school student who, in 1980, after suffering physical assaults and a public court trial, eventually won the right to take a male date to his senior prom in Cumberland, Rhode Island. Before her prom, Jessica was anxious about the response of others in her high school of over two thousand students, and she did not make the final decision until she chose someone to ask. "I didn't have a 'girlfriend' at the time, so I asked my good friend Josie Gold [a cofounder of the Gay/Straight Alliance at nearby Belmont High School] who also asked me to her prom."

Happie Byers (Jessica's grandmother with whom she has been living since the death of her mother three years ago), was supportive, but also concerned for the young women's safety. "I didn't really know what to expect," she recalls. "I really didn't know if they would get more than stares or rude comments. Since neither school had had same-sex dates at the senior proms, I feared the unknown."

On the days of the proms, the young women dressed in their finest party dresses, exchanged corsages, and entered the hall like all the other couples. Aside for one rude remark made by a male student at the Belmont High prom, who apparently had come intoxicated, and by some rather uncomfortable and prolonged glances from some individuals, both proms were quite remarkable in that they were not at all remarkable. The young women danced, drank punch, stood hand-in-hand having their pictures taken, laughed and chatted with one another, with other students, and with the staff chaperons, and left taking with them the material of fond memories. Responding to the remark made by the young man at her prom, Josie told me: "I was surprised and happy to know that a lot of his friends got angry at him."

Jessica did not want her actions to be taken solely as a political statement, but conscious of the reality, she knew this would be inevitable. Jessica reflects: "I'm glad I did it for a lot of the closeted people at both schools. I think it was important for everyone to see that we could do it, and it wasn't a big deal." Happie Byers said that Jessica has taught her much, adding: "We need to support young people who have the courage to change society."

Indeed, change has been a visible by-product. Rachel Mazor sees real progress as a result of her group at Brookline High School. "There has been a change in the general atmosphere of the school," she points out. "There is an enormous awareness of what homophobia is, and that there are homosexual and bisexual students." She said that, since the creation of the Gay/Straight Alliance, teachers have attended workshops to manage their own homophobia and that of their students, and are learning how to help students who are struggling with issues of sexual identity. "People are now willing to interrupt homophobic jokes and slurs," she continues. "People now include sexual orientation when talking about diversity." In fact, during last June's commencement address, the class valedictorian proclaimed: "I was proud to be a member of Brookline High School when I heard that thirty of my classmates went on the March in Washington under the Brookline High School banner."

Rachel was one of the students who participated in that historic "March for Lesbian, Gay, and Bi Equal Rights and Liberation," Sunday, April 25, 1993. "I went to Washington with about thirty students, some parents and five or six teachers and their spouses and friends." This group marched behind a banner announcing, "BROOKLINE HIGH SCHOOL" which also included two linked female and two linked male symbols connected by a linked male and female symbol, which, when taken together, represents the sexual orientation continuum. A number of people came up to the group with expressions of support and encouragement: "I went to Brookline High School in 1953," said one observer; "I graduated in 1949," said a second; "I was there in 1971," said yet another; and all agreed, "It's so great that you are here and that you have a Gay/Straight Alliance now."

Brookline and other high school gay/straight alliances also took part in the recent annual Gay, Lesbian, and Bi Pride Parade in Boston. It was a brilliantly sunny, though rather cool, mid-June, New England afternoon. Banners flying, music blasting, people of all walks of life assembled, reuniting, greeting, kissing, embracing, catching up on lives lived in the space in between. The signal was given with a contagious cheer rising from the crowd, and for the next few hours the streets would be theirs: Dykes on Bikes revving their engines; shirtless muscled young men dancing to a disco beat atop flatbed floats winding their way down Boylston Street en route to Boston's South End; dazzling drag queens in red and gold and silver; the Freedom Trail Marching Band trumpeting the call; a black-and-white cocker spaniel wearing a sign announcing "DON'T ASSUME I'M STRAIGHT"; lesbian mothers and gay fathers pushing strollers or walking beside children of all ages; Gays for Patsy decked out in their finest country duds, two-stepping down the boulevard; AIDS activists falling to the pavement of those same boulevards in mock death to expose governmental and societal inaction, which is killing so many; Parents, Friends, and Families of Lesbians and Gays (P-FLAG) proclaiming "WE ARE PROUD OF OUR GAY AND LESBIAN SONS AND DAUGHTERS," alongside political, social, and service organizations, business and religious caucuses of all stripes and denominations; and of course, bystanders watching the procession, holding court from the sidelines.

And in the midst of this merriment and this protest, the humorous posters and angry placards, the enormous rainbow balloon sculptures arching overhead, and the colorful streamers and glistening "fairy dust" wafting from open windows, amid the shinny black leather and shimmering lamé, the multicolored T-shirts and the drab business suits—came the students, their radiant young faces catching the rays of the sun, marching side by side, hand in hand, their high school Gay/Straight Alliance banners waving exaltedly in this storm of humanity, announcing their entry, their solidarity, their feisty outrage, and yes, their pride—Brookline, Concord and Carlisle, Milton, Cambridge, Lincoln and Sudbury, Belmont, Newton, and those unnamed—chanting "two, four, six, eight, Gay is Just as Good as Straight, three, five, seven, nine, Lesbians and Bi's are Mighty Fine;" then, gaining intensity, singing: "Hey Hey, Ho Ho, Homophobia Has Got to Go;" and then, as if hit by an all-consuming revelation, shouting "We're Here, We're Queer, We're Not Going Back, We're NOT Going Back, WE'RE NOT GOING BACK."

And indeed they will not go back. Oh, they will physically return to their schools and their homes. They will continue to study and play sports, to watch television and movies. Some will most likely become community leaders, parents, and teachers once their own school days are behind. The place they *will* go back to, though, is nowhere that can be seen. It is a place of consciousness that teaches those who have entered that everyone is diminished when any one of us is demeaned; that homophobia (as well as all the other forms of oppression) has no place in a just society.

From the sidelines of the parade, beginning as a whisper and ending as a mighty roar of support: "We are so glad you are here," came voices from the crowd, "We wish we could have done this when we were in high school," cried others too numerous to count. "Thank you so much for your courage."

From where has this courage come, and how has this change actually come about? It seems that a great many factors have merged to make this happen. In addition to support for student and staff gay/straight alliance groups, schools are now inviting professional trainers to lead workshops to sensitize and educate members of the campus community on issues related to homophobia, homosexuality, and bisexuality. Administrators are adopting policies to reduce harassment and violence, to increase LBG visibility, and to provide equal access to campus services and benefits. Schools are beginning to provide services to meet the health, counseling, academic, and social needs of students and staff of all sexual identifications, and are beginning to redesign curricula and provide other academic means of incorporating issues addressing the LBG experience.

Peter Atlas, CCRHS math teacher, reflects back over the past year: "Massachusetts hit critical mass in the year 1992 to 1993. Something was different in the schools." Asked what that was, he could not quite put his finger on it, but when I questioned him on what it takes for a gay/straight alliance to form and function successfully, especially in a traditionally conservative community, he said that building coalitions is a necessary first step. To a LBG faculty member, he suggests "Find a straight-identified faculty member and do the work with that person. For a student, find other students and find the faculty member you trust the most." He continued, "It also helps to have a principal with principles."

He also realizes that, especially with the right-wing political backlash spreading in areas of the country, some faculty and students do not yet feel safe enough to organize openly. "If you are working for change and support and health in the schools and you just have no clue about how to do it," he said, "then work for it in the community outside the schools, and then you will reach critical mass, and you will be able to do it inside the schools. And if you are a student, hang on.... It *does* get better."

REFERENCES

Bidwell, R.J. (1988). "The Gay and Lesbian Teen: A Case of Denied Adolescence." *Journal of Pediatric Care, 2* (10), pp. 3–8.

Blumenfeld, W.J. (1992). *Homophobia: How We All Pay the Price*. Boston: Beacon Press.

Elze, D. (1992). "It Has Nothing to Do With Me." In *Homophobia: How We All Pay the Price*. Warren J. Blumenfeld, ed. Boston: Beacon Press.

Finn, P. and McNeil, T. (1987). *The Response of the Criminal Justice System to Bias Crime: An Exploratory Review*. Washington, DC: U.S. Department of Justice.

Fricke, A. (1981). *Reflections of a Rock Lobster: A Story about Growing Up Gay*. Boston, MA: Alyson Publications.

Gibson, P. (1989). "Gay Male and Lesbian Youth Suicide." In U.S. Department of Health and Human Services, *Report of the Secretary's Task Force on Youth Suicide*. Washington, DC: U.S. Government Printing Office.

Governor's Commission on Gay and Lesbian Youth (1992). *Excerpts from public testimony heard in Boston, MA*.

Miller, B.J. (1992). "From Silence to Suicide: Measuring a Mother's Loss." In *Homophobia: How We All Pay the Price*. Warren J. Blumenfeld, ed. Boston, MA: Beacon Press.

National Gay and Lesbian Task Force (1984). *National Anti-Gay/Lesbian Victimization Report*. New York.

Pollak, M. (1985). "Male Homosexuality." In *Western Sexuality*. Phillipe Aries and Andre Bejin, eds. New York: Blackwell.

Remafedi, G. (1985). *Male Homosexuality: The Adolescent's Perspective*. Minneapolis, MN: Unpublished Manuscript, University of Minnesota Adolescent Health Program.

Winship, B. (1992). Quotation, Back Cover, in *Homophobia, How We All Pay the Price*. Warren J. Blumenfeld, ed. Boston, MA: Beacon Press.

Ziebold, T. (1979). "Alcoholism and Recovery: Gays Helping Gays." *Christopher Street*, January, pp. 36–44.

17

OutRight!

Reflections on an Out-of-School Gay Youth Group

Hugh Singerline

> Someday, maybe, there will exist a well-informed, well considered and yet fervent public conviction that the most deadly of all possible sins is the mutilation of a child's spirit.
>
> —*Erik Erikson* (In Rofes, 1989, p. 444)

OutRight! is the name of an out-of-school gay youth group located in Durham, North Carolina. We who work with OutRight! share Erikson's hope, because we are all too aware that there are many ways to mutilate a child's spirit, including on the basis of sexual orientation. It can be done slowly and insidiously, or quickly and brutally. It can even be done in such a way that the child helps with the ongoing mutilation, believing that he or she is deserving of the pain, the suffering, or the punishment. Dedicated to the belief that no young person should be subjected to this abuse, OutRight! exists to provide support for gay youth.[1]

OutRight! was founded in 1990 by a group of people who saw that something needed to be done to help adolescents who were struggling with issues of sexuality, particularly those issues which surround homosexuality and bisexuality.[2] Although there were resources for adults in our community, until the founding of OutRight! there was no informed, caring, and safe source of support to which teens and young adults could turn for help.

The people who started OutRight! came from a variety of backgrounds. Some worked in the fields of therapy, counseling, public health, and social work. Some were associated with local churches. Some were parents. Some, but not all, were gay. Whatever the source of their knowledge, these people were all aware of the sometimes desperate condition of gay adolescents in general. Many knew personally of individuals in troubled situations.

OutRight! is administered by a board which undertakes long-term planning, solicits funding, maintains contacts with other organizations (both within and outside the gay community), publishes a newsletter, and provides speakers for outreaches on the subject of OutRight! or on gay youth more broadly. The officers consist of female and male cochairs, a treasurer, and a secretary.

The facilitators are involved with the youth meetings, held weekly on Saturday afternoons in the meeting room of a local church. Meetings are scheduled to last two hours, and participants are encouraged to arrive on time in order to minimize disruption, although they are made welcome whenever they come. Most meetings consist of discussion sessions based on subjects which they bring up themselves or which the facilitators have prepared.[3] A specified weekend each month is set aside for a more involved activity such as bowling, a movie, or a hike in a local park. OutRight! has attempted to provide role-model images through, among other things, a series of informal presentations by adult gay men, bisexuals, and lesbians on the types of work they do, their relationships, and their involvement in the local gay community. Meetings are often followed by a visit to a local, lesbian-owned, ice cream shop, at which conversation on the day's topic tends to continue.

To the question: "Is an OutRight! needed in my community?" the only response, judging from our experience is: "Yes." Gay people live in all parts of the country, a fact which is daily reinforced by the increasing visibility of lesbians, bisexuals, and gay men, not only in New York and San Francisco, but also in Minneapolis, Houston, Annapolis, and even in Durham, North Carolina. If there are gay adults in these places, there are gay adolescents, and if there are gay adolescents, then there are the special problems which an OutRight! can help them face.

OutRight! works with teens and young adults who are dealing with troubling aspects of their sexuality. They find it possible to be gay in a positive way, using the safe space created by the group to explore their identities and feelings without having to worry—if only for a short time—about negative reactions. OutRight! helps them to realize that being gay is not bad or sick, but that they, too, can have whole, satisfying, and rich lives.

Because the founders of OutRight! were mostly gay people themselves, they were intimately aware of the heterosexism and homophobia which exist in this society. They were, therefore, in a position to recognize the suffering and hurt inflicted on gay youth. While this kind of personal understanding and knowledge is valuable, there is also a growing network of hotlines, health projects, and documentation projects which can help provide this background information. Whether gay or nongay, counselors, teachers, clergy, parents, and others who are likely to interact with adolescents can now find access to the information they need to help young bisexuals, gay men, and lesbians.

It is this sort of knowledge which informed the claim, in the Department of Health and Human Services 1989 report on youth suicide, that "[g]ay and lesbian youth belong to two groups at high risk of suicide: youth and homosexuals" (Gibson, 1989, p. 110). Adolescence, in and of itself, is not a carefree period. The ongoing fundamental challenges of adolescence—establishing self-identity and finding one's own place in society—are often rendered more difficult by other pressures:

> The period defined as adolescence encompasses a number of tasks leading from the physical, psychological, and emotional dependence of childhood to the independence of adult maturity. (Cates, 1987, p. 354)

Gay youth face all of these same issues, but with extra burdens. Basic development is greatly complicated by an environment which stigmatizes gay identities, forbids the dissemination of accurate information on (homo)sexuality, and rejects positive gay role models. Gay adolescents are thus caught in an untenable position: trapped by confusion, ignorance, guilt, and fear, and lacking the guidance necessary to escape to healthier, more self-accepting lives, they are often driven by both external and internalized homophobia to self-destructive attitudes and actions.

In their efforts to support the young people dealing with these burdens, the founders of OutRight! soon realized the importance of already existing organizations, which could be tapped for their resources, personnel, and experience. They were able to obtain funding from several sources, including the local Episcopalian diocese. They could provide a phone line, because volunteers at the local lesbian and gay health project agreed to answer it as part of their own hotline service. And, if the need ever arose, they could turn to members of the gay community for special expertise, such as therapy and counseling skills, or legal advice.

These existing groups provided a sense of legitimacy, a "track record" so to speak, which the new organization could not have had on its own. This was of immense aid to a project such as OutRight!, which of necessity and design would operate in a zone of ever-possible controversy because it dealt with young people and homosexuality. The potential fallout was worrisome enough that some organizations and many individuals would have nothing to do with the new group. Constant effort on the part of those associated with OutRight!, and ongoing support by well-regarded bodies, has enabled its mission to continue and to expand. For example, members of OutRight!, adults and adolescents, have increasingly been invited to conduct outreaches to area schools.

Once the structure was put into place, the youth of the area were alerted to its presence. OutRight! began with those whom individual adults happened to know. Word of mouth was credited with locating a few more teens, but the isolation which is a major problem for many of these young people has tended to keep this method of contact to a minimum. Notices in local gay or gay-friendly papers are another possible method of contact, and one which OutRight! has indeed used, but some individuals are fearful of exposure should they be discovered with a gay paper.

High school papers have also been a means of communication, but because of hostility on the part of principals, teachers, or newspaper advisors, or the anticipation of parental response, OutRight! often has its requests rejected. Some papers have, however, accepted and printed the small advertisement which provides a phone number for further information. In one incident, the students on the paper wished to print the notice, but the nervous principal overrode their decision and pulled it, sparking a student protest against censorship lively enough to be covered by local newspapers. Referrals from local counselors, therapists, clergy, and the gay student organizations at the local universities account for a number of other youth.

Occasionally, OutRight! has not had to reach out in order to make itself known. Individuals have learned of the organization from unexpected sources. One young woman learned about the group by calling a hotline listed in an article she read in *Mademoiselle.* The lack of resources in many local areas frequently demands that these youth search far afield. It is not unusual to find individuals who have traveled for an hour or more to reach meetings, and people from out of state are not unknown. The recent experience of a similar group in Texas, Out Youth Austin—in which its national toll-free number was swamped with enough phone calls to run the organization into debt—is indicative of both the need for such groups and the lengths to which young gay people often need to go.

Informing people of the existence of OutRight! was only the first problem; others soon become apparent. Some of OutRight!'s potential clientele have been too young to drive themselves to the meeting site, and many lack access to automobiles for other reasons. Less-than-adequate public transportation, coupled with the wide area needing support services, has made it simply impossible for some to get to the meetings. The board was able to improve the situation marginally by moving the meeting time from a weekday evening to Saturday afternoon, but this has not solved the difficulty for everyone.

OutRight!'s response to problems varies, but sometimes the only thing that can be done is to accept the fact that the organization just cannot provide certain services. For example, it was decided long ago that, as a rule, facilitators would not offer rides to the meetings. For one thing, we cannot reach all the places from which we have been contacted. There are also questions of liability and, again, the ever-present fear that the charge of recruitment will be leveled at the organization or at a single facilitator. As another example, our toll-free number has been blocked to calls from outside our own area code for budgetary reasons. One alternative available to us is to maintain referral lists to relevant services and contacts for outlying areas, but the inability more directly to help some who go through rather strenuous efforts to contact us has been very frustrating. [4]

Still other problems come through the door with those who can make it to meetings. We have found that little can be assumed about those who need OutRight!. They are male and female, Asian, African-American, and Caucasian. Their educational backgrounds, sexual experiences, relationships with family, political beliefs, and general level of comfort range widely across the spectrum. As a result, what works for one individual may not work for another.

Those who come to the meetings rarely face questions only of sexuality, even if these are what bring them to OutRight!. This diversity has given us a formidable challenge. OutRight! makes a concerted effort to provide several facilitators at every meeting, and we try to assemble a pool of facilitators with diverse backgrounds in order to bridge whatever gaps these youth bring with them. We obviously cannot solve all of their problems, but we attempt to create an atmosphere comfortable enough to encourage as many as possible to work through their particular concerns.

In the past, facilitators heard about OutRight! through word of mouth. Recently the board has been working on making the process of finding and training new facilitators somewhat more formal. A notice concerning an upcoming training session was placed in the local gay and gay-friendly press. Experienced facilitators led the respondents through a day-long series of exercises, explained to them the history and purpose of the group, and made them aware of what would be expected of them. Those who decided to stay were required to observe at a youth meeting before assuming full facilitator responsibilities. We hope to offer occasional training sessions on particular topics which are relevant to people who attend OutRight!.

The commitment level asked of volunteers includes the monthly gathering of board members and facilitators, at which the previous month's meetings are discussed. In this way everyone can be kept abreast of developments in the lives of individual youths. We have found this particular practice to be very beneficial, as it allows us to conduct youth meetings with some degree of continuity from week to week, and facilitator to facilitator. The larger number of perspectives brought to bear may also note things which individual facilitators can miss, or which could go unnoticed at a single youth meeting. These discussions are kept within the circle of OutRight! volunteers, so as to maintain our pledge of confidentiality.

There is a divided sense among board members about the necessity of having only bisexuals, lesbians, and gay men as facilitators. Some consider it more important that an adult who works with OutRight! adolescents be able to listen to what they say and to respond in a way to which they can relate, while others see more significance in the impact which adult gay people could provide as role models. In one sense this has remained a moot point, since there has not yet been a nongay applicant for facilitator. The issue remains, however, quietly in the background.

In each of us working with OutRight!, there are memories of our own adolescence, of our own struggles with gay identities in a world which is predominantly nongay. OutRight! provides an opportunity for us to help someone else through the assorted difficulties which we ourselves faced.

While we certainly appreciate and welcome relevant skills which many non-gay individuals possess, we are at the same time drawn to the image of the role model who is the embodiment of hope.

And hope is, after all, what OutRight! offers.

NOTES

To those members of OutRight! who shared their experiences with me for the purposes of this article, I am thankful. To all those who work with OutRight, I am indebted for the ongoing lessons in community. To Barbara Lippa, whose sharp reading helped to shape this article, I am grateful.

1. There is no uniformly accepted terminology used to refer to gay people. To many, *homosexual* sounds too clinical, and it is often considered quaint, even derogatory in a faint way, a gay equivalent to Negro. *Faggot*, *dyke*, and *queer* are sometimes used by gay people to refer to themselves, but this is by no means universal, and their use by nongay people is generally assumed to be meant in a negative way. Although *gay* has been criticized as subsuming lesbians and bisexuals under the shadow of the gay male (much as the pronoun he or the noun man is so criticized when used to refer to all humans), I will use *gay* for the collective, and *bisexual*, *lesbian*, and *gay man/male* as specifics dictate.
2. These issues include questions of identity, gender roles, societal expectations, family relations, fear of violence, and health problems. It should be noted that these (and other) difficulties are a part of homosexuality and bisexuality *as they are experienced in this society*, and not in and of themselves.
3. The youth are encouraged to take as much responsibility for the meetings as they wish. The role of the facilitators is emphasized if, for example, a recent incident or the sense that a given individual may need to hear more on some specific topic suggests a more guided discussion.
4. Once again, other organizations can be a boon. Their contacts, coupled with those of individual board members and facilitators with knowledge of other gay communities, may turn up a phone number or address of some agency, group, or hotline which can better help a distant youth. National bodies, particularly, but not only, Parents and

Friends of Lesbians and Gays (P-FLAG), are often a great resource for the beleaguered local support group.

REFERENCES

Cates, J.A. (1987). "Adolescent Sexuality: Gay and Lesbian Issues." *Child Welfare, 66* (4), pp. 353–364.

Coleman, E. and Remafedi, G. (1989). "Gay, Lesbian, and Bisexual Adolescents: A Critical Challenge to Counselors." *Journal of Counseling and Development, 68* (1), pp. 36–40.

Dunham, K. (1989). *Educated to Be Invisible: The Gay and Lesbian Adolescent.* ERIC ED 336 676.

Gibson, P. (1989). "Gay Male and Lesbian Youth Suicide." In *Report of the Secretary's Task Force on Youth Suicide.* Volume 3: *Prevention and Interventions in Youth Suicide.* DHHS Pub. No. (ADM), pp. 89-1623. Washington, DC: Supt. of Docs., U.S. Govt. Printing Office.

Hunter, J. and Schaecher, R. (1987). "Stresses on Lesbian and Gay Adolescents in Schools." *Social Work in Education, 9* (3), pp. 180–190.

Kissen, R.M. (1991). "Listening to Gay and Lesbian Teenagers." Paper presented at the *81st Annual Meeting of the National Council of Teachers of English,* Seattle, WA. ERIC ED 344 220.

Kourany, R.F.C. (1987). "Suicide Among Homosexual Adolescents." *Journal of Homosexuality, 13* (4), pp. 111–117.

Rofes, E. (1989). "Opening Up the Classroom Closet: Responding to the Educational Needs of Gay and Lesbian Youth." *Harvard Educational Review, 59* (4), pp. 444–453.

Sears, J.T. (1987). "Peering into the Well of Loneliness: The Responsibility of Educators to Gay and Lesbian Youth." In *Social Issues and Education: Challenge and Responsibility.* Alex Molnar, ed. Alexandria, VA: Association for Supervision and Curriculum Development. ERIC ED 280 781.

Selected Resources

ORGANIZATIONS

Campaign to End Homophobia
PO Box 819
Cambridge, MA 02139

Association for Gay, Lesbian, and Bisexual Issues in Counseling (AGLBIC)
PO Box 216
Jenkintown, PA 19046

Association for Lesbian and Gay Psychologists
2336 Market St., Number 8
San Francisco, CA 94114

Bisexual People of Color Caucus/BiPol
584 Castro St., No 422
San Francisco, CA 94114
(415) 775–1990

Black Gay and Lesbian Leadership Forum
3924 W. Sunset Boulevard
Los Angeles, CA 90029

Federation of Parents and Friends of Lesbians and Gays
(P-FLAG)
PO Box 27605
Washington, DC 20038–7605

Gay Teachers Association
Box 435, Van Brunt Station
Brooklyn, NY 11215

National Bisexual Network
584 Castro St., No 422
San Francisco, CA 94114

(415) 775–1990

National Gay and Lesbian Task Force
1517 U Street, NW
Washington, DC 20009
(202) 332–6483

National Gay Youth Network
PO Box 846
San Francisco, CA 94101

You Are Not Alone. National Lesbian, Gay, and Bisexual Youth Organization Directory, published by:
The Hetrick-Martin Institute
401 West Street
New York, NY 10014-2587

CURRICULAR UNITS
Available from the Harvard Graduate School of Education Gay and Lesbian High School Curriculum and Staff Development Project:
- A Staff Development Manual for Anti-Homophobia Education in the Secondary Schools
- Strategies for the Teacher Using Gay/Lesbian-Related Materials in the High School Classroom
- The Stonewall Riots and the History of Gays and Lesbians in the United States
- The History and Nature of Homosexuality (and its "Causes")
- Looking at Gay and Lesbian Literature (Packet 1)
- Reading List: Some Works of Noted Authors with Gay/Lesbian Content
- Reading List: Books about Homosexuality and Coming Out for Young Gay People

For ordering information, write to Dr. Arthur Lipkin, Harvard Graduate School of Education, Longfellow Hall 210, Cambridge, MA, 02138.

BIBLIOGRAPHY OF WORKS FOR ADDITIONAL READING AND RESEARCH

Abelove, Henry, Michele Aina Barale, and David M. Halperin, eds. *The Lesbian and Gay Studies Reader*. New York: Routledge, 1993.

Allport, Gordon W. *The Nature of Prejudice*. New York: Doubleday/Anchor, 1958.

Baird, Robert M. and Stuart E. Rosenbaum, eds. *Bigotry, Prejudice and Hatred: Definitions, Causes and Solutions*. Buffalo: Prometheus, 1992.

Bawer, Bruce. *A Place at the Table: The Gay Individual in American Society*. New York: Poseidon, 1993.

Beam, Joseph, ed. *In the Life: A Black Gay Anthology*. Boston: Alyson, 1986.

Berzon, Betty, ed. *Positively Gay: New Approaches to Gay and Lesbian Life*. Berkeley: Celestial Arts, 1992.

Blumenfeld, Warren J., ed. *Homophobia: How We All Pay the Price*. Boston: Beacon Press, 1992.

Blumenfeld, Warren J. and Diane Raymond, eds. *Looking at Gay and Lesbian Life*. Updated and expanded edition. Boston: Beacon Press, 1993.

Borhek, Mary V. *Coming Out to Parents: A Two-Way Survival Guide for Lesbians and Gay Men and Their Parents*. Cleveland: Pilgrim, 1983. (Revised and updated 1993.)

Boswell, John. *Christianity, Social Tolerance, and Homosexuality*. Chicago: University of Chicago Press, 1980.

Browning, Frank. *The Culture of Desire: Paradox and Perversity in Gay Lives Today*. New York: Crown, 1993.

Cohen, Susan and Daniel. *When Someone You Know Is Gay*. New York: Laurel Leaf, 1989.

D'Emilio, John. *Sexual Politics, Sexual Communities: The Making of a Homosexual Minority in the United States, 1940-1970*. Chicago: University of Chicago Press, 1983.

Duberman, Martin, Martha Vicinus, and George Chauncey, Jr., eds. *Hidden From History: Reclaiming the Gay and Lesbian Past*. New York: Meridian, 1990.

Fricke, Aaron. *Reflections of a Rock Lobster: A Story About Growing Up Gay*. Boston: Alyson, 1981.

Garnets, Linda D. and Douglas C. Kimmel, eds. *Psychological Perspectives on Lesbian and Gay Male Experiences*. New York: Columbia University Press, 1993.

Gonsiorek, John C. and James D. Weinrich, eds. *Homosexuality: Research*

Implications for Public Policy. Newbury Park: Sage, 1991.

Harbeck, Karen M., ed. *Coming Out of the Classroom Closet: Gay and Lesbian Students, Teachers and Curricula*. New York: Harrington Park, 1992.

Herdt, Gilbert and Andrew Boxer. *Children of Horizons: How Gay and Lesbian Teens Are Leading the Way Out of the Closet*. Boston: Beacon Press, 1993.

Herdt, Gilbert, ed. *Gay and Lesbian Youth*. New York: Harrington Park, 1989.

Herek, Gregory M. and Kevin T. Berrill, eds. *Hate Crimes: Confronting Violence Against Lesbians and Gay Men*. Newbury Park: Sage, 1992.

Heron, Ann, ed. *One Teenager in Ten: Writings by Gay and Lesbian Youth*. Boston: Alyson, 1983.

———. *Two Teenagers in Twenty*. Boston: Alyson, 1993.

Hilton, Bruce. *Can Homophobia Be Cured?* Nashville: Abingdon, 1992.

Jennings, Kevin, ed. *Becoming Visible: A Reader in Gay and Lesbian History for High School and College Students*. Boston: Alyson, 1994.

———. *One Teacher in Ten*. Boston: Alyson, 1994.

Katz, Jonathan Ned. *Gay American History: Lesbians and Gay Men in the USA*. New York: Meridian, 1992.

McConnell-Celi, Sue, ed. *Twenty-First Century Challenge: Lesbians and Gays in Education, Bridging the Gap*. Red Bank, NJ: Lavender Crystal Press, 1993.

McDonald, Helen B. and Audrey I. Steinhorn. *Understanding Homosexuality: A Guide for Those Who Know, Love, or Counsel Gay and Lesbian Individuals*. New York: Crossroad, 1993.

McNaught, Brian. *On Being Gay: Thoughts on Family, Faith, and Love*. New York: St. Martin's Press, 1988.

McNeill, John J. *The Church and the Homosexual*. Boston: Beacon Press, 1988.

Mohr, Richard D. *A More Perfect Union: Why Straight America Must Stand Up for Gay Rights*. Boston: Beacon Press, 1994.

Nava, Michael and Robert Dawidoff. *Created Equal: Why Gay Rights Matter to America*. New York: St. Martin's Press, 1994.

Nelson, Emmanuel S., ed. *Critical Essays: Gay and Lesbian Writers of Color*. New York: Haworth, 1994.

Nugent, Robert and Jeannine Gramick. *Building Bridges: Gay and Lesbian Reality in the Catholic Church*. Mystic: Twenty-Third Publications, 1992.

Pharr, Suzanne. *Homophobia: A Weapon of Sexism*. Little Rock: Chardon Press, 1988.

Pronger, Brian. *The Arena of Masculinity: Sports, Homosexuality, and the Meaning of Sex.* New York: St. Martin's Press, 1990.

Rench, Janice E. *Understanding Sexual Identity: A Book for Gay and Lesbian Teens and Their Friends.* Minneapolis: Lerner Publications, 1990.

Savin-Williams, Ritch C. *Gay and Lesbian Youth: Expressions of Identity.* New York: Hemisphere, 1990.

Scanzoni, Letha and Virginia Ramey Mollenkott. *Is the Homosexual My Neighbor: Another Christian View.* San Francisco: HarperCollins, 1980. (Revised and updated 1994.)

Scroggs, Robin. *The New Testament and Homosexuality.* Philadelphia: fortress, 1983.

Sears, James T. *Growing Up Gay in the South: Race, Gender, and Journeys of the Spirit.* New York: Harrington Park, 1991.

Sedgwick, Eve Kosofsky. *Epistemology of the Closet.* Berkeley: University of California Press, 1990.

———. *Tendencies.* Durham: Duke University Press, 1993.

Shilts, Randy. *Conduct Unbecoming: Gays and Lesbians in the U.S. Military.* New York: Fawcett, 1993 and 1994.

Signorile, Michelangelo. *Queer in America: Sex, the Media, and the Closets of Power.* New York: Random House, 1993.

Singer, Bennett. *Growing Up Gay.* New York: New Press, 1993.

Spong, John Shelby. *Living in Sin? A Bishop Rethinks Human Sexuality.* San Francisco: HarperCollins, 1990.

White, Mel. *Stranger at the Gate: To Be Gay and Christian in America.* New York: Simon and Schuster, 1994.

Whitlock, Katherine. *Bridges of Respect: Creating Support for Lesbian and Gay Youth.* Philadelphia: American Friends Service Committee, 1989.

Contributors

Dennis A. Anderson, M.D., is Assistant Professor of Psychiatry at the Albert Einstein College of Medicine and Unit Chief of the Child and Adolescent Day Hospital at Long Island Jewish Medical Center in New York City. Dr. Anderson also serves on the Board of Directors of the Hetrick-Martin Institute which operates the Harvey Milk School. He also serves on the Homosexual Issues Committee of the American Academy of Child and Adolescent Psychiatry. Dr. Anderson's clinical and research interests include gender identity development and sexual development in children and adolescents. He has spoken at numerous scientific meetings and has written several book chapters and journal articles on these subjects, as well as on the experiences of lesbian and gay adolescents. His address is: Hillside Hospital, Long Island Jewish Medical Center, Glen Oaks, NY 11004. Telephone: (718) 470-8061.

Warren J. Blumenfeld facilitates diversity Workshops specializing in issues related to sexual orientation for educational, business, religious, community, and government organizations. He also travels extensively, giving lectures in the area of LBG studies. He is coauthor, with Diane Raymond, of the book *Looking at Gay and Lesbian Life* (Boston: Beacon Press, 1988, 1993), editor of the book *Homophobia: How We All Pay the Price* (Boston: Beacon Press, 1992), has also authored *AIDS and Your Religious Community: A Hands-On Guide for Local Programs for the Unitarian Universalist Association* (1991), and is the principal author of *Making Colleges and Universities Safe for Gay and Lesbian Students*, a report for the Massachusetts Governor's Commission on Gay and Lesbian Youth. In addition, he is the coproducer of the documentary film *Pink Triangles* (Cambridge Documentary Films, 1982), and associate editor of *Empathy*. He is a steering committee member and trainer for the Gay, Lesbian, and Bisexual Speakers Bureau of Boston, and former features editor for *Gay Community News*. Mr. Blumenfeld is also a former Outreach Educator for the Public Broadcasting Service series *The AIDS Quarterly*, and a former classroom teacher and peripatologist at Perkins High School for the Blind, 1973–1990, where he coauthored that school's Sex Education and Family Life Curriculum. In 1971 he founded the National Gay Student Center of the National Student Association in Washington, DC. His address is: 136 Hancock Street, Cambridge, MA 02139. Telephone: (617) 492-4639.

James E. Brogan is Professor of English at San Francisco State University. He has taught gay and lesbian literature there since 1972. He has recently developed courses on E.M. Forster, Christopher Isherwood, and gay cinema, all of which are now part of the university's new Lesbian/Gay/Bisexual minor. He has published an autobiography, *Jack and Jim: A Personal Journal of the Seventies* (1981) and a novel, *Casey: The Bi-Coastal Kid* (1986). Currently he is concluding work on a novel about contemporary gay life in San Francisco. He is interested in the Men's Movement and has conducted many workshops at the California Men's Gathering. Glaring omissions in his article? His address is: SFU, English Department, San Francisco, CA 94132. Telephone: (415) 338-1886 (work) or (415) 868-0872 (home).

Vincent Fuqua is a student at San Francisco State University and a Research Associate with the AIDS Office, City and County of San Francisco. He is a coauthor of a study concerning AIDS prevalence and risk behaviors among young men, ages 17 to 22, who have sex with men. Correspondence can be directed to him at the Department of Psychology, San Francisco State University, 1600 Holloway Avenue, San Francisco, CA 94132.

Pat Griffin is Associate Professor in the Social Justice Education Program in the School of Education at the University of Massachusetts, Amherst. She is a former high school and college coach and physical education teacher. Her research interests focus on lesbian and gay teachers and students and on homophobia and heterosexism in women's athletics. She conducts workshops for teachers and coaches on homophobia in schools and in athletics, and has written several articles on these topics. Her address is: 368 Hills South, University of Massachusetts, Amherst, MA 01003. Telephone: (413) 545-0211. E-mail: Griffin@educ.umass.edu.

Karen M. Harbeck, Ph.D., JD, as both an attorney and an educator, is a nationally recognized author, scholar, and consultant on the concerns of gay, lesbian, and bisexual youth and adults in educational and employment settings. She is the editor of and major contributing author to the award-winning new book entitled *Coming Out of the Classroom Closet: Gay and Lesbian Students, Teachers, and Curricula* (Haworth Press, 1992). Dr. Harbeck is an adjunct assistant professor at Boston College, and she practices law on behalf of gay and lesbian clients throughout Massachusetts, in addition to her nationwide lecturing and consulting. Dr. Harbeck is also a partner and consultant with Life Management for Gays and Lesbians, a Georgia-based corporation committed to providing educational information to gay, lesbian, and bisexual individuals. Her address is: P.O. Box 1809, Brookline, MA, 02146. Telephone: (617) 321-3569. Fax: (617) 321-9901.

Michael J. Koski is a guidance counselor at the Bayard Rustin High School for the Humanities in New York City. He is a doctoral candidate in Counseling Psychology at Teachers College, Columbia University, where he is a member of the teaching staff who prepare graduate students to provide individual and group counseling. He is also a volunteer group therapist at the Gay Men's Health Crisis, where he coleads a therapy/support group for care-partners of people with AIDS. Mr. Koski has twice presented at meetings of the American Psychological Association concerning his AIDS-related group work, and has conducted workshops to train counselors to deal more effectively with lesbian, gay, and bisexual youth. His address is: Box 102, Teachers College, Columbia University, 525 W. 120th St., New York, NY 10027. Telephone: (212) 678-3397.

Glorianne M. Leck is a Professor of Foundations of Education at Youngstown State University and a past president of the American Educational Studies Association. Dr. Leck identifies as a teacher-scholar-activist, a queer, a lesbian, and a crone. Her work involves coalition-building around civil rights, diversity and justice issues. She is actively involved now as the Chair of the Lesbian, Gay and Bisexual Coalition of Ohio, known as OUTVoice, and as a Commissioner on the Youngstown Human Relations Commission. Your communication is invited: College of Education, Youngstown State University, Youngstown, Ohio, 44555. Telephone: (216) 742-1935.

Arthur Lipkin, Ed.D., is a Research Associate, Instructor, and head of the Gay and Lesbian Curriculum and Staff Development Project at the Harvard Graduate School of Education, a center for curriculum writing and teacher training in lesbian and gay studies for grades K–12 and a clearinghouse for antihomophobia work in schools. Prior to coming to Harvard, he taught for twenty years at the public high school in Cambridge, MA. His course, Staff and Curriculum Development for Anti-Homophobia Education, is the first gay-themed course to be offered at the School of Education. His address is: 210 Longfellow Hall, Cambridge, MA 02138. Telephone: (617) 491-5301. Fax: (617) 495-8510.

Peter McLaren is formerly Renowned Scholar-in-Residence, Miami University of Ohio, and Director, Center for Education and Cultural Studies. He is currently Associate Professor, Graduate School of Education, University of California, Los Angeles. His essays have appeared in such journals as *The Harvard Educational Review, Educational Theory, The American Journal of Semiotics, Polygraph, Curriculum Inquiry, Philosophy and Social Criticism, Journal of Education, Cultural Studies, Strategies, Journal of Curriculum Theorizing,* and *College Literature.* Coedited books include *Paulo Freire: A Critical Encounter* (with Peter Leonard), *Politics of Liberation* (with Colin Lankshear), *Critical Literacy* (with Colin Lankshear), *Critical Pedagogy, the State and Cultural Struggle* (with Henry Giroux) and *Between Borders* (with Henry Giroux). He is the author of the award-winning *Life in Schools* and the highly acclaimed ethnography, *Schooling as a Ritual Performance.* Professor McLaren lectures widely in the U.S., Latin America, and Europe, where he is involved in school reform efforts.

Dr. Kenneth P. Monteiro is a Full Professor of Psychology at San Francisco State University. He received his Ph.D. from Stanford University and held teaching positions at Rutgers University—New Brunswick and the University of Illinois at Urbana-Champaign prior to his current position. He has published in the areas of emotion and cognition, African-American literacy and scholastic achievement and is currently the principle investigator on a study concerning the stress and coping processes of African-American men with AIDS and their caregivers. Correspondence can be directed to him at the Department of Psychology, San Francisco State University, 1600 Holloway Avenue, San Francisco, CA 94132.

Andi O'Conor is a Ph.D. Candidate in Educational Foundations, Policy and Practice at the University of Colorado at Boulder. For her dissertation research, she is conducting an in-depth ethnographic study of gay, lesbian, and bisexual teenagers, and examining the structuring of high school homophobia as it relates to social reproduction, resistance and social change. She welcomes any correspondence regarding this subject. Her address is: The University of Colorado, School of Education, PO Box 249, Boulder, Colorado, 80309. Telephone: (303) 492-7265.

Amy L. Reynolds is an Assistant Professor of Counseling Psychology at Fordham University-Lincoln Center in New York City. She is the past Chair of the American College Personnel Association Standing Committee for Lesbian, Gay, and Bisexual Awareness and is the coauthor (with Raechele L. Pope) of a chapter in *Beyond Tolerance: Gays, Lesbians, and Bisexuals on Campus* (AACD, 1991) as well as an article from the *Journal of Counseling and Development* (1991, 70) entitled "The Complexities of Diversity: Exploring Multiple Oppressions." She is also a coauthor (with Christine Browning and Sari Dworkin) of an article, "Affirmative Counseling for Lesbians" which was published in *The Counseling Psychologist* (1991, 19). Dr. Reynolds has taught courses, presented at national conferences, and delivered numerous training sessions and workshops on combating homophobia and counseling LGB clients. Her address is: Counseling Psychology Program, Fordham University-Lincoln Center, Rm. 1008J, 113 W. 60th St., New York, NY 10023–7478. Telephone: (212) 636-6463.

Eric Rofes directed the middle-school program at the Fayerweather Street School (Cambridge, Massachusetts) and is the author of seven books including *The Kids' Book of Divorce* and *Socrates, Plato and Guys Like Me: Confessions of a Gay Teacher*. He serves on the Board of the National Gay and Lesbian Task Force. Correspondence may be directed to him at 2775 Market Street #108, San Francisco, CA 94114.

James T. Sears is an associate professor in the Department of Educational Leadership and Policies at the University of South Carolina and a teaching professor for the South Carolina Honors College. Professor Sears's specialties are curriculum and sexuality. He has authored nearly 100 book chapters, articles, essays, and scholarly papers and has written or edited five books: the critically acclaimed *Growing up Gay in the South: Race, Gender, and Journeys of the Spirit* (New York: Haworth Press, 1991); *Sexuality and the Curriculum: The Politics and Practices of Sexuality Education* (New York: Teachers College Press, 1992); *Teaching and Thinking About Curriculum* (New York: Teachers College Press, 1990); *Teaching Sex in America: Communities, Cultures and Identities* (San Francisco: Jossey-Bass, forthcoming); and *Why Not the Best?* (New York: Teachers College Press, in press). Professor Sears also serves as coeditor of an international journal, *Teaching Education* and is the Director for the biannual international conference on Enhancing Teaching in Colleges and Universities.

A frequent speaker on college campuses, Professor Sears is the founder of the Lesbian and Gay Studies special interest group of the American

Educational Research Association and the developer and instructor for the first gay and lesbian studies course offered in South Carolina. He is editor of *Empathy: An Interdisciplinary Journal for Professionals Working to End Discrimination on the Basis of Sexual Orientation*, and has served as a consultant for a variety of agencies and organizations, including the J. Paul Getty Foundation for Education and the Arts (Los Angeles), Office of Education Research (Washington DC), Far West Laboratory (San Francisco).

Hugh Singerline is a graduate student in the Department of Political Science at the University of North Carolina at Chapel Hill, and is planning to write a dissertation on the topic of the gay community as imagined community. He has been a facilitator at OutRight! for more than a year, and is also currently on the board. His present address is Davis Library Reference, CB# 3922, University of North Carolina, Chapel Hill, NC 27514–8890. OutRight! can be reached directly at P.O. Box 3203, Durham, NC 27715–3203. Telephone: (919) 286-2396.

Gerald Unks is Professor of Social Foundations of Education at the University of North Carolina at Chapel Hill where he teaches undergraduate and graduate courses in educational policy and social analysis. His pioneering education course for noneducation majors has gained him numerous awards for outstanding teaching and a national reputation. The editor of *The High School Journal*, his research interests include school design and delivery systems and academic freedom. He can be contacted at: School of Education, 212D Peabody Hall, University of North Carolina, CB #3500, Chapel Hill, NC 27599–3500. Telephone: (919) 962-1395.

Virginia Uribe, Ph.D., is a teacher and founder of the school-based intervention program for gay and lesbian youth called Project 10, which has been featured in many news articles and educational journals, including the *Harvard Educational Review, Education Week, Focal Point,* and *Theory into Practice.* Dr. Uribe is the author of the *Project 10 Handbook: Addressing Lesbian and Gay Issues in Our Schools, A Resource Directory for Teachers, Guidance Counselors, and School-Based Adolescent Care Providers* (1989, fifth edition, 1993). She is a speaker, consultant, and workshop presenter throughout the United States and Canada. Dr. Uribe can be reached at Fairfax High School, 7850 Melrose Avenue, Los Angeles, CA, 90046. Telephone: (213) 651–5200, Ext. 244 or (818) 577-4553.

Index